Remembering My Indic Heritage

PERSONAL RECOLLECTIONS

Varadaraja V. Raman

ISBN 978-1-956001-94-5 (paperback)
ISBN 978-1-956001-95-2 (eBook)

Copyright © 2021 by Varadaraja V. Raman

All rights reserved. No part of this publication may be reproduced, distributed, or transmitted in any form or by any means, including photocopying, recording, or other electronic or mechanical methods without the prior written permission of the publisher.

Printed in the United States of America

This book is dedicated to the countless sages, thinkers, poets, artists, and activists who have contributed to making India's culture and civilization what they are today.

Breathes there the man with soul so dead
Who never to himself hath said,
This is my own, my native land?
Whose heart has ne'er within him burn'd
As home his thoughts have often turned
While living in a foreign land?

- Adapted from *The Lay of the Last Minstrel*
by Sir Walter Scott

Acknowledgments

I am indebted to the spirit of India that courses through my veins, to countless authors some of whose books I have listed under *Select Bibliography*, to Professors Arvind Sharma and Jeffery D. Long for their gracious words at the beginning of the book, and to M. L. Raman, my dear wife of more than fifty years, whose love of India and Indic culture prompted me to write this book.

Contents

Acknowledgments vii
Introduction to the Book by McGill University 1
Introduction to the Book by Jeffery D. Long 3
Preface 5
I. The Varied Expanse: Remembering the Subcontinent 9
II. Sounds and Structures: The Languages of India 35
III. Epic of the Ideal Hero: The Ramayana 98
IV. The Longest Epic: The Mahabharata 169
V. Song Divine: The Bhagavad Gita 211
VI. Thoughts Sublime: The Upanishads 229
VII. The Puranas (Puránas): Lore and legends
      nourishing the Culture 255
VIII. Sage-Poets: Rishis of Ancient India 299
IX. On the Past and the Future 343
Select Bibliography 359

Introduction to the Book

Professor Arvind Sharma
McGill University

I would like to congratulate the author for this delightful read. I had no idea what to expect when I was requested to write this foreword, except a confidence born of our association extending over several years, that it would be something remarkable. It has turned out to be something more than remarkable -it borders on the sensational, as something inspired and inspiring; inspired in the unique approach of the author in weaving the right tapestry of Indian history and culture from the threads of his own lived experience of it, and inspiring in demonstrating that not just Hinduism but India itself is a way of life -a way of life distinguished by a warm and willing embrace of diversity.

This book also possesses the quality of a novel without being one; it is a page-turner. This is all the more remarkable because the book is difficult to categorize as travelogue, or autobiography, or cultural essay, or encyclopedic survey, or a book on Hinduism because it is all of them, sharing specially with the latter its recalcitrance to definition. But its attitude towards Hinduism is like Hinduism's attitude to the world, which a French Indologist has described as one of "fascination."

The reader should perhaps be gently warned that the book -charming and anecdotal- is deceptively informal in style while astonishingly rich in content. It carries its learning lightly, even as it teems with epigrams. George Eliot famously mourned the loss of wisdom in knowledge and of knowledge in information. He would have been more optimistic about information leading to knowledge, and knowledge to wisdom, had this book about Indian culture, in its most refined understanding, fallen into his hands.

I recommend this book unreservedly but with a warning to the reader: once you flirt with reading it, you might be tempted to go all the way.

Introduction to the Book

Jeffery D. Long
Elizabethtown College
Professor of Religion and Asian Studies
Author of *A Vision for Hinduism: Beyond Hindu Nationalism* and *Jainism: An Introduction*

This book is a presentation of various key elements of classical Hindu thought, without chauvinistic enthusiasm or superficial second hand information. It is based on scholarly research and presented from contemporary perspectives. Its distinguishing features are a pan-Indian perspective (Sanskritic as well as Tamil), extensive bibliography, and references to other cultures as well. It is interspersed with personal encounters with the topics as well as some reminiscences

In this rich and wide-ranging intellectual memoir, Dr. V.V. Raman, a highly respected progressive voice within the global Hindu community, gives his readers a firsthand view of the enormous variety and depth of Indian culture. Written in a highly accessible, conversational style, Dr. Raman's book touches upon topics ranging from the tensions between religion and science, and tradition and modernity, to India's linguistic diversity, to the wisdom of the ancient Hindu scriptures and the great reformers of contemporary Hinduism, such as Swami Vivekananda and Mahatma Gandhi. Insights leap off of every page, and the reader is treated to a panoramic view of Dr. Raman's Hindu heritage. This book will provide enjoyable and fruitful reading for Hindus and non-Hindus alike.

Preface

No matter how far from home and for how long, the land and culture of our birth keep beckoning us homewards. So it has been with me and India: a country and culture that taught me to experience the world in all its richness, to think with sensitivity, and to be respectful of other cultures. I am quite at home and quite attached to the great nation of the USA, but India has always been close to my heart, Like India, the United States has also had a rich past and it too has welcomed people from all over the world. It too has made and continues to make significant contributions to human welfare and culture. It too is facing, like India and many other nations today, difficult challenges to its well-being and integrity.

India and the United States have much to be proud of and quite a few things to be embarrassed about. But it is not of pride and predicaments that I wish to write in these pages. I want to re-live the cultural enrichments I received during the first two decades of my life. I am a Tamil who grew up in Bengal and is fully Hindu in heritage. Linguistically I am at ease with Tamil, Bengali, Hindi, Sanskrit, and a few European languages including English. As to perspectives, as a Hindu I view religious tolerance as an enlightened and necessary virtue for the modern world, and as a physicist I respect reason and expanding worldviews. As a humanist I try to see all cultures as flowers in a bouquet that is Humanity, Spiritually and intellectually I am a product of both the East and the West. I have benefited from the abundant literature, philosophy, culture, and science of both traditions.

The following chapters are largely personal reflections, but I am indebted to countless authors on the topics. Most of my remembrances here belong to Classical India whose echoes continue to reverberate overtly and subtly in the soul and spirit of modern India. May they continue to do so for all times to come!

I have reminisced in this book on some of the literatures, names, and ideas that inspired me as I was growing up in India decades ago. Unexpected and unplanned events took me away from the land of my birth. During these years I have been keeping in touch with Indian culture in various ways, including periodic visits to different cities and regions.

As a modern dynamic nation India has been changing in many ways since the days it was my home. The nation's infrastructure has been modernized, its educational system has expanded, there are now lots more academic institutions, scientific centers and productive factories. The standard of living of an increasing number of citizens has been steadily rising. There are more cars on the roads, more planes in the air, more highways and luxury hotels, and more pollution in land, air and waters than when I was growing up as a lad in the 1930s. There are pubs and drinking joints, yoga classes on TV, and racy stuff in movies such as I could never have imagined as a youth six decades ago. Dating—in the American sense of the term—is not uncommon, and reports of rapes and bribes abound in newspapers and on TV.

In a sense, all this is inevitable in an open and evolving society. There are nations which strive to filter out what they regard as the morally negative aspects of modernity, which is commendable. But some insist on reverting to or continuing the unconscionable values and anachronistic modes of the past at great cost to human life and liberty and the experience of happiness. Modernity and technology, like life itself, is a package deal: the good and the bad come together. Sometimes, whether we like it or not, they are thrust upon us. It is for us to handle them wisely.

It is ironic that in this age of freedom, individuals and societies seem to have lost their freedom to choose and reject their lifestyles and values. They are dragged by technology, media, and peer-pressures along roads which, left to themselves, they might not have chosen. It would seem that we are all in it together, zooming with time on one global ski-slope, riding deliriously, even uncontrollably, downhill towards what appears to be a perilous precipice.

In the meanwhile, in the context of Indic culture and the Hindu world, the most ominous change I have been observing in recent years in private conversations as well as in letters to editors, on list serves, in internet postings, lectures, symposiums, books, and other public forums is a growing concern that the very existence of Hindu culture and religion is at stake. The integrity of the Hindu world is challenged, its foundations diluted, and its essence distorted. Most seriously, its survival is threatened by what many see as concerted moves from within India, and by intrusions from the outside. Because of all this, there has surfaced widespread suspicions, if not hatred, between Hindus and others. These fears are also articulated with sensitivity and consternation by a good many Hindus residing beyond the shores of India. I fear that the threats to Hindu identity and culture are genuine. In the midst of all this I well remember the good old days when our family had Christian, Muslim, Sikh, Jain, Buddhist, and Theosophy friends as well.

I like to think and I often pray that ugly inter-religious dissensions will dissolve with time all over the world, though at this point this seems to many to be unrealizable in the next few decades. All religions, not just in India but all over the world, will have to recognize before it is too late that mutual respect is the only enlightened vision that offers hope for peace and harmony. This has to be based on the principle that all individuals and groups must be allowed to choose their own paths to spiritual and cultural fulfillment: the tenet of *polyodosism*. It is more urgent to work together as brothers and sisters to resolve the growing planetary problems our species is facing than to be fighting about which God will take us to heaven or which culture is superior to which.

In this context, millions of Hindus in India and abroad, can be enriched by reading and reflecting on the literary, spiritual, and philosophical legacy that our ancestors in classical India have left for all of us. That is what I have tried to offer in this book.

Varadaraja V. Raman
http://acharyavidyasagar.wordpress.com/

I

The Varied Expanse: Remembering the Subcontinent

Mountains and meadows, lakes and rivers in regions without people do not a country make, but they offer homes to civilizations.

- Anonymous

The land and its southernmost tip

I remember reading in my geography text in school that the Indian subcontinent is a vast territory, covering an area of more than three million square kilometers. It is bounded in its northern regions by mighty mountain ranges: the snow-capped Himalayas that have for ages filled the people of India with awe and reverence. (Gansser, 1987) An inspired poet by the name of Ramdhari Singh Dinker wrote an ode to the Himalayas which begins with the lines: (George, 1992)

> My king of mountains! My magnificent one!
> Radiant embodiment of great glory!

> Flame of fierce, accumulated prowess!
> Snowy diadem of my motherland!
> Effulgent brow of my Bharat!
> My king of mountains! My magnificent one!

India's shoreline is embraced by the blue expanse: the Arabian Sea, the Indian Ocean, and the Bay of Bengal, across which ships and boats have come and gone for trades and forming settlements since ancient times. As a youngster I used to want to get a glimpse of all these aquatic expanses. Over the years I have had the privilege of being in many parts of India, surveying at one time the slopes of the hallowed Himalayas that provide a natural bulwark for the subcontinent in the north, and at other times, dipping my feet in the Ocean waters, the Bay, and the Sea that guard the triangular landmass.

I recall a visit to Kanyakumari in 1959. I spent a few minutes in the famed rock at the southern-most tip of the subcontinent. The town is named after the Maiden Goddess who, per Hindu sacred history, once waited for the deity from Suchindram, some six miles away, whom she was to wed. Mounds of precious gifts and hallowed edibles came for the occasion, but for various reasons, the arrival of the groom at the auspicious hour was thwarted. The marriage did not come to pass. The goddess cursed the articles of gifts to become sand grains and sea-shells, and she has remained Kanyakumari (*Maiden Princess*) forever. (Das, 1964, 1-4)

The sand at the beach is of different hues, made up of monazite which contains uranium. I remember going into the temple of this goddess, and admiring the sparkling diamond nose-ring on the beautiful icon bearing a garland. Deities in Hindu temples are adorned in multicolored costumes and glittering jewelry to reflect the effulgent splendor of the Divine. Personified gods of the religion have an eerie grandeur that evokes an ecstatic reverence that faceless abstraction rarely provides. Aesthetics merges with spirituality in Hindu iconic worship.

When I was there, I thought of the Kali temple in Kolkata with which I was more familiar. As per another episode in the lore, once when the demons Baan and Muja were wreaking havoc, the deities appealed to Lord Shiva in Varanasi for help. By his magical powers, Shiva actualized his consort Shakhty into Kali in Kalighat in Kolkata and Kanyakumari in the deep south as powerful guardians.

I was in Kanyakumari before they built the massive statue of Tiruvalluvar, my favorite Tamil poet, and the majestic meditation hall (*Dhyána Mandapam*) to memorialize Swami Vivekananda, the orator-sage who brought Hinduism within global reach, transforming it from what seemed to the outside world as pure exotica into a virtual lighthouse, as it were, that illumines distant lands and beckons one and all to her bosom. It was exhilarating to recall that Vivekananda sat there some sixty years earlier in meditation before taking off to Chicago to preach and propagate the ideas and ideals of Hindu thought at the Parliament of World Religions in 1893.

Vivekananda was elated by India's spiritual strength, but he was also acutely aware of her material backwardness at that time. He realized that the West needed the religious outlook and sensitivity which it was fast losing and which the Hindu world still cherished. But he also felt that India could benefit from the scientific awakening in the West. His writings made Indians aware of the painful chasm between the spiritual ideals on the one hand and some of the awful conditions and appalling practices on the other: as true when he spoke a hundred years ago as perhaps it is still today in many respects in many parts of India.

Facing north from that historic rock, I closed my eyes and visualized, as millions of others had done before me, and millions more still do, the vast stretch of land stretching all the way to hoary Himalayas. Facing south, I felt the merger of the Bay of Bengal and the Arabian Sea with the Indian Ocean which has a link with sacred history. It was across this strait that, per the Ramayana, Hanuman took his grand leap into Sri Lanka to locate Sita who had been kidnapped by Ravana. Nearby on the islet of Ramesvaram stands a large temple with impressively long corridors. Consecrated to Shiva and Parvati, known here as Ramanathar and Parvatavardini, Rama had this temple built, so says the lore, to redeem himself of the sin of slaughtering the Brahmin but brutal Ravana. Non-traditional scholarship tells us that the temple was constructed in the twelfth century of the Common Era by a Panydyan king. (Bhatt, 2006)

There are not a great many ancient historical monuments in India, but many precious relics of the Indus Valley Civilization have been unearthed. Scholars have been able to draw a good deal of interesting information about the people who lived in these regions (most of which are now in Pakistan). (Gupta, 1996) The countless temples, old and new, that adorn the Indian landscape, as also the mosques and churches of alien vintage, are constant reminders of spirituality and sacred history which play a major role in the lives of millions of Indians.

Physical geography and lore

Sloping from the Himalayas are vast plains, whose gentle gradient from west to east causes the flow of rivers and rivulets that bring silt from the high mountains and nourish abundant fields of rice and wheat. The region is also blessed with regular rains. The majestic Ganga and her companion Yamuna are two great rivers which have played a dominant role in the culture of the people and the agriculture of the region. There is reason to believe that at one time there was also a third river, the sacred

Sarasvati, as part of a triune of rivers which had their confluence in Triveni. (Lal, 2002). This junction is now one of the major pilgrimage-spots with which the land is studded.

Yamuna which has its source in Himalayan glaciers meanders in the plains through Vrindhavan and Mathura. I was about six when I first heard of Yamuna, and this was in a bhajan song dedicated to Lord Krishna:

> yamuna thíra vihári - vrindhávana sanchári
> govardana giri dhári - gopi hridaya vihári

As per Hindu sacred history, Krishna as lad and youth used to sport on the banks of this river. It was across Yamuna that Krishna's father Vasudeva stealthily transported baby Krishna to protect the child from his monstrous uncle who had vowed to kill every offspring of his sister.

When little Krishna slipped in the waters by accident, Yamuna cleansed his Divine feet, and this is how it became a sacred river. When in my twenties, I rode in a car on the *Lohe ka Pul*, as the old iron bridge over the Yamuna is called in New Delhi. I recalled to myself the Bhagavatam story, and reflected on the power of the Purana which had transformed what seemed like an indifferent flow into something so supremely significant in the Hindu world. In the minds of people poetic visions, especially when touched by religion, are more real than scientific theories. Henry Wardsworth Longfellow reminded us in *The Day Is Done* of

> The bards sublime
> Whose distant footsteps echo
> Through the corridors of Time.

A tributary of Ganga, called the Hughli (spelled variously) which is often identified with Ganga, is on the edge of Kolkata, separating the city from its principal railway station. About the Port Office there many decades ago, Rudyard Kipling wrote in *The City of Dreadful Night*: "(It) owns enormous wealth; and spends huge sums on the frontaging of river banks, the expansion of jetties, and the manufacture of docks costing two hundred lakhs of rupees. Two million tons of sea-going shippage yearly find their way up and down the river by the guidance of the Port Office, and the men of the Port Office know more than it is good for men to hold in their heads. They can without reference to telegraphic bulletins give the position of all the big steamers, coming up or going down, from the Hughli to the sea, day by day, with their tonnage, the names of their captains and the nature of their cargo."

The rivers in India were safe and sacred in my youthful days. They still are sacred. I have taken pious plunges in the time-honored waters of more than one Indian river. But with industrialization, urbanization, increased population, and consequent pollution, the once clear waters have drastically deteriorated. In 1998 there was a BBC report to the effect that the good people of Delhi dump more than 3 billion liters of sewage every day into this sacred river whose waters, after appropriate treatment, serve 60% of the Indian capital's residents for drinking, bathing, and more. I also read, to my shock and sadness, that at one time some 50,000 migratory birds used to hover around the Yamuna in Delhi during the winter months, but now there aren't any. Projects are under way to restore the rivers to reasonable pollution-free levels.

In the central regions of the body of India rises another mountain chain which divides the southern triangle from the northern mainland. These are the Vindhya mountains. Valmiki's

Ramayana lists Mahendra, Himalaya, Vindhya, Kailash and Mandara as the five tallest mountains. It is said that once the sage Narada teased the Vindhya range by praising the much loftier legendary Mount Meru, whereupon the slighted Vindhyas grew high as the sky, making it difficult for sun and moon to rise and set. Rishi Agasthya was dispatched from Varanasi, with Tamil language and all, to the south. The Vindhyas were on the path of the sage, and they bowed down reverentially to a smaller size, and let the holy scholar climb over and cross. (Mahabharata, III: 103) Since Agasthya settled down in the Tamil country and did not return, the shrunk mountains have maintained their modest altitudes. Hindu imagination has always been fertile and fantastic, sometimes funny also.

The southern sector gives India its characteristic beautiful shape on the map. I may be biased, but I have often felt, upon inspecting the maps of nations on the globe, that the Indian subcontinent has one of the most beautiful contours, with a broad and well-sketched upper zigzag and graceful entry into the blues of the sea. The southern segment is known as the Deccan, an anglicized form of the Sanskrit *dakshin* meaning south.

On the western coast rise other slopes, known as the *Western Ghats*. In a train ride to Mumbai I once got a glimpse of some of the most picturesque and breath-taking sceneries in these mountainous regions where evergreen forests thrive in regions like Amboli and Radhanagari, bearing lush tropical vegetation, including the hog plum, coral tree, and jamun. Oh, the variety of fruits one finds in India!

Nature has blessed the subcontinent with many bounties. How the inhabitants take care of them is another matter. For in India, as elsewhere in the world, there are serious threats to land and air, to plants and trees. A population that has excceded a billion is hungry for food and thirsty for water. It is amazing that, even amidst serious growing scarcities, the land is producing enough fruits and grains, leaves and roots, to feed all its people and the millions more of animals that also thrive in those lush regions.

Forests, flora, and fauna

Many years ago I went as a tourist to El Yunque: a rainforest in Puerto Rico. I was impressed by its coolness, waded bare-feet in a stream, and admired a mini-waterfall there. Until then, I did not even know that there were rainforests in the world. Then I discovered that I had myself been living for many years not far from one. The Sundarban (Beautiful Forest), which I had known only as a jungle, is in fact a rainforest of great complexity. There are rainforests in the Western Ghats of India as well.

The vast Sundarban is exposed to heavy monsoon rains, huge tidal waves, and much erosion. It spreads out in both India and Bangladesh. Nature knows no national boundaries. The Sundarban is where the famous Bengal Tigers live: those beautiful and majestic creatures with an orange coat lined with black or white stripes. [I never imagined as a lad that one day there would be a picture of me with a statute of the Bengal tiger in the *New York Times* (November 23, 1991).] The still surviving wild boar and the spotted deer help sustain the diminishing tiger population. Other beasts like the rhinoceros and the water buffalo have become almost extinct there. The Sundarban is also home to lots of monkeys and birds and fish, snakes and crocodiles; not to mention the mudskipper, an incredible fish that lives in water, but can come out on land and climb on trees too!

Historians say that there was an ancient township in the Sundarban back in the 3rd century C.E., and that some rulers used to take refuge there in the face of advancing armies. The folks inhabiting the adjoining villages today - fishermen, lumberjacks, people who work in the forest for the government, and their families mostly - worship Goddess Banbibi of whom few Hindus elsewhere may have even heard. She is unique among goddesses in that the Muslims of the region also pray to her; both Hindus and Muslims celebrate her in a festival. The Rig Veda too speaks of a Forest Goddess: *Aranyáni*. A hymn in the Rig Veda is dedicated to her: (Griffith, 1890: Hymn CXLVI)

> Goddess of wild and forest who seemest to vanish from the sight.
> How is it that thou seekest not the village? Art thou not afraid?
> What time the grasshopper replies and swells the shrill cicala's voice, Seeming to sound with tinkling bells, the Lady of the Wood exults.
> And, yonder, cattle seem to graze, what seems a dwelling-place appears: Or else at eve the Lady of the Forest seems to free the wains.
> Here one is calling to his cow, another there hath felled a tree:
> At eve the dweller in the wood fancies that somebody hath screamed.
> The Goddess never slays, unless some murderous enemy approach.
> Man eats of savoury fruit and then takes, even as he wills, his rest.
> Now have I praised the Forest Queen, sweet-scented, redolent of balm, The Mother of all sylvan things, who tills not but hath stores of food.

A whole corpus of Vedic literature is known as the *Áranyakas* (Forest Texts). It was meant only for those who had retreated to sylvan seclusion. They were the inspiration for the Upanishads. The most important Upanishad (Brihadáranyaka) is an Áranyaka.

The epic Ramayana begins with the poet Valmiki strolling in the forest and hearing the agonizing wail of a bird whose mate had been killed by a hunter. Sages like Vishvamitra and Buddha retreated to the forest to meditate on unfathomable mysteries. Many gurus established ashrams (hermitages) in the forests where they instructed the young. In the classical Hindu view of the stages of life, one was expected to retire to the forest in the evening of one's life to feel at home with the fullness of nature.

India has a plethora of flora and fauna. This reminds me of the famous Botanical Garden on the other side of the Hugli River. On one occasion our science teachers took us there for a picnic. The entire noisy group of students boarded a steam launch called *Cossipore* from Chandpal Ghat. This was a fair sized ferry with a cover to protect the passengers from the sun. It was operated by a couple of men who were wearing pointed and embroidered caps. We students were boisterous, but not unruly.

We observed birds flying here and there, some perched briefly on boats, indifferent to or unaware of the fun we were having. I saw men and women taking dips in the river: they looked skyward with folded hands before taking a plunge. They were imbued in the profound conviction that they were heard by divine spirits in the ethereal world above.

I spotted narrow boats plying the river, some were fishing boats, and other vessels were part covered and part open. They carried people from one bank of the Hugli to the other. We waved at them, and they waved back, as per an unwritten convention among people in boats and ships. I stared at the brownish waters right below: even with all its dirt and mud, the river was holy in my worldview, for Hugli was from the Ganga. Those waters had their origins in Himalayan peaks, they were of molten snow, flowing for countless miles, accumulating silt and filth as they meandered along the banks of places made holy by their course, and now heading towards the saline sea: the Bay of Bengal.

When we landed on the Sibpur side and proceeded to the Botanical Garden, we were given instructions as to how to behave. Professor Bose informed us that we were in one of the most important botanical gardens in the world, and that it spanned more than 250 acres of tropical greenery. Thousands of species of plants and trees were there, he proclaimed, while most students were chatting away on unrelated topics. I was in the habit of taking notes on trivia to fill the pages of my diary. That is how I remember to this day that the Botanical Garden in Calcutta was established in the last quarter of the eighteenth century (which already seemed a very long time ago). As we strolled along, Botany Bose (as we called our professor) often walked backwards in front of us, wanting our attention.

He would stop to point to this plant or that tree, and explain the peculiarities of those noteworthy members of the green kingdom. He showed us Poa and Chamaerops, Tropaeolum majus, Mimosa pudica and Acacia heterophylla, and many more. He asked us to pay particular attention to the variety of leaf forms. I jotted down such words as ovate, peltate, pinnate, and palmate, all of which we had seen in our text-book. Until then, however, I had never related those classifications to real leaves on plants and trees, and unconsciously imagined they belonged only to the pages of botany textbooks. I was impressed with Professor Bose's familiarity with it all, although I secretly wondered how a grown man could get that ecstatic about the shape of leaves. Yes, this was geometry in the woods, symmetry in nature, variety in the world of plants and trees. While Bose was eloquent about leaf forms and plant varieties, I was enjoying the strange words used to qualify them: words which did not mean much at the time, but which sounded profoundly scientific all the same.

Botonay Bose listed the names of dozens of plants and shrubs and trees, in their Latin and Indian names. I was impressed by his fund of knowledge when he rattled off names like Prosopis cineraria (*Jand*), Acacia jaoguemontil, Benth (*babool*), Ficus religiosa (*peepal*), and many more. Ajay Rawat of Kumaon University informs us that some 45,000 species of the plant kingdom and 65,000 of the animal are thriving on Indian soil. (Rawat, 1991)

Gardens and orchards have always been prized in India, as testified by many writers and in works of art. In his famous play *Shakuntala*, the playwright Kalidasa lists the names of a number of plants and trees in a pleasure garden: like *madhavi, kadamba, parijata*, etc.

I can never forget the flower stalls at the approach of temples in India, busy and noisy and full of life. The flowers, white and pink and red and yellow, rich in fragrance and beauty, that are offered with piety to the Divine or pinned with elegance on the abundant hair of women on joyous occasions must impress even the most casual on-looker. I bring back to mind my visits to the *Lake Market* in Kolkata where I used to be fascinated by the extraordinary variety of fruits and vegetables of every shape, size, and taste: gourds and stalks, roots and nuts, grains and spices: one can go on and on.

Over the ages, the people of India understood the role, and respected the presence, of bio-diversity. That is why the rodent, the peacock, the cobra and the monkey have all gained places in Hindu lore, legends, and places of worship. The cow, the elephant, margosa and tulasi plants have attained sacred status too.

Such is the terrain of India: plain here, mountainous there, rich and abundant in one place, parched and sparse in another, waterfall in Kottralam and desert in Rajasthan, valleys and jungles and more. In this grand backdrop, human-made structures may be seen everywhere: from humble hutments to lavish palaces, and much in between. In the modern frenzy to build apartment complexes and multi-storied structures, many archaeological treasures are buried deeper still, as if to forget forever India's ancient history.

The fate of Nature is hanging mightily in a delicate balance in our age of technology. There are increasing demands to produce and build for more than the billion people who make their living on the ancient land which once supported just a few million. The intrusion of modern civilization into every domain of Nature to quench its ever increasing needs is threatening the balance and beauty that existed in the Indian subcontinent for millennia, as it does in practically every corner of the so-called civilized world.

Variety in India's people, and controversies on origins

Once, at the end of a talk I gave, someone came to me and asked, "Do all Indians have a sense of humor?" I don't know the answer to this question, but I do know that the people of India are of a tremendous variety, not just in external features, but in creeds and convictions, in attitudes and values, and in other respects too. If I have to say anything general about them, I will say that they are, by and large, friendly and hospitable, and tolerant at heart towards all religious modes; and that educated Indians have more than their share of ethnic pride.

In the course of her long history, India has witnessed many of the triumphs and tribulations that humanity is heir to. The subcontinent has witnessed countless political struggles and conflicts, wars and battles, victories and defeats, joyous celebrations and days of harshness. In the midst of all this, the people have created and nurtured great poetry and philosophy, sublime art and music, mathematics and science too.

The inhabitants of India range from the so-called *tribals*, who still guard their pristine ways (though this is fast disappearing), to an array of sophisticated groups who speak a variety of languages and contribute as much to international debates as to modern science. The tribals in India are, like other pristine people, simple in their ways and joyful in their festivities, but have been victims of marginalization and victimization since very ancient times. (Dube, Shyama Charan, 1977) In addition to this, they have also suffered under political turmoil and religious conflicts. According to a report published in 2009, "A total of 401,425 tribals have been displaced due to armed conflicts and ethnic conflicts across India," Asian Indigenous and Tribal People's Network (AITPN), which has special consultative status with the UN's Economic and Social Council (ECOSOC), claimed in its report that "These displaced persons (tribals) have been living miserable lives without basic amenities including food, water, shelter, medical services, sanitation and livelihood opportunities." (The Times of India, 24 May 2009)

I once saw the sacrifice of bleating goats at the altar of Maa Kali, and it was not a pretty sight for a faint-hearted vegetarian like myself. The shining ax was lifted high, and in one strong stroke the creature was decapitated. A man took the bleeding severed head into the sanctum sanctorum to offer it to the mother goddess. This sight made me think twice about the sanctity of religious rituals, Hindu or any other. Butchering animals in the name of God is an ancient and widespread practice that persists to this day in more than one religious tradition. I decided to move away from the temple mode and took to meditating on an impersonal Cosmic Mystery for spiritual fulfillment, which too – thank goodness – is part of the Hindu tradition.

The variety within the Hindu fold is incredibly rich. I have friends whose travel plans are regulated by prohibitions in the astrological almanac and who fast on New Moon days. I also have friends who make complex calculations for long-range missiles and nuclear reactions, devise electronic instruments and perform heart surgery. Many Hindus still arrange marital partners on the basis of sect and sub-sect and horoscope compatibility, but Hindus also fall in love in college or elsewhere, and choose partners from other faiths and nations. The emergence from traditional enclosure to total openness has occurred only during the past hundred and odd years.

Hindus of the twenty-first century, notwithstanding their caste consciousness and lingering obsession with racial purity (expressed more openly in small groups, and seldom done any more in public), are the product of healthy mixtures that have resulted from waves upon waves of immigrants to the subcontinent. Present day Indians include descendents from Vedic rishis, from Negroid Africans, from ancient Greeks and medieval Mongols, and from the Portuguese, Persians and Afghans also. Periodic chromosomal studies to trace the racial connections of very ancient Indians with people from beyond (Wells, 2002) tend to anger people who have little interest in determining these matters through scientific studies. All Indians are of purely indigenous origins, is their assertion, and that's it.

Be that as it may, in no other nation is there a greater variety of facial features, skin pigmentation, and English accents than one finds in India. Countries like the United States, Canada, and France, with large numbers of immigrants are slowly undergoing changes in the features of their average citizen, but the difference in appearance between Caucasians and others is all too glaring in these countries. In places like China and Korea people are far more homogeneous. But in India, the change in appearance is a continuous spectrum. Yet, one can tell a person from India by facial appearance, although there are also striking similarities with people referred to as Latinos in the Americas.

Nineteenth century Indologists, inspired largely by phonetic/linguistic similarities between Sanskrit and some European languages came up with a theory according to which a horde of nomadic peoples from Central Asia entered India via the perilous Khyber Pass in the Afghan borders, and established Vedic civilization in the northern plains of India. This so-called Aryan Invasion Theory (AIT) has had a long history, and is one of the few hypotheses in ancient history that has spilled over from genuine scientific quest to the ugly arena of political name-calling. It has been subjected to severe critical analyses, both at the scholarly level and in ad hominem attacks. The general consensus among scholars is to either reject it as not convincing at all, or to look upon it with some caution with need for considerable revision. Some Hindus have contended that it was a sinister scheme, a trickery on the part of the British, to justify their occupation of India as simply another instance in a long pattern of invasions. This is the refrain even in many valid attacks on the AIT. The newly emerging paradigm is that of an Indus-Sarasvati culture as the original Indic civilization which emerged in the northern river valleys (Lal, 2002).

These are important discoveries and changing perspectives, linked as much to archeology and historical scholarship as to cultural sensitivities and historical rancor. For me personally, it makes little difference from where my most distant ancestors came, given that we all came from Africa anyway. They could have been from Hardwar or Holland or from what is now

Mylapore in Chennai. I rejoice in the inspiring poetry and enlightened visions that arose from India's spiritual, intellectual, and moral roots. The worldviews and values enshrined in the Vedas and the Upanishads, in Tolkappiyam and Tirukkural, in Valmiki and Kamban have all enriched my life, as they have the lives of countless others, and I am grateful for that. Linguistic connections between ancient Sanskrit and Latvian or Lithuanian may be interesting, but they don't stir me to the point of getting emotional. I enjoy the plays of Shakespeare whether or not they were written by the man whose supposed home I once visited at Stratford Upon Avon, or by an altogether different person who might have lived near the South Pole.

What seems to be well established on the basis of literary and other records is that ancient Indic culture was nurtured by two principal streams, the Sanskritic and the Tamil, and enhanced in later centuries by many others. The first two interacted and mutually enriched each other. Whether both of these had yet another common root is another issue of interest and debate among historians. However, it too touches many political and cultural raw nerves, and has lost its academic virginity, and so will not interest me any further in these reflections.

Particular individuals

Rama Sastrigal was our family priest: *Sástrigal*, we used to call him. He showed up periodically to remind my father of upcoming events which needed to be observed at home: a child's birthday, a son's *upanayanam* (investiture of the sacred thread), the death anniversary of a departed grandparent, and other such occasions that call for rites and rituals. My father used to be meticulous in remembering his departed parents with due ceremony. There was something beautiful and gracious in this recall: It was a symbolic and continuing expression of gratitude to those who had cared for him at one stage of his life.

Clad in immaculate dhoti and sporting a hefty pigtail, RS was an alert and cheerful man, remarkably efficient at whatever he did. He used to set up the *havan* (fire-altar) with twigs for burning, arrange *darbha* (sacred grass) and other paraphernalia for the rituals, often with an assistant, and enunciate the appropriate mantras with impressive clarity. He was one of the millions of *purohits*, thanks to whom sacraments in the Hindu world have been carried on from generation to generation over many centuries, serving as indispensable links in a cultural continuity that dates back to very distant times.

The *purohit* is different from the *pujari* whose role is mainly in the temple, offering periodic worship (*puja*) to the icons which are consecrated there. Traditionally, unlike the purohit, the pujari was not formally schooled. He learned by rote the canonical mantras with the associated rituals, that is about all. Few pujaris had the training in Sanskrit diction and intonation that the purohits normally get. This might have changed. In Hindu temples outside of India, the same person is often both purohit and pujari.

There are lots of other individuals in the Hindu world who are identified as persons of religious standing. They bear honorifics like *guru, swamiji, sadhu, muni, sannyasin, yogi*, and more. I rather doubt that in any other culture there are as many different categories of god-men as in the Hindu world. All of them command respect from the populace, not only because they generally (used to) lead simple lives, and are believed to abstain from the normal temptations of secular life, but also because they are believed to have a closer link to God.

Some of them are affiliated to a religious order, and hold the title of swami. Swamijis are often more learned than purohits, and they seldom perform domestic rituals or temple services, because they have, in principle, renounced the world. Indeed, they don't even have the right to perform rituals, although I knew at least one eminent swamiji who used to conduct weddings outside of India. Generally, but not always, swamijis sport a saffron attire. The more eloquent ones go on lecture tours to speak on Hindu philosophy and religion, both within India and Europe, America and other secular nations. Not many go to Africa or China, and perhaps no one ventures into countries where Islam holds sway.

Another person I got to know as a youngster was Mr. LM, father of one of my college mates. LM was an I.C.S. (Indian Civil Service) officer. In those days, these were the elite in society. The family lived in an upper-class neighborhood in Calcutta. They had cooks, servants, and a chauffeur, all in white uniforms. I saw LM only in shirts and trousers, sometimes with jacket and tie, but never in Indian attire. He used to smoke a pipe, and spoke with what sounded like an alien accent: British, perhaps. His wife was very *modern*, as they used to say in those days, referring to women whose hair was cut and bobbed in the Western style. Her blouse was often sleeveless, and though clad in sari, she wore lipstick which was not very common in India then. Mr. and Mrs. LM had Indian faces, yet did not at all look Indian to me. They were, to use an old phrase, brown sahibs.

In conversations I had with LM, I often detected scant respect for things Hindu. He once told me that India was still living in the Middle Ages, and he doubted very much (in the 1950s) if the country would ever enter the twentieth century. How surprised he would be if he were alive today! He expressed the view that India's future depended on how well its people assimilated the English language and learned to think in Western ways. He thought the British had brought in a lot of education, science, and modern values to India. He was what some Indians today (inspired by a French Indophile) derisively call a Macaulayite. Yet, it was people like him who, for the good or for the bad, contributed significantly to the functioning of modern India.

Mr. PKD was another man I well remember. He was well-read, versed in Bengali literature and in popularizations of science in English. He was a constant thinker, and he liked to talk about Bengali poetry, modern science, and Indian philosophy. He lived in a spacious house in South Calcutta. He was one of many educated Hindus, channeled by chance to non-academic professions, but who kept an active interest in purely intellectual matters. There were (are) millions like him all over the country, but in Bengal (in those days) there were perhaps more of them than elsewhere. PKD's hero was Sri Aurobindo, and he insisted I go through *Savitri* and *Life Divine* which are not easy reads for a college kid. But thanks to him, I plodded through them. PKD was convinced that India's spiritual message would be recognized by the West sooner or later, and then her former glory would be re-established in the world. I never understood then, and I still don't understand now, why India's glory, past or present, should be connected to its being recognized by the West. To this day there are Indians griping about not receiving sufficient well-deserved pat on the back from Europeans and Americans.

Next, I recall SB, one of my professors at the university. He was a remarkable man. He could solve any problem in analytical mechanics, hydrodynamics, and complex variables. He kept technical books in German and French in his office. He was invariably dressed in Indian clothes of the Bengali version: half-sleeved shirt and dhoti. He told me once that he performed puja at home every day, and was very fond of Alfred Hitchcock movies.

Then there was PH, the man who used to come every Sunday morning to our house, bringing back in neat, ironed, and folded version the dirty linen he had taken for washing the previous week, and collecting a new set of clothes the family had used during the week. We would list the items given and count them when they were returned. We knew him only as the *dhobi*, until one day, out of sheer curiosity I asked him for his name. What I now recall with a sense of irony – but which never struck me as anything odd at the time – was that, along with the barber and the toilet cleaner – the dhobi was also regarded as so impure a human being that it was sinful to come in physical contact with him. I have had great difficulty in my later years reconciling myself to the fact that for the first two decades of my life I practiced this abominable degradation of fellow human beings without so much as being aware of the unconscionable nature of that worldview. How the world has changed for the better in this regard! I am grateful I have lived long enough to see this transformation in values in many parts of the world.

I have mentioned these different people to bring to mind the incredible variety among the people of India. The ones I have recalled represent but a small sample from the traditional purohit to the totally Westernized Hindu, from the culture-sensitive scholar to the well-adjusted professor of modern mathematics who was respectful and appreciative of his tradition. They all live normally at peace with many others who had different faces and features. They loved their culture, even if some of them were anglophiles. They might not have had a good sense of history, but they were never an unhappy or frustrated lot. I don't recall any of them feeling religiously insecure or culturally persecuted at home or abroad, or virulently anti-this and anti-that. Today, Indians number more than a billion with considerable achievements in industry and technology, and far more economic potential.

Nevertheless internet exchanges and patriotic books are sullied with ethnic hatred, religious bigotry, bitterness towards the West and Western scholars, and arguments to the effect that our ancients knew all about modern science.

All this seems to reflect a deep sense of intellectual, moral, and spiritual insecurity. The irony is that much of this has happened after millions of Hindus voluntarily emigrated to Western countries, after securing sound English-based education in India, often in Jesuit schools. These are among the louder voices of discontent, cultural malaise, and West-baiting. Perhaps they have difficulty living in the Western world which they unconsciously contrast with what strikes them as the relative backwardness of their native land, every aspect of which retarded state they attribute to Western colonialism.

Example of cultural continuity: *adhyáyanam*

The rote learning of Vedic verses is called *adhyáyanam*. This is the basis of the oral tradition by which hundreds of thousands of precious literature and sacred verses of the ancient world have been preserved.

At fifteen I was initiated into the *adhyáyanam* of some hymns. I recall, in particular, *Purusha Súktam*, *Rudram* and *Shri Súktam* which were taught to me by a pandit who came to our house every evening. He would recite the lines with the proper intonation:

sahasra sírishá purushah; sahasráksha sahasra pád;
sa bhúmim visvato vrtvá; atyatishtad dasángulam....

A rough translation of some of the lines would be:

> The Cosmic Person, with a thousand heads,
> A thousand eyes, and a thousand feet,
> He pervades the earth and envelops space ten fingers wide.
> He is all there was, is, and ever will be.
> ...
> All creatures together form a fourth of Him,
> And three fourths is life eternal in Heaven.
> From there he strode on all sides over those that eat and that eat not.
> ...

We used to repeat the lines rhythmically. Our goal was to learn the stanzas with proper diction and tone, not studying them in the sense of knowing or interpreting their contents. When I came to understand their meanings, I was fascinated by the imagery of the cosmology which reflects a sweep of space and season, of man and animal, and of all of Creation. It was grand poetry, transporting us to sublime thoughts.

There is also here a passage narrating the origin of the castes. When I read that Brahmins arose from the mouth of the Supreme Person while the Shudras were engendered from his feet, I began to wonder how a Shudra might feel about this: a thought that has never ceased to trouble me for decades.

I liked and enjoyed the verses. While taking walks around the Dhakuria Lake in South Calcutta (as it used to be called then) or while lying in bed in the dark before going to sleep I used repeat some of these lines. Their spiritual content did not touch me as much as the rhythm of the meters. The mystery in sacred syllables arises from their antiquity. There is magic in sounds because sounds bind us all as human beings. How isolated we would feel in a world where silence reigned!

Indic civilization is so ancient and diverse that practically every perspective has been expressed in it: from the most liberal to the most narrow. Though Hindus generally believe that their religion allows for other paths to the Divine, one of the lines in the Purusha Súktam says there is no other path to liberation but this: *nánya panthá ayanáya vidhmahe*. Perhaps what is meant is that the experience of the Divine is the only way we can apprehend it. I also like to interpret this line to mean that if one wishes to understand Hindu (Vedic) culture and philosophy at any significant level, there is no other path but to learn at least some of the Vedic verses in the original Sanskrit.

In the recitation of *Rudram* I enjoyed the frequent repetition of *cha* as in *"namo bhaváya cha rudráya cha nama śarváya cha paśupataye cha namo nīlagrīváya cha śitikaháya cha ...,"* not knowing then that *cha* was simply the conjunction and like the Latin *que* as in *virginibus puerisque*. I learnt from my father that this invocation to Shiva (who was regarded here as another aspect of Vishnu) is the foremost principle in the Shaiva tradition. It is here that the five-syllabic mantra *na-ma-shi-vá-ya* occurs, as it does in the Tamil Siva Puranam. I liked *Chamakam* in which another sound occurs frequently: *chame* (to me), meaning "May various favors be granted to me."

Vedic hymns must be learned with the proper intonation from an accredited guru. Their continued cultural power resides precisely in this dynamic and living aspect, not in the countless scholarly works that have been published on them in various languages.

There is an aphorism which says:

> *Gití síghree sirahkampí tatha likhita pátakah*
> *anarthajnah alpakanthascha shabdate pátakádhamah.*

Roughly translated, it means that there are six inferior modes of reciting the Vedas: reciting musically, reciting fast, reciting while shaking one's head, reciting from books, reciting without knowing the meaning, and reciting with a feeble voice. I must confess that, like many others I have engaged in all these prohibited modes. In some traditions one recites the scripture while swaying the whole body. This is known as *shokeling* in Yiddish.

Vedic recitation by priests in the context of sacraments is called *prayogam* - practice in rituals - which is different from *adhyáyanam*. Of course, one needs to be trained in adhyáyanam to engage in prayogam. Vedic culture was sophisticated not only in its insights and artistic expressions but also in its prescriptions and proscriptions of religious modes. It distinguishes between individual spiritual pursuits and collective ritualistic rules.

I am grateful to my father for insisting that I learn these magnificent hymns by rote. I studied them is slightly more depth after gaining some knowledge of Sanskrit, and I have derived fulfillment from the fact that I can recite them even as I read them in the original.

But I never experienced the profound spiritual thrill that more pious individuals feel in these matters. Much less have I understood the deeper esoteric meanings that are said to be couched in them, as explained in the writings of seers like Sri Aurobindo. I respect, but never envy, the heights from which mystics and masters speak and write about these. I am quite content with the modest light that is available to me from the lower non-mystical plane from which alone I am able to appreciate these. I am inclined to think that the Almighty will understand and excuse my situation.

That one needs to be trained for conducting religious services is appropriate, but that such training used to be (perhaps still is) available only to people born in certain families (castes) has always struck me as quite unfortunate. Such esotericism was practiced by the Pythagoreans of ancient Greece and the priest-class of ancient Egyptian religion. Whether it was needed or relevant in the distant past, it is no longer relevant. It is simply unacceptable in the value framework of the age in which we live. Thus, both in the context of our Zeitgeist and yugadharma, and in the interest of an evolving tradition one would hope that religious chanting will become the birthright of all Hindus, male and female. A culture that does not transform with time is bound to stagnate, if not die away. Given the dynamic nature of Hindu history, this change will also certainly.

II

Sounds and Structures: The Languages of India

Every language is a temple in which the soul of those who speak it is enshrined.

-Oliver Wendel Holmes

L'accent du pays où l'on est né demeure dans l'esprit et dans le coeur, comme dans le langage. (The accent of one's native country dwells in the mind and in the heart, as well as in the tongue.)

-La Rochefoucauld

Introduction

During a train ride from Calcutta to Madras (Chennai) along the eastern coast of India, I passed through regions where I heard four different languages: Bengali, Odiya, Telugu, and Tamil. A similar thing happened when I took a train from Amsterdam to Madrid: Dutch, Flemish, French, and Spanish. However, in

India each language has its own alphabet as different from each other as Cyrillic is from the Roman or Greek is from Hebrew.

Europeans understand this linguistic multiplicity better than Americans some of whom have asked me: "Do you speak Indian?" or "Do you speak Hindu?" But let us not laugh at others too quickly. Not many (even educated) Indians from the northern regions of India - some of whom are shocked by the ignorance of Westerners about India - can even list the principal languages spoken in South India, let alone name writers from these traditions. Not many Indians know where Kota and Konkani are spoken.

Like its lush tropical vegetation, India's linguistic tradition is also rich and variegated. At least thirty different languages are spoken in India, with some two thousand distinct dialects. In the words of a famous historian, "The Indian linguistic area is one of the larger areas involving hundreds of languages from four major language families — Indo-Aryan (a branch of Indo-European), Dravidian, Munda (Austro-Asiatic) and Tibeto-Burman (Sino-Tibetan); of these the first two have been the major contributors to the development of Indian culture and society and rich data of historical wealth are available from these." (Thapar, 1995, 62)

The major Indian languages which have deep roots in India are put under two broad categories. To the first group belong the ones with clearly Sanskritic roots, such as Hindi, Bengali, Odiya, Marathi, Gujarati, Punjabi, and Kashmiri. Their phonetics and alphabets have similarities. The second group of major Indian languages include Tamil, Telugu, Malayalam, and Kannada, each with its own alphabet. All the languages of India have impressive literary histories. Up until the nineteenth century much of this was religious poetry. During the past 150 years there has been an enormous output of literature of other genres as well.

Urdu is an enrichment of Hindi through Persian-Arabic influences. (Rai, 1984) The name Urdu is of Turkish origin, meaning an army or a tent. The language evolved during the centuries of Mogul rule in India. Aside from practically doubling the vocabulary of Hindi through Hindustani (as French did to English), Urdu has added much to Indic poetry, especially of the romantic kind. When one uses phrases like *meherbáni* (please) and *tashreef rakhiyé* (place your honor: please have a seat), one is using Urdu words.

Languages of what philologists call the Tibeto-Burman and the Munda groups are also spoken in India.

Some concerned Hindi lovers have been bemoaning the fact that Urdu and English are corrupting Hindi and making it obsolete. Though their complaints may sound xenophobic to some, one should not forget that sometimes cultural enrichment can stifle and extinguish the original culture which is being enriched. Some Amerindian languages have been victims of English intrusion.

This variety in the linguistic landscape of India may be compared to Europe where also there are two principal language groups - the Germanic and the Romance - geographically divided into northern and southern, as well as a number of others, like Celtic, Basque, Finnish, and the Slav languages outside of the two principal groups.

Language, race, and religion are the three most cementing forces in human culture. But they also become quite divisive. As in other polyglot nations, linguistic chauvinism separates the people of India more emphatically than would be the case if there had been only a single language. Thus, there have been language-based riots between Assamese and Bengalis, Marathis and Tamils. In 1952 Potti Sriramulu fasted to death for a separate state for people of his language group (Telugu), and posthumously achieved his goal. The perceived hegemony of Hindi which has the largest number of speakers (more than 400 million) once caused some resentment, provoking resistance to efforts to make Hindi the national language.

Even with all that, the languages of India are like flowers in a bouquet, each with its unique color, fragrance, and richness. To appreciate these qualities in any language, one needs to be acquainted with at least some of its sounds and songs. It has been my good fortune to run into people of different linguistic traditions. I have been touched by the beauty and wisdom in a few of them, but I don't believe that one language is inherently more melodious than another. Whether it is the sweetness of Bengali, the richness of Tamil, the lilting melody of Telugu, the nasal nuances of Malayalam, the Sanskritic coloration of Marathi, or the majesty of Hindi, each language is like a different musical instrument. The melodies created depend not just on the instrument, but one who wields it, and to some degree on how often one has listened to what is being played.

When one hears in Punjabi *tusee kado'n tak ávoge* (when will you return?); or in Marathi *usher karu náko!* (don't be late!); or in Bengali *kothai theke áschen?* (where are you coming from?); or in Guajarati *hun patra váchto ho'eesh* (I will read the letter); or in Malayalam *orálukku English padikkán eluppamánu* (it is easy for one to learn English); or in Hindi *yah bahút acchá hai* (this is very good); or in Telugu *ikkada rá!* (come here!); or in Kannada *návu yávágalu sathyavannu helabéku* (one should always speak the truth); or in Tamil *enakku onnumm puriyallai* (I don't understand anything); how one appreciates the sounds will depend on one's familiarity with them, and not to anything intrinsic in the language itself.

On Sanskrit

In my boyhood days I used to sit with my older brother when father did his daily puja. This often involved the rhythmic repetition of an *astottara shatha námávali* which consisted of a hundred and eight laudation of the Divine. This was my first exposure to Sanskrit sounds. Then there were bhajan songs and shlokas which I recited, without knowing what they meant. [Technically, a shloka refers to a prosodic meter – like the iambic tetrameter - developed in the Vedas, and used in the Ramayana and the Mahabharata. It is made up of four parts each of which has eight syllables. Thus, a shloka consists of sixteen syllables, generally in two lines.

When I was thirteen I had my *upanayanam* (investiture of the sacred thread), and this initiated me into mantras which I learned and repeated by rote.

When I was taking my first course in Latin I learned the word *ignis* for fire (root of the English word to ignite). I was struck by the similarity in the sounds *agni* and *ignis*. I decided to learn Sanskrit systematically. I bought a used copy of A. A. Macdonnell's Sanskrit Grammar (MacDonell, 1927) for less than a rupee, and began to study the language on my own. This was not too difficult, since I was familiar with the script through Hindi. I discovered that, as with Latin, one has to memorize declensions and conjugations in Sanskrit. Aside from the six cases of Latin, Sanskrit has instrumental and locative cases as well; like classical Greek, it has three numbers: singular, dual and plural. I was struck by the similarity between Sanskrit and Latin in *asti* and *est* (he is), between *smah* and *sumus* (we are), *santi* and *sunt* (they are). Some years later I discovered that William Jones had been struck by such similarities already in the eighteenth century.

The oft-repeated prayer:

> tvameva mátá ca pitá tvameva
> tvameva bandbhus ca sakhá tvameva
> tvameva vidyám dravinam tvameva
> tvameva sarvam mama deva deva:
> You are my mother and my father,
> You are my kin, and you are friend.
> You are knowledge, you are a treasure,
> You are the All, my Divine, O Divine

became more interesting now.

I began to translate every Sanskrit prayer I came across into English. The result was that what once sounded serene and magical now became merely descriptive and interesting. It occurred to me that the reverence for religious invocations arises in the Hindu world and probably elsewhere too, not so much from their meanings as from intonation and the hoary cultural context. Some of our prayers, if translated into Engligh, would sound strange, if not meaningless. A treatise on quantum physics may sound less strange in Swahili than *Om padmanábháya namah* does in English. Likewise, for some things there is an appropriate language. It is difficult to evoke religious feelings for ancient utterances in modern languages because our thought processes have been profoundly modified. Whenever I participate in an *Akhand Pát* (the continuous reading of Tulsidas's *Ramacharitramanas*) session or in the recitation of *Hanuman Chalisa* (the Forty Four-syllabic meters consecrated to Hanuman), I choose to simply partake of the spiritual experience that comes from the reading, and not bring their meanings to mind. Mantras are for utterance, not for analysis.

Sanskrit is an ancient language, but still is very vibrant. Like Latin and Greek, it has an impressive body of literature which is studied and commented upon by scholars and students all over the world. Speaking of Latin and Greek, one may recall the oft-quoted hearty appraisal of Sanskrit by William Jones, the founder of the Royal Asiatic Society. Jones famously declared:

> "The Sanskrit language, whatever be its antiquity, is of a wonderful structure; more perfect than the Greek, more copious than the Latin, and more exquisitely refined than either, yet bearing to both of them a stronger affinity, both in the roots of verbs and in the forms of grammar, than could possibly have been produced by accident; so strong, indeed, that no philologer could examine them all three, without believing them to have sprung from some common source, which, perhaps, no longer exists."

This was long before the allegedly mischievous motivation for dreaming up the *Aryan Invasion Theory* came into effect. Today, people with little knowledge of other languages or cultural history pontificate on the Internet on the roots of languages in emotionally charged ways.

Like Hebrew, Greek, and Arabic, Sanskrit is closely linked to the scriptures of a major religion. For this reason, it is regarded by the devout as the language of the Gods: through it, Divinity is said to have communicated with mortals. To me, all languages are sacred, and none more divine than another.

Sanskrit is, more importantly, the backbone of Indic culture. Hymns in sacred Sanskrit are recited with precision on festive occasions and it is used in solemn sacraments everywhere in the Hindu world. Even to an untrained ear, it is a supremely uplifting experience to listen to Sanskrit verses chanted by skilled pundits who have mastered the phonetics, prosody, and rhythm of the language. The grandeur of Sanskrit *shlokas* deeply touches the accustomed Hindu heart. There is a magic in ancient tongues in which the Divine has been invoked generation after generation, that minds molded solely by modernity have difficulty experiencing.

Contrary to what some have said, Sanskrit is by no means a dead language. If anything, it is culturally very much alive. It is recognized as one of more than two scores of official languages of India. What is true is that Sanskrit is not mother-tongue to any child. But it is also true that it is mother tongue to a whole culture. Sanskrit compositions more than 3500 years old have not just survived, they continue to have profound cultural impact. A great many philosophical works, religious poetry, plays and maxims, as well as technical writings in mathematics and medicine exist in classical Sanskrit. The great poets and philosophers who have written in the language, including the authors of the epics, have had enormous spiritual and aesthetic impact on Indic civilization and beyond.

To this day, experts lecture and debate in Sanskrit with ease and intellectual elevation, like Latin at the Vatican. Not long ago I attended a Vedanta Conference held at Miami University in Oxford, Ohio, where, in one session, all the papers read and the ensuing discussions were in Sanskrit. Even radio broadcasts are now made in Sanskrit. As an ancient language that has flourished for millennia, Sanskrit has undergone modifications over time. Vedic Sanskrit is not the same as that of a later poet like Kalidasa, nor is Kalidasa's Sanskrit the same as that of some modern writers.

Sanskrit is one of the few languages whose name is not affiliated to a people or a place. The name Sanskrit literally means that which is made, polished, or cultured. The culture of a people is known in Sanskrit (and derived languages) as a people's *sanskriti*. Echoes of Sanskrit can certainly be heard in many modern languages, both Indian and Non-Indian. Sanskrit roots may be detected in a number of English words. For instance, the words *punch, door, royal, pedestal,* and *center* are all cognate to Sanskrit words.

Tamil

Tamil (*Tamizh* as it is called by its speakers) is the first language I learned. So, I have a special fondness for it. It is a very interesting and unusual language in syntax, vocabulary, and idiomatic genius. The classification on Indian languages into Dravidian and other groups was the work of a scholar by the name of Robert Caldwell, inspired primarily by linguistic considerations.

Tamil is spoken primarily by the inhabitants of the state of Tamil Nadu in India, and by millions more in other regions of the world where Tamils have settled down in large numbers. Some scholars say that the language is as old as Latin and Greek. This may be true, but I have never been persuaded that the greatness of a culture or tradition or language for that matter is proportional to its antiquity. So claims to the effect that Tamil or Hindu culture goes back to ten thousand years, as asserted by some inspired patriots, have never moved me to thump my chest.

In classical times, the Tamil people were cautious in adopting words of foreign vintage. Rules were spelled out for borrowing words into Tamil, not unlike the *Académie Française* that stipulates which words can enter French dictionaries. There have been movements to preserve the chastity of Tamil from what is regarded as Sanskritic verbal contamination. (Ramaswami,

1997) But today, practically every third word spoken by many so-called educated Tamilians is English or an Americanism.

The link between Sanskrit and Tamil is intriguing. In some ways the languages look like distant cousins. In other ways they are like old and very close friends. It has been argued, usually by people who have no knowledge of Tamil, that attempts to view Sanskrit and Tamil as belonging to different language-families arose from sinister motives on the part of cunning Europeans to divide and rule the people of India, and that only Indian victims of Eurocentric brainwashing continue to uphold this theory. On the other hand, some scholars have suggested that Tamil has ancient Sumerian origins.

I am unable to understand the annoyance among (Tamil-ignorant) North Indian Hindus who fear that such a division would acknowledge a cultural separateness of the Tamils from the Vedic-Sanskritic culture that has always prevailed in the North. Given that millions of Africans and Indonesians, Iranians and Pakistanis – all belonging to different ethnic and linguistic groups are devout Muslims and feel a transnational religious brotherhood, I don't see why Tamils and Gujaratis cannot form as similar cultural bond, even if they were speaking languages belonging to different families. In any case, I have lost interest in these insidious and hate-mongering cultural quarrels which are driven more by unpleasant political forces and confused ethnic pride than by any scientific understanding of languages or their evolution.

The Tamil language is rich in synonyms: Often a pure Tamil word has a Sanskrit-derived equivalent. Thus, we have the following examples of pure Tamil = Sanskritized Tamil = English:

sakala = ella = all; nádu = désam = country; araci = ráni = queen; piranda nádu = janma bhúmi = native land.

So we can write two perfectly correct Tamil sentences one of which can be more or less understood by a North Indian language speaker, while the other will be totally opaque to one who knows no Tamil:

Tamil 1 (Pure): ellá náttugalikkum araci ennudaiya piranda nádu.

Tamil 2 (Sanskritized): sakala désangalukkum ráni, en janma bhúmi.

Bengali: shokol déshé ráni amár jonma bhúmi.

English: The queen of all nations, my native land (is).

My father (Shree P. S. Varadaraja Aiyar) was a Tamil scholar. He had authored books on Siva Puranam and Tamil culture. He deepened my love for Tamil. I studied Kamba Ramayanam and Tirukkural with him, and used to attend his lectures on various aspects of Tamil literature at the Bharati Tamil Sangam in Kolkata (of which he was a founding member). I had a Tamil teacher (Aramudam Iyengar) who inspired me to learn Tamil grammar and poetry. I remember his quoting the verse:

> yádum úr yávarum kélír
> tídum nandrum pirartara vará
> nódalum tanidalum avatrór anna
> cádalum puduvu andré.
> It is all my town, where I'm in.
> Whoever they are, they too are my kin.
> Evil and good do not ensue
> From what others may, or may not do
> Aching and relief are likewise too,
> Even death is not something new.

These are the first few lines of a poem thrice as long, written by a little known poet called Kanian Púnkundran. The first

Tamil line above (which I have translated in two English lines) is known even to some Non-Tamils. It expresses an enlightened vision that occurred to very few in the ancient world.

Kaniyan was a poet of the Sangkam (ancient Tamil) age. It was a time when many poets sang the glories of chieftains and kings, of the territories and kingdom where they lived. Kaniyan lived in the town of Púngkundru. He felt that a poet ought to write about ideas, principles, and nature, rather than extol the local ruler. He had no affiliation for any particular place or potentate. So he wrote this poem which essentially says that he regarded every place as his own, and all human beings as his own kin. Like Shakespeare's "To be or not to be," this line is known to practically all Tamils who have even a modicum of education in their language and culture, except that not all may know the name of the author. The pithy motto of this poem deserves to be reflected upon by people of all castes and faiths, of all races and nations, for it expresses quite simply the humanity that binds us all. Later in the poem Kaniyan goes on to say that he will not pay homage to people simply because they are rich, nor look down upon those that are not.

We are reminded of the Latin playwright Terence who had written in a similar vein, *Homo sum, humani nil a me alienum puto*: I am a man, and nothing of the human condition can be foreign to me.

I remember reflecting a lot on a line of another poet called Náladiyár. His line was written in the seventh or eighth: *nalla kulam endrum tíya kulam endrum cholluvadu allál porul illai*. It is meaningless to say that one is of a good or of a bad lineage: an obvious criticism of the caste system. I have often wondered why thinkers like this had only marginal impact on the practice of the people of India. These were perhaps simply expressions of anger and frustration by bold minds at a system that was unjust to a great many members of society.

Tamil poets and philosophers have composed an enormous body of fascinating works. Works of spiritual value in Tamil have inspired millions of people. Their impact on the culture and temple-life of the Tamil country has been immense too. Outsiders – some of them Christian missionaries - have also contributed to the growth and propagation of Tamil language and literature. Practically every foreign scholar who has studied Tamil has had only the highest praise for the language and its literature. In Rev. Percival's view: "Perhaps no language combines greater force with equal brevity than Tamil, and it may be asserted that no human speech is more close and philosophic in its expression as an exponent of the mind." (Percival, 1854).

For a few months in 1957 it was my privilege to teach conversational Tamil to some students at the *Institut des Langues Orientales* in Paris while I was taking a course in Russian there.

I have often felt that the richness and insights of Tamil sages have not received the universal attention, let alone acclamation they deserve, even within India. To this day, there are Hindus of the Northern tradition who have not even heard of Murugan and Máriyamman, much less of the Azhvárs and the Náyanmárs. Even erudite scholars who write knowledgeably on Hinduism for the English-speaking world make only scant reference, if they do at all, to its Tamil dimensions. This is because they themselves know little on the subject.

A global view of Indic culture must recognize the Tamil components of India's rich traditions, because they offer some superb poetry and philosophy of the Hindu-Jain world. Unfortunately, they are clothed in a language that is regarded as difficult by many people. Though many Tamil classics have been translated, it is not easy to derive the same aesthetic experience in another language as from the originals. Translations are pale echoes, like amateurish copies of a Rubens or a Raphael, or a papier-maché version of the Pietá of Michelangelo, the Thinker of Rodin or the sculptures of Khajuraho: only a little of the glory of the originals is reflected in imitations.

On Banglabhasha and Bengal

Since I grew up in Kolkata, I learned to speak Banglabhasha (as the language is called by its speakers) with friends, vegetable vendors, grocery shopkeepers, and eventually with some professors at the university. During the first decade of my life, I began to familiarize myself with the Bengali script by looking at sign boards on Calcutta stores, where they are (used to be) inscribed both in Bengali and in English (Latin) characters. Then one summer I took a systematic course with a Bengali primer, which enabled me to read little books in the language. Since I have always loved Bengal, it was an honor for me to serve for a year as President of the *Bengali Association of Rochester*, New York, in the 1980s.

Aside from acquiring more than a smattering of Bangla to carry on decent conversations, I learned to appreciate Rabindra Sangeet (or *Robindro Shongeet*, as it is pronounced in Bengali). No one who has experienced the sweetness of Bengali poetry and heard this marvelous music can be insensitive to the charming intonations of this mellifluous idiom, which, in beauty of sound and richness of heritage, let alone in the linguistic pride of its practitioners, has been called "the French language of the East." (Ganathe, 1997). On February 21, 1952, many students in Bangladesh, in their demand that their language be made the national language of (the then) East Pakistan, exposed themselves to bullets from the army, and quite a few of them died as language-martyrs. (Uddin, 2006)

Bangla is abundant in prose, poetry and plays, and graced by the works of countless creative writers. One of the earliest of them was Baru Chandidas who like others of the time, wrote of the Radha-Krishna amour (*Sri Krishna Kírtan*). Chandidas is perhaps best known for his strikingly modern assertion *Shobar upor manush shotto tahar upore nai*: Above all is human, truly nothing is above that. This reminds us of Walt Whitman's line in *Leaves of Grass*, "If anything is sacred, the human body is sacred."

The religious spirit, powerful in shaping the culture and outlook of the Indian people, found grand expressions in Bengal through devotional singers, eloquent interpreters and revered saints. These may be found in the poetic outpourings of Joydeb, the Krishna songs of Shree Chaitanya Mahaprapbhu, the saintliness of Sri Ramakrishna, the inspired speeches of Swami Vivekananda, and the mystic visions of Sri Aurobindo. In the nineteenth century, Bengal gave rise to religious reform movements, which tried to forge new paths and patterns in a changing world. In this context, we recall Raja Ram Mohun Roy, the Brahmo Samaj, and Keshab Chandra Sen.

I am sure Bengal continues to produce great men and women, but truth to say, we have not seen of late many of the stature of the nineteenth and early twentieth century Bengali cultural, literary, and political giants.

Hindi

My Hindi teacher at school was a Gandhian. He only wore khadi (home-spun cloth), and he always had a Gandhi cap. Those were the days when the British still ruled India and nationalist feelings were strong. We took pride in learning Hindi. Lads in white shorts and shirts used to shout *Jai Hind!* with great fervor. Our teacher taught us to sing Iqbal's patriotic song, "*sáré jahán sé achchá Hindustan hamárá…*" (Of all the world, our India is the best!) It is not unlike *Deutschland über Alles, Que Viva España, America the Beautiful,* and other similar patriotic songs which fill the hearts of people with parochial pride.

This is fine as long as it doesn't provoke one into disrespectful attitudes towards others. Although I loved that song when I used to sing it, and like to hear it even now, in my more mature years I seldom appreciate expressions of nationalistic comparative greatness of cultures. To say that our country is great is acceptable. But to say that our country is greater than any other may sound fine to people of the nation, but ridiculous to outsiders. But it seldom becomes as dangerous as the conviction that one's religion is the best or the only valid religion that all must embrace.

Our teacher was fond of reciting Hindi poems, both classical and modern. His favorite poet was the 14th century saint Kabir. I remember our teacher's quote one day from the saint: *Játi pati púchai na koi, hari ko bhaje so hari hoi* (Ask not for one's caste; one who recites the Lord's name becomes one with him)."

Hindi is the major language of India. It is one of the most widely spoken languages in the world: According to the 2001 census some 422 million people claim Hindi or one of its variants as their mother tongue. It is also the national language of India.

A descendent of Sanskrit through Prakrit, some scholars have traced the origins of Hindi back to seventh century Bhutanese monks. From the fourth century C.E. on, Hindi used the Brahmi script, but since the eleventh century it has been written with the Devanagari alphabet.

Modern Hindi has many local variants and dialects, generally divided into the Eastern and the Western modes of expression, bearing such names as Bhojpuri, Maithili, Rajasthani,

Braj, and more. Prior to the nineteenth century, literature in Hindi consisted largely of poetry and religious songs. (Shapiro, 2001, 305-309) Modern Hindi literature, however, is rich in many other ways also. Poetry, prose, novels, essays, short stories, biographies, criticisms, and scientific works, may all be found today in Hindi books and journals. But the old works of Bhakta Kabir, Tulsi Das and Sur Das continue to be read, and they still evoke joy and admiration from the masses.

In a strange sort of way the history of the development of Hindi is associated with the name of an Englishman by the name of John Gilchrist who arrived in India in the 1780's as a surgeon in the service of the British East India Company. This man was fascinated by Indian languages. He adopted the costume of the people and traveled widely in India. In 1796 he published the first *Grammar of the Hindoostanee Language*. In 1800 the Fort William College was established, and Gilchrist became the Head of that institution. He brought together a number of native scholars and asked them to develop a series of works to assist the British in their study of local languages. (Kidwai, 1972). It was in this context that the eminent Pundit Sri Lallu Lal wrote works which were truly trail blazers in modern Hindi literature. (Jindal, 1955).

Hindi has its simple forms in the village dialects, and its sophisticated modes among writers and public speakers. It has a majesty when it is spoken with the purity of Sanskrit-derived words alone - as was presented in the Ramayana and Mahabharata TV series which had only a few anachronistic Urdu words here and there. When Hindi is fused with Urdu words and delivered in political speeches, it acquires another kind of charm all its own which is no less pleasing to hear.

I once sat in the Calcutta *Maidan*, one among several thousands, listening to Pundit Jawaharlal Nehru orate in

Hindustani. It was a thrilling experience. As I noted earlier, there are Hindi enthusiasts who lament the dilution of chaste (Sanskritic) Hindi with impure words of Urdu vintage. Though there is merit to the fear that Hindi may ultimately become a bastardized linguistic mélange of languages with radically different cultural roots, such concerns often reflect a naiveté regarding languages: Like organisms and cultures, languages evolve, and in that very process become enriched. Languages that don't do this become stagnant and sterile.

I recall reading some *dohe* (couplets) of Vrind Kavi of medieval times as part of our prescribed texts, but I enriched my vocabulary when I plodded through Premchand's *Nirmala* with a Hindi-English dictionary for frequent consultation. Recently I came across an English edition of this work. (Premchand, 2008)

The novel is a powerful portrayal of social evils. Nirmala was to marry a young man, but when her father died unexpectedly, the prospective groom left her for a woman who brought him a heftier dowry. This left the heroine to marry a much older widower who would settle for much less. The theme is ancient, and current too. There have always been thinkers and writers exposing the corruption in their societies, but their impact tends to be slow, often too slow.

Once it was hoped that Hindi would completely replace English in India by the 1960s, and would become the sole national language. But there were severe protests to this plan in some parts of India, notably in the south and in Bengal. Because these sometimes became violent, it was decided not to impose Hindi on those who are reluctant to adopt it. But Hindi continues to be one of the major official languages of India. Given its vitality, richness, and potential, it can certainly be a proud representative of the Indian people in the international arena. It is very likely that if and when India becomes a permanent member of the

U.N. Security Council, its representatives will (may have to) speak in Hindi. But I am not sure that, as of now, all members of the Indian bureaucracy speak Hindi fluently.

On Konkani and Konkanis

I recall a heated exchange more than five decades ago, in the coffee room of the *Maison Internationale* at the Cité Universitaire in Paris. I asked a new-made friend from Goa what languages he spoke besides English and French. Portuguese and Marathi, he told me, and added that his own mother tongue was Konkani. A Marathi student who was also there added, "Konkani is a dialect of Marathi." A small portion of hell broke loose. The student from Goa, became furious, and said this was pure nonsense, and that though there are commonalties between Marathi and a version of Konkani spoken in Maharashta, the latter was as much a language as Marathi. Later I discovered that the marginalization of Konkani by Maharashtrians has a long history.

The name of the student in question was Manoharrai Sar Desai. He was to become an eminent scholar and highly respected professor and propagator of Konkani, receiving the title of "Chevalier de L'Ordre des Palmes Académiques" from the French government for his contributions to the spread of French language.

While browsing in a bookstore in India some years later, I chanced to see a book by him, entitled *On the History of Konkani Literature* (Sar Desai, 2000). He has become one of the activists who had worked for the recognition of his language. Two lines from this poet reminded me of the exchange between Marathi and Konkani:

> *Phulak Sangle Phulunaka*
> *Phulan Sangle Ullovnaka.*

> The flower was asked not to blossom
> The flower said, Keep quiet!

In two simple lines the poet has compressed two great truths: More dominant cultures often try to snub less powerful ones, and the latter often say, "To hell with you!" and develop all the same.

Since I was brought up as a strict Tamil vegetarian, I used to wonder about Brahmins in Bengal eating fish liberally. I discovered that Konkani Brahmins do the same.

At one time Konkani was spoken primarily by large numbers of people in and around the Goa region. There are references to this in the Mahabharata. This was before the Portuguese came to the scene. Their intrusion led to many unhappy things for the Konkani people. Many of them, out of fear of being converted to Christianity or of facing other dire consequences, moved to Karnataka, Kerala, and elsewhere. They served their culture by spreading it far and wide. But those who stayed and survived in Goa also served their language in a different way. For it is thanks to them that there is now a state in India - Goa - whose official language is Konkani. The hand of history can compose utterly unexpected narratives. Who could have imagined that the landing of Vasco da Gama on Indian shores would lead one day to the dispersal of the Konkani people to different regions in India, or to the creation of an Indian State whose language would be Konkani?

Some say that Konkani derives its name from the words *kum*: Mother earth and *kana*: dust. It has therefore been argued that Konkanis were worshippers of Mother Earth because they were farmers for the most part. It is difficult to be too sure of the etymology of many Indian names. It is also said by other scholars that Konkani used to be called *Brahmananchi Bhas*: language of the Brahmins, because it was the language of the so-called Sarasvat-Brahmins. Their name derives from the ancient River Sarasvati which is now playing a major role in the resurgence of Hindu culture.

Konkani is unique in being perhaps the only language in the world which is written in four different scripts: Devanagari, Kannada, Malayalam, and English (Roman). Goan Konkini may be the only Indian language which uses Roman script. Once, during a trip to Lisbon, I discovered that there is a Konkani version of the Mahabharata, entirely in Roman script, in a library there.

Because of their Diaspora, Konkani writers have contributed to the literature of five different languages: Konkani, Portuguese, Kannada, Malayalam, and English. Speaking of contributions by people of Konkan origin, I am reminded of The *Consortium of the Americas for Interdisciplinary Science* founded by the prolific Konkani physicist Vasudev M. Kenkre at the University of New Mexico. (http://consortium.unm.edu/BasicIdea.html)

The purpose of this unique institution is to serve scientific investigators of the Spanish-Portuguese speaking world in Latin America. We may recall that Europeans have gone to distant lands and established schools, hospitals, sanatoriums and such. But there are not too many instances in modern times of people from India going beyond their shores and establishing centers and institutions that serve people not of their own kind, and not for the purpose of spreading Vedanta. The center established by the Konkani physicist is a prime example of this unusual kind.

Punjabi

A close friend in my boyhood days was a Sikh whose father was a well known figure in the local Punjabi community. I learnt a good deal about the Sikh tradition and a little about the Punjabi language from my association with his family. It was during a visit to the Gurudwara on Rash Behary Avenue in Calcutta that I first saw the Gurmukhi script and learned about it. What struck me when I got acquainted with it are the following: Unlike most alphabets, Gurmukhi does not start with the a-sound. Its first letter is pronounced as *oorhá*. Unlike other Indian languages, the Punjabi alphabet has only three vowels. Every letter of the alphabet, except for one, is sounded with an *a*-ending: oorha, erha, sa or sussa, ha or haha, ..., la or lulla, va or vava, ... Secondly, the alphabetical system was artificially constructed in the sixteenth century by a known historical personality: Guru Angad Dev who was the second Guru of the tradition. The only other alphabet (that I know of) whose origin is clearly known, is that of Russian. The Russian alphabet is named after Saint Cyril. It was invented by St. Kliment of Ohrid in the tenth century.

Another feature of the Punjabi language is that, like Konkani, it is written in more than one script: Gurumukhi (or Gurmukhi) and Urdu. Equally interesting, some Muslim Punjabis in India read and write Gurmukhi while many Hindu Punjabis still read and write in the Urdu script.

The emergence of early Punjabi literature has been traced to Perso-Arabic sources on one hand, and to the Sanskritic currents on the other. The finest ideals of Islamic brotherhood and Sufi mysticism merged with the age-old visions of Vedic wisdom to create the earliest literary expressions of the Punjabi language. Thus, the richness of the Punjabi literary heritage arose from the fertilization of two different cultural streams and the synthesis of two major religious traditions. Guru Nanak, founding father of Sikhism, was a prophet who was both preacher and poet. His aesthetic sensibilities were as keenly developed as his sense of religious mission. So his prayer for the morning, known as *Jap Sahib*, is as much poetry as praise of the Lord. All the Gurus were poetically inclined, and so the scriptural treasure of Sikhism, called the *Guru Granth Sahib*, is sublime literature as much as uttered religion. The theme of unity in diversity is expressed beautifully in Sikh scripture in the line: "There are six schools of philosophy, six teachers, and six sets of teachings. But the Teacher of teachers is the One, who appears in so many forms." That teacher of teachers is the Divine.

There also evolved in Punjabi the biographical genre of hagiography. Known as *Janam Sakhis* these combine history with the life-stories of the Gurus. Seva Ram and Gyan Singh are counted among the great authors of those works. In the eighteenth century some Muslim writers also began to compose in Punjabi. Today Punjabi authors write works in Punjabi and also in Hindi and English.

Every history of Punjabi literature mentions Bhai Vir Singh, an incredibly prolific writer by any standard. He was the founder of the *Singh Sabha* or Punjabi Society. His literary output spans a vast array of writings that include prose and poetry, fiction and theological dissertations. (Talib, Singh, 1973) Through his writings Vir Singh infused a sense of enormous cultural pride and identity in the Sikh people who, in the face of British occupation and well-meaning big-brotherly Hindu embrace, were much inspired by his works.

Of the many other members of the *Singh Sabha*, one often mentions Kahan Singh as one of the most illustrious. He authored an *Encyclopedia of Sikhism*, a mammoth scholarly achievement in any language. (McLeod, W. H., 1989) Charan Singh gained popularity through his sense of humor, while countless others published verses and inspired poetry of varying worth.

Recently I came across an interesting book entitled *The Rise of Sikhs Abroad*. (Singh, 2003) Its author perceptively reminds his Punjabi readers: "Punjabi's capacity to affect our thinking is shrinking every day and conversely our ability to conceptualize and memorize English is increasing every day. If this approach holds ground then we will become less and less Punjabi and more and more English or *modern*." Gurumukh Singh's worry may be valid only for the children of NRI Punjabis.

On the other hand, this statement is equally applicable to other languages of India and not only of the Non-Western world. Whatever communicational convenience the global spread of English might be bringing, thoughtful people have expressed the fear that it has serious implications for the preservation of cultural identities. Many thinkers all over the world - from France and Russia to India and China - are worried about this unintended negative impact of English on other cultures. And yet, ironically, the languages of India, including Punjabi, have been flourishing and growing as never before in their history *after* their contact with English.

As to languages molding our modes of thought it is not the language that does this, but the ideas, values and worldviews which change with breakthroughs in science, innovations in technology, and broadening of perspectives. If this happens in any language, so much the better for it.

Telugu

When war broke out in Europe in 1939, India was also affected because it was part of the British Empire. Japan joined in and encroached into Burma. Calcutta was exposed to nightly bombings from Japanese planes. During this evacuation (as it was called) many people left the city. Our family moved to a town called Berhampur in Ganjam district in what is now Odisha State. At that time, this was a place where Telugu was spoken by a large number of people.

During our stay in Berhampur Ganjam, a Telugu gentleman used to come to our home thrice a week to give me private lessons. I used to squat on the shady porch of the Gangaraj Bungalow where we stayed. This teacher taught me some English, arithmetic, and a few Telugu letters, words and phrases. I was struck by the fact that the Telugu *a* is almost a mirror image of the Tamil *a*. Through contacts with neighbors, servants, shopkeepers, and others, I acquired a smattering of the language, a little more than simple words like *ikkada* (here), *akkada* (there) and *ekkada* (where), *émandi* (what, sir?) *kúchchandi* (sit, sir!) and *cheppandi* (say, sir!) I was struck by the fact that except for a few initial consonants, there was no straight line in any letter of the Telugu alphabet.

This teacher told me stories about Tanali Raman, a prankster who is said to have entertained with his wit and wisecracks Krishna Deva Raya, the sixteenth century emperor of Vijayanagaram kingdom, who is said to have described Telugu as the sweetest of all Indian languages. In the Telugu tradition, Tanali Raman is one of the eight poets who graced the court of the famous king who was himself a poet. I recall a quip this teacher told me. Once, a Sanskrit scholar at the king's court said something to the effect that compared to the golden chain of Sanskrit poetry Telugu ones were like iron chains. Before he could explain what he meant, Tenali Raman replied that such a chain would be ideal to control the pundits who prowl like wild elephants through the jungles of Sanskrit.

During the glory days of the Vijayanagaram Empire, language, literature, art and culture reached a zenith (Majumdar, 1951). It was during this time that *Prabhandha*, a new literary genre evolved in the language. It could be in prose or in poetry form, often a story about some royal or divine personage of ancient times. It is composed with great literary skill and imagination.

Telugu literature had started a few centuries earlier. Nannaya Bhattu, Tikkana Somayaji, and Errapragada are regarded as the Kavi Trayamu (Triumvirate of Poets) who began the Telugu literary tradition. All three rendered the Mahabharata in Telugu, one after the other, between the tenth and the thirteenth centuries. Nannaya is called the Adi Kavi or first poet: a title conferred on Valmiki, the author of the Sanskrit Ramayana (Chenchiah, Rao, 1988).

In my later years I came across the name of another Telugu poet, by the name of Vemana who is said to have lived in the fifteenth century. Little is known about the man. The collection of his sayings covers a wide range of topics (Narla, 1969). It embodies much commonsensical wisdom, like:

> "Cows may come in different colors, but the milk they give is always white."
> "Flowers vary in forms and fragrance, but they all may be used to worship God."
> "Faiths may be different in forms, but the God they preach is one and the same."

Vemana spoke out against traditional modes: "Not in earth or metal, not in wood or stone, nor in painted walls or images, can we perceive the great Spirit." Long before Thomas Jefferson, Vemana wrote, "If we look through all the earth, Men, we see, have equal birth, made in one great brotherhood, and equal in the sight of God."

Here are a few more nuggets in the Telugu originals with translations:

> *Anuvu gani chota Nadhikulamanaradu*
> *Kochmayina nadiyu kodava gadu*

konda addamandu knochami undada
Viswadhaabhiraama, Vinura Vema
When it is not our place or time, we cannot win
You have not become small because of this.
Don't you know the hill looks small in a mirror
Beloved of the Bounteous, Vema, listen!
Apadiana velanarasi bandhula judu
bhayamuvela judu bantu tanamu
Pedavela judu pendlamu gunamu
Viswadhaabhuraama, Vinura Vema
In times of distress, observe the attitude of relatives.
In times of fear, observe the behavior of the army.
In times of poverty, observe the nature of the wife.
Beloved of the Bounteous, Vema, listen!
Chippalonabadda chinuku mutyambayye
nitabadda chinuku nita galise
Brapti galugu chota phalamela tappura
Viswadhaabhiraama, Vinura Vema
The rain drop that fell on the shell became a pearl.
The one that fell in water merged with water
If something is yours, you are sure to get it.
Beloved of the Bounteous, Vema, listen!
(Brown, 2007).

But here is an unhappy note on history. They called Vemana a non-Hindu because of his rebellious stance on mindless orthodoxy, but he was as much a Hindu as any Veda-chanting, yajña-performing, caste-respecting dharmi. Herein lies the strength, sanctity, and security of Hinduism. Every thinker, writer, and worshiper of every mode has a place in the culture. The guardians of the traditional mode cannot keep errant thinkers suppressed for long. If the likes of Vemana had held the day, who knows what intellectual revolutions Hindu society might have undergone in earlier centuries! The battles in human civilization are not just military, nor even only between good and evil. Often they are between enlightened and obscurantist ways of looking at the world. And Vemana was on the side of light.

Because of his unorthodox views, not only were Vemana's poems scrupulously excluded from general publications of Telugu poetry, his name was not even mentioned by scholars and compendia of great Telugu writers. Sadly for West-baiters, it was a European scholar (C. P. Brown) who re-discovered Vemana and brought him to the attention of the modern world that it deserves. It is shocking to read that when "The Verses of Vemana: Moral, Religious and Satirical" was first published in 1829, 450 of the 500 copies "were rolled up as waste paper and tucked away in the lumber room of the College library" by orthodox guardians of culture.

In his satire and *écrasez l'infâme* attitude, Vemana was a Voltaire of his times. Instead of the Bastille, he suffered oblivion. He was cryptic in his sayings, and was not without a touch of humor. Yet, he was no cold rationalist. Only he who has compassion for his fellow-men's sufferings deserves to be called a human being, he declared.

Compositions of a religious nature also abound in Telugu literature. The most illustrious name here is Thyagaraja, poet and musical composer extraordinaire, the Hindu Johann Sebastian Bach. His melodious expressions of intense piety have moved the hearts and touched the souls of millions even beyond the Telugu-speaking world. Thyagaraja's music flowed from his heart. Through his sublime music he not only experienced but also communicated to others the Divine, especially in its incarnation as Sri Rama. Incidents from the saga of Rama and from the Puranas were translated into ragas that move the devout to tears of joy (Raghvan, 2007).

I recall hearing about his music for the first time when I used to eavesdrop on my sister's music lessons, and the staid teacher used to instruct her on Thaygaraja and the richness of Carnatic music. One of my favorite Thyagaraja songs is *ninuvinà nàmadi*, in the *navarasa kannada raga* with *rúpaka tàlam*. I used to listen enraptured to the words in mellifluous Telugu:

> *ninnu viná námadi endu niluvadé shrí hari*
> *kanulaku ní sogasentó grammi unnadi ganuka ...*
> Other than Thou, my mind rests on nothing else, Oh Shri Hari,
> My eyes are filled with Thy beauty...
> Your stories fill my ears, Rama
> Your name is constantly resonating in my mouth, because...
> Wherever I look I see only you ...

But printed words do little justice to the divine music of the saintly composer. That musical joy can be experienced only when one hears them actualized by a trained human voice.

Telugu also came into the modern age in the nineteenth century. In this context, Viresalingam is unanimously regarded as one of the founders of modern Telugu literature. As with other pioneering writers, he used his talents to expose and condemn prevailing social evils. In the 1930s some Telugu writers began to experiment with new forms such as blank verse and surrealist modes of expression. Just as Marxists urge us to think of the forced labor involved in the construction of Pyramids rather than admire their impressive dimensions, so too some Telugu writers suggested a similar approach in our admiration of the Taj

Mahal. Works in the more usual forms of literature, such as the novel and the short story, drama and essays, continue to grow. At the same time, English education in India notwithstanding the Telugu publishing world brings out books on science, politics, economics and sociology.

As an instance of intertwining multiculturalism, bilingualism is quite common in India. Many people speak Tamil and Telugu with equal ease. The saint Ramana Maharishi—a Tamil by birth—is known to have composed verses in Telugu.

An irony of history: Andhrapradesh was carved out because of protests demanding a separate state for people who speak Telugu. This was good, but the capital of then state, Hyderabad, was named after a Muslim king. Formerly Tamil and Telugu were the major languages of the so-called Madras Presidency. Now Urdu and Telugu are co-equal languages in that capital. This may not have been what the Andhra patriot Sri Potti Sriramulu who fasted unto death for a Telugu Desam and his many followers had in mind. Incidentally, the formation of this explicitly language-based state put an end to a fresh dream of the founders of modern India: to form a country where linguistic differences would not be part of a sub-national identity, and where there would be true national integration transcending people's mother tongues.

Marathi

My contacts with Marathi arose from my father's involvement with the Shirdi Sai Baba movement. It was a Maharashtrian who brought this saint of the first decades of the twentieth century to our family's attention. I was about eleven years old then. We used to attend bhajans in the home of that Maharashtrian family where I heard the refrain: "*jaya, jaya Panduranga Rakhumaayee, jaya jaya Pandaripura Rakhumaayee.*" The tune still rings in my years. At that time, I had no idea what these names meant.

Many years later I discovered that Panduranga refers to an aspect of Krishna as worshiped in Maharashtra. Devotion to Panduranga is an extremely powerful factor in the cultural framework of the Maharashtrian people, but it has also spread to other regions of South India. I found it interesting, but also surprising that this name means: *One Who is White*. Rakhumai is the Mahatrashtrian version of Rukmani, Krishna's wife. Thus one was paying homage to the White Rukmani. Pandaripura is one of the most frequented places of pilgrimage in Maharashtra.

Generally speaking, Shiva is represented as white, and Vishnu as dark (black or blue). This is because Shiva is regarded as the essence of *tamas:* dark and destructive; while Vishnu represents *sattva*: shining and bright. But in order to remind us that the two are reciprocally valid and mutually complementary, and that one cannot be without the other, their representations are sometimes given colors which are opposite to the essences each represents. Some say that initially the name Panduranga was used only for Shiva.

Marathi, the language of the Maharashtrian people is as close to Sanskrit as any Indian language, though some have traced its origins elsewhere. It uses the Devanagiri script with a few additions. The earliest literature of Marathi dates back to the hymns of Namdev (thirteenth to fourteenth century), an important saint-poet of the tradition (Karandikar, 1985). They are dedicated to the incarnation of Vishnu known as Vithoba, which literally means Father Vitthala. This is the name by which Vishnu is called in the Kannada language. Krishna worship in Maharashtra was inspired by the transcription of the Bhagavad Gita in Marathi by another great saint-poet, Jñanadeva, during the thirteenth century (Bahirat, 1956).

Perhaps the greatest of all Marathi saints was the seventeenth century Tukaram whose long and beautiful religious poems were to have great impact (Ranade, 1994). I remember listening to a talk on him in Calcutta by a visiting scholar. I was moved when I heard that he came from a so-called low-caste. When I mentioned this to my father, he told me this was not uncommon. Many saint-poets in India in other linguistic traditions had also arisen from Non-Brahmin castes. Swami Vivekananda and Sri Aurobindo were not Brahmins either.

Tukaram's *abhangas* enjoy high esteem among Marathis. *Abhanga* simply means *unbroken*, and it refers to the continuous flow of the hymns. A contemporary of Tukaram was Ramdas who, through his work on religious responsibility called *Dasbodh*, inspired the great Shivaji to become the brave nationalist leader who was to fight against the occupying Muslim rulers of the time. Shivaji's name is sacrosanct in Maharashtra.

Other great names in Marathi literature include Kavivarya Moropant and Mahipati. There is a genre of folk songs in the tradition which conveys the sadness of a woman when her husband has gone to war. Known as *Pawada*, it is often presented as a story in lyric form. There is another classical mode of rural theater in Maharashtra, known as *Lavani*. It is said that during the reign of Peshva Bajirao II this took on erotic dimensions. There has been a revival in this art-form these days.

Marathi was one of the first Indian languages to bring out an English-Indian language dictionary. This was compiled by J. T. Molesworth in the nineteenth century. R. Navalkar's grammar of Marathi is regarded by many linguists as one of the best modern grammars of any Indian language.

In the course of the nineteenth century there appeared a major novel, indeed the first of its kind, in Marathi. This work by Baba Padmanji was revolutionary in that it condemned in frank terms Hindu orthodoxy, and advocated the adoption of Western social norms. Another influential writer, Vishnu Shastri Chiplunkar, wrote in a nationalistic vein and in beautiful prose. Already in the nineteenth century a thinker like Gopal Ganesh Agarkar spoke out against untouchability and pleaded the cause of women.

Not unlike the adjective *Great* in Great Britain, Maharashtrians describe their country as *Maha Rashtra:* Mega-State, Great State. They seem to have been prescient about India's future. In recent years commentators have been writing that in the course of the twenty-first century India will become the *megastate* of South Asia. Maharashtra is a more secular name than Bharat or Hindustan, and could well be used as a name for India as a whole. But it is not as easy to change the name of a country as to change the name of a city.

Kannada and Karnataka

When I was in my fifth grade, the headmaster of our school was a very strict gentleman from Mysore. One day, because I was talking with a class-mate while the teacher was explaining how to solve an equation, I was ordered to go to his office. This used to be standard punishment in those days, stricter than having to stand up on the bench. This headmaster asked me to stretch out my left palm, and inflicted a harsh stroke on it with his cane, with the words: "As we say in Mysore, *classille neenu máthádabáradu.* He translated this by saying that I shouldn't be talking in class. Actually he was following Samuel Butler's dictum, "Spare the rod and spoil the child." One may think that this Victorian British mode of punishing children is a thing of the past, but it was reported recently that according to a survey commissioned by the *Times Educational Supplement,* "Almost half of parents believe caning should be brought back to the classroom" (Huffington Post, 15 November 2011).

In any case, such was my painful introduction to Kannada. Till then I had associated Mysore with only a sweet concoction (*mysúrpák*). Now I had a taste of *my sore part*.

When I started learning the alphabets of Indian languages as a hobby, I found Kannada to be somewhat difficult: I was confused by the fact that a mere dot and a twirl distinguished *gha* from *pha*, and a curl made all the difference between *ma* and *ya*. But the letters were pretty and Kannada has many words and sounds similar to Tamil.

The Kannada language, which is the state language of Karnataka (where other languages are also widely spoken), is categorized by philologists as Dravidian. Like Telugu and Malayalam, it has incorporated abundant Sanskrit words. I understand that here, as in Tamil, the difference between spoken and literary language is considerable. Linguists call this phenomenon *diglossia*. In Kannada too there are clearly distinguishable differences between the Brahmin, Non-Brahmin, and Dalit versions of the language (Kamath, 2002).

One of the most enlightened thinkers of the classical Hindu world was born in Karnataka. (twelfth century) His name was Basava (or Basavanna). He rejected orthodoxy, the superiority of Brahmins, and casteism. No less importantly, he stressed social work as part of religious practice, and preached gender equality. His call for love of fellow humans and service to others came to be called *Anubhava Mantapa*. Like other religious leaders, he established his own sect called *Veerashaivism*. It was dedicated to Lord Shiva. His followers, known as Lingáyats, are perhaps the only Hindus who do not cremate their corpses (Ishwaran, 1992).

Karnataka produced many eminent mathematicians in classical India, such as the great Bhaskara. Mokshagundam

Visweswaraiah (1861 – 1962), who had built the first dam in India, was the greatest modern engineer in India. He was a brilliant and productive Indian who spanned two centuries, living to the ripe age of 101. Though he received many honors in his lifetime he is one of those great Indians who are not as well known throughout India as he deserves to be. He was a creative thinker who established factories and universities, and wanted India to come into the industrial age (Husain, 1966).

As early as in the first quarter of the tenth century there was a work in Kannada on the art of poetry (Mugali, 1975). Scholars call the period from about 925 to 1150 the golden age for epics because it was then that portions of the Mahabharata and some Puranas found expression in Kannada. The three great writers of the period were Pampa, Ponna and Ranna. During the era of the Vijayanagaram kingdom religious poetry again reached a zenith. Kumara Vyasa and Ratnakaravarni are remembered among the many names that have left a mark of those times. In the seventeenth century the satirist Sarvajna wrote on the social scene resulting from the collapse of Vijayanagaram. It is said that it was during this time in the sixteenth century that the internationally famous city of Bangalore was founded, commemorated now by the Bugle Rock. Today it is a cosmopolitan city of science and technology, of art and culture, growing at a faster rate than one can handle. A Kannadika friend once told me that the first part of the name Bangalúru means *baked beans*.

The nineteenth century witnessed a transformation of Kannada literature from its medieval modes to more modern ones. A work entitled *Mudra Manjusha* (1823) by Kempu Narayana is said to have initiated this transition. Christian missionaries and English literature played their usual roles in instigating new styles and formats. Perceptive Kannada thinkers who voraciously read Western authors brought in many new perspectives of the world and fresh ideas into their own language. The intellectual elite began to rediscover Sanskrit wisdom, and reworked much of it in more meaningful terms. Thus, both Shakespeare and Kalidasa, both Biblical thought and Upanishadic philosophy, were recast in a Kannada that was more accessible to the masses.

If Bangaluru has become world renowned for information technology, another spot in Karnataka was famous in India and in the world even before that. Udupi is culturally rich and proud of its Krishna temple and international university. It has also become synonymous with excellent South Indian vegetarian cuisine (Rajalakshmi, 2006).

We generally associate only the Kannada language with the state of Karnataka because that is spoken by the majority in that state. But a number of other languages are also there. Tulu is another Dravidian language spoken in Karnataka by a couple of million people at least (Steever, 1998). It is a born-again language in that, after being marginalized for a long time, it is now springing back with writers and poets. I once chatted with a Tulu woman in Mumbai, and she sounded defensive about her language. This is natural when one's language has only a secondary place within a larger community. Life is often more difficult, culturally speaking, for people who belong to a linguistic, racial, or religious minority in any country. A mark of enlightenment is when a society, through laws, education, and the attitudes of its citizens strives to make minorities feel more included and respected than their sense of insecurity enables them to feel. The Tuluvas have a saying that is followed by millions of people today who migrate to Western countries: *Oorudu nanjaanda paarad badkodu*: "If it's tough at home; run away (elsewhere) and live."

Gujarati and Gujarat

Gujarati is another major language of India. It is spoken in one form or another in the State of Gujarat as well as in Maharashtra. Already in the thirteenth century it had developed into an independent linguistic entity. Innumerable poets and singers have enriched the language since that time.

My introduction to Gujarati was through a fellow student in my French class at the *Alliance Française* in Calcutta in 1953-54. NP was a *pukka* Gujarati, as she described herself one day, because she spoke only Gujarati at home and ate only Gujarati food: always vegetarian and very fond of *dhokla*. She added that they did not have a *maharaj* at home. A *maharaj*, she explained, was a cook of the Brahmin caste. Her family fasted on certain days. When she scribbled for me the Gujarati alphabet on a piece of paper, I said that some letters looked like incomplete Hindi letters. She did not appreciate this observation, though I did not mean anything bad. Innocuous comments about another culture can sometimes be misconstrued as intended to be offensive. I once told a Portuguese professor in Porto that I could understand many phrases in his language because it sounded like a dialect of Spanish. He was mildly upset, and gave me a short lecture on how mistaken I was. But he was generous enough to let me know that this was a common mistake. When I told NP that *ka* and *pha* looked only slightly different, she agreed, but she had never noticed that.

Another friend told me about a scholar in Bombay who had done research on Apabhramsa which was a widely spoken language between the sixth and the thirteenth centuries. It was the immediate parent of most North Indian languages. At one time, Gujarati itself was known as Gaurjara Apabhramsa. It was only in the seventeenth century that the language acquired its present name. Because of influences from foreign traders, some Gujarati dialects have incorporated a number of alien words. One seldom realizes the role that tradesmen have played in contributing to word-enrichment of languages.

To an untrained ear spoken Gujarati seems to have too many *che*-sounds, just as French seems to have too many –s sounds. Actually che simply means to be, or is, or are, and is not unlike the Bengali *aache*.

NP was ecstatic when she talked to me one day about Dwaraka. That was where, as per the Mahabharata, Krishna once reigned with brother Balarama. She told me about the magnificent temples there. In fact, in *Srimad Bhagavatam* there is a picturesque description of Dwaraka which, it says, was constructed by no other than Vishvakarma, with the most precious gems, gold, and corals. NP said that the ancient capital of Krishna had been swallowed by a tidal wave. We did not know then that archeologists would uncover the relics of the ancient Dwaraka someday or that I would have the privilege of meeting the eminent archeologist Dr. S.R. Rao at a UNESCO 15th International Congress of History of Science, held at Edinburgh in 1979. In his book, Professor Rao wrote: "The discovery is an important landmark in the history of India. It has set to rest the doubts expressed by historians about the historicity of Mahabharata and the very existence of Dwaraka city. It has greatly narrowed the gap in Indian history by establishing the continuity of the Indian civilization from the Vedic Age to the present day" (Rao, 1999).

According to the Mahabharata, it was in (present day) Gujarat that Lord Krishna died. Though we have no monuments for historical personages like Valmiki and Patañjali, in the lore of the tradition we do have the place where Krishna is said to have left his mortal frame. This was near Somnath where Arjuna came all the way from Hastinapura to cremate Krishna's body. There is the famed temple dedicated to Lord Shiva in this place (Van der Veer, 1992). NP also told me about a Sun temple in a place called Modhera which was so constructed that on the day of the winter solstice sun rays shine directly on the deity there, reminding one of Stonehenge in England.

Contrary to general impression, not all Jains are Gujaratis. In fact there are more Jains in some other parts of India than in Gujarat. But a great many Parsis are Gujaratis, as also Muslims. Thus Gujarat is among the more religiously diverse states of India.

Aside from many eminent writers, five major personages from Gujarat lend luster to the state, and four of them are the pride of India. K. M. Munshi—scholar, philosopher, politician, and educationist—was perhaps the most illustrious student of Sri Aurobindo. He founded not only a Gujarati literary society (*Gujarati Sahitya Sansad*) but also the *Bharatiya Vidya Bhavan* (Sharma, 2008). The mission of the Bhavan is to spread knowledge and understanding of Indian culture and history both within India and beyond. During its many decades of existence the Bharatiya Vidyabhavan has spread to many countries, with at least fifty branches all over the world. It was my privilege to speak at the inauguration of its New York branch in 1981 under the leadership of the Tamil-Hindi-Sanskrit scholar Dr. P. Jayaraman.

Then there was Sardar Vallabhai Patel, a brilliant lawyer and freedom fighter who was the first Deputy Prime Minister of India (Gandhi, 1990). His firmness was enormously valuable in the first years of the new India. Third, and most importantly, there was Mohandas Karamchand Gandhi, reckoned as one of the greatest figures of the twentieth century, respected and admired to this day all over the world for his adherence to truth and non-violence (Chadha, 1998). Sadly he is being criticized, chastised, and bad-mouthed by many in India for what they estimate as the unintended ill-effects of his religious tolerance and largesse towards those who had/have little regard for Hindus. All these three were stars of the first magnitude in a constellation of extraordinarily gifted and selfless patriots of the pre-independence decades in India. Those leaders were charismatic and unusual; India has not produced any leader of their eminence in recent decades.

The fourth great Gujarati of the twentieth century was Mohammed Ali Jinnah, the Father of Pakistan. It is an irony of history that Mahatma Gandhi, a devout Hindu who was faithful to his tradition became the father of secular democratic India, whereas Mohammed Ali Jinnah, a consummate Westernized Oriental Gentleman, became the father of the theocratic Islamic nation of Pakistan. Both were Gujaratis.

The fifth great pan-Indian Gujarati leader belongs to the twenty-first century. Narendra Modi was elected Prime Minister of India by an overwhelming majority of the Indian people in May 2014. A man of integrity who loves his Hindu heritage no less than India's secular democratic ideals, he does not hesitate to refer to the sacredness of the River Ganga any more than his determination to purify its waters. He goes to Hindu places of pilgrimage to show respect for his tradition, as well as to distant secular capitals to extend India's hand of friendship to others. He addressed the U. N. General Assembly in Hindi, and persuaded the organization to declare on day as Yoga Day.

Odiya (Odiya) and Odisha

Once when I had some difficulty with a technical problem in the equation of continuity in hydrodynamics, my professor (a serene Bengali gentleman) invited me to his home where, he said, he would give me special instruction. I discovered that this professor—who had authored a widely used textbook on calculus—lived in a mansion. While he was in the thick of his explanation of the Euler's equations, a cook came with two cups of tea. "Not now, not now," he curtly told the man in Bengali, and added in a hushed voice to me, "These Odiyas never understand the most elementary things." I was accustomed to inter-provincial gibes in India, but this struck me because one of my bright class-mates was from Orissa (as the state used to be called then).

I mentioned this comment to my friend, and he laughed, saying he was not surprised. "Bengalis think we are all a notch inferior," he said, and added that he knew many Bengali families with cooks from his state. He reminded me that once Odisha was the center of the Kalinga Empire, of which Ashoka was the most illustrious monarch. I learned much from this friend about his state. All this was in the 1950s, and I like to think that things have changed a lot by now.

In the nineteenth century some Bengali thinkers refused to recognize Odiya as a separate language. One scholar said that Odiyas would remain backward unless they adopted Bengali as their language. It was the English linguist John Beames who argued that Odiya was an older linguistic entity than Bengali.

Fakirmohan Senapati (1843-1918) was the pioneer of modern Odiya literature. He translated the epics and wrote poems, essays, short stories and novels. Like Charles Dickens, Senapati portrayed the social condition of the poor, painting powerfully how society tended to exploit them (Mohanty, 2007).

Odissi, a great Indian dance form, emerged from Odisha. I had a taste of it a few years ago at Nazareth College in Rochester, New York, in a performance by a group touring the United States. It was one of the most beautiful and intricate dances I have seen.

Its remarkable impact arises from the subtle coordination of head, bust, and torso. This is an ancient system of dance which was once confined to temples and royal courts. The dances are around themes relating to Krishna whose worship has influenced Odiya culture in profound ways. I read in a pamphlet that there are three schools of this dance, and that Odissi would have disappeared altogether but for the dedication of a few devoted enthusiasts in the twentieth century.

Puri is a city of considerable renown in Odisha. It stands vibrant on the Bay of Bengal. It is said to have been an important center in the hoary days of Indian Buddhism. The majestic temple for which the city is famous began its origins in the twelfth century: the Temple of Jagannath (Lord of Universe), another name for Vishnu. Jagannath is enshrined here with Balarama and Subhadra, brother and sister of Krishna.

Per a time-honored Puranic legend, when Lord Krishna gave up his mortal coil, succumbing to the arrows of a hunter, his physical body was left to rot under an abandoned tree. A passerby noticed the scattered bones. He carefully put them in a box. Vishnu directed King Indradyumna to have the bones properly arranged within a grand image of Jagannath. The task was entrusted to Vishvakarma, the divine architect who is also credited with the construction of the temple in Dwaraka. He agreed to do this on condition he would not be disturbed. Weeks passed, and the impatient king asked when the work would be completed. The upset Vishvakarma left the image without hands or feet. The king appealed to Brahma who gave the image eyes and soul, but no hand or foot, and officiated at the consecration of the temple, promising to make it famous.

Such are the temple lore (*sthala purana*) of the Hindu world. Fascinating, imaginative, and thrilling in the recall. To some it may seem a cultural wonder that many take them to be literally true in this day and age. But it must be remembered that human beings live on several planes: the logical, the emotional, the psychological, the material, the cultural, the spiritual, and more. It is as if our existence is a mansion with many rooms. When we are in the kitchen, we may taste the delicious food without looking into the history of the recipe. When we are in the library, we may read a book on astronomy and come to know about the stars without peeking through a telescope. When in the bedroom, we make ourselves comfortable on a mattress and recede into a world of dreams.

Every summer the icons from the temple are taken in a procession in a magnificent chariot, 45 feet high, to a summer home known as *Gundicha ghara*. The chariots of Krishna's siblings are somewhat smaller. These richly decorated sacred vehicles are pulled by ropes by thousands of pilgrims. Sometimes fatal accidents occur. The English word *Juggernaut* (a corruption of Jagannath) refers to a terrible force, something that demands blind obedience, and exacts merciless sacrifice. It is a corruption of the name of this temple. The occasion, during which there are fairs and festivities, games and music and toy-vending, is known as *rathajatra* or chariot festival.

This magnificent temple in Puri is a major place of pilgrimage in India. Its architectural splendor is great, and its spiritual significance considerable. There is a rule which prohibits Non-Hindus from entering this sacred temple. This is understandable, and shows how in some ways Hindus are like their Muslim brothers, for in Islam too some mosques are no-entry zones for Non-Muslims. But the exclusivism by which its guardians jealously protect the sanctity of the temple of Jagannath by not allowing people of the so-called lower castes to enter its precincts diminishes its claims of spirituality, at least in the estimation of some thoughtful and spiritually awakened

Hindus. What place of worship can be so sacred that members of the faith are excluded from it because of their lineage and birth!

As recently as 2011, when the eminent Yoga-guru Baba Ramdev said something to the effect that all Hindus should be permitted to enter the temple there was a huge protest, asking for the arrest of the Baba and to deport him from the state (*Daily News Analysis*, January 21, 2011). The spiritual cousins of the Taliban may be found in every religion. Their resurgence is among the most dangerous developments in recent decades.

Odisha can boast of the largest inland salt-water lake: Chilka, which is said to have a unique eco-system. Here white-bellied sea eagles, graylag geese, purple moorhen, jacana, herons and flamingos thrive.

In the eighteenth century a gifted artist painted on palm leaves several episodes from the Bhagavada Purana. These have been collected and put together in a marvelous book that is illustrative of the enormous cultural richness of India (Mishra, 1987).

The archeological remains of the medieval Sun Temple of Konarak, which was described in an article in the 1911 edition of the *Britannica* as "the most richly ornamented building—externally at least—in the world," is not far from Puri. Mythic history says it was built by Krishna's son Samba who had been cursed with leprosy for casting his longing eyes at one of Krishna's spouses, and was later cured. It is interesting that just as corresponding to the Krishna Temple in Dwaraka in the West facing the Arabian Sea there is one in Puri facing the Bay of Bengal; so too, like the Sun Temple at Modhera in the West, there is one in Konarak in the East. If these are mere coincidences, they are very interesting coincidences indeed. The wonders of the classical Indian temple landscape are both fascinating and remarkable.

Malayalam and Kerala

The spouses of my older brother and sister were both from Palakkadu, a region in Kerala. Thus, their Tamil has a touch of the sweet Malayalam accent and also many Malayalam expressions. Thanks to them, I gained some acquaintance with this language. Once it was called *manipravalám*: diamond and coral.

Like Sanskrit-enriched languages, Malayalam has hard and soft versions of the consonants as well as aspirate and non-aspirate ones, plus some additional sounds. Some of the letters resemble Tamil, but I discovered that the alphabet can be misleading to one who is accustomed to Tamil. For example, in Malayalam, the Tamil *va* is *kha*, the Tamil *ma* is *tha*, and *dha* looks almost like the Tamil *ya*.

A Malayalee friend once told me that Malayalam has the longest name of all languages. "How about Gujarati?" I asked. "I mean in the number of letters used to spell it," he said. "How about Portuguese?" I asked. "I mean of all Indian languages," he said. We all like to attribute some uniqueness to our own language and culture. What is unique with the name Malayalam is that when spelt in English, it becomes a palindrome.

I recall a brief stay in Trichur many years ago. It used to be called Thrissivaperúr: *Big City of Three Shivas*. It is a cultural capital of Kerala where Malayalam is the main language. It is said that Adi Shankaracharya's parents made pilgrimages from Kalady to pray to Vadakkunathan, as Lord Shiva is referred to here. This name could mean in Tamil *Lord of the North*. One might think this suggests that Shiva worship originated in north India. But Mr. P. K. Ramakrishnan, an internet scholar friend of mine, has pointed out that:

> There was a temple dedicated to Vrishabhamuni on the hillock where the Siva temple stands now.

In Malayalam Mesham becomes Medam, and Vrishabham becomes *Edavam*. The hillock was originally *Vrishabhakkunnu* named after the Jain Vrishabha Muni. This became *edavakkunnu*. This got further changed as *vadakkunnu* The lord of this *kunnu* came to be called *Vadakkunnunathan* which became shortened as vadakkunathan.

How the gradual transformation of words can change the meaning altogether!

Though people of the Kerala region have been speaking the language since time immemorial, and are known to have traded with ancient Greece and Rome (it was all part of the Chera kingdom), the earliest works of Malayalam literature belong only to the fifteenth century.

Folk songs and legends in the language have existed from much earlier times. By the fifteenth century, as with Telugu, Sanskrit influences had become considerable. Cherusseri Nambudiri's lyrics on Krishna, known as *Krishna Gatha*, are reckoned as the first creations of Malayalam literature. Another eminent writer was Mahakavi Ulloor S. Parameshwara Iyer. (Asher and Kumari, 1997)

As with all the languages of India, the Ramayana and the Mahabharata were among the first to be introduced into Malayalam literature. What is remarkable here is that one and the same illustrious poet and initiator of Malayalee literature accomplished this dual task, writing many other works also, some of them of a philosophical nature. His name was Thunjattu Ezhuttachan. He is one of the few ancient Indian poets for whom there is a geographical marker. A sacred spot in Kerala is said to commemorate where the poet died. I am not aware of any such place for Valluvar or Kalidasa, let alone Valmiki or Vyasa.

In the twentieth century, Vallathol Narayana Menon wrote an epic poem called *Chitrayogam* in Malayalam. He channeled his poetic gifts to give a clarion call to his countrymen to rebel against the British, and went on to become the greatest nationalist poet of the language. But he was no narrow nationalist, no mindless hater of all that is alien. For he also wrote a magnificent work called *Magdalana Mariam* which depicts Mary Magdalene's conversion with touching sensitivity. According to Thomas Palakeel, this work "paved way for a new tradition of Christian symbolism in Malayalam. A literary tradition attempting to disengage itself from the mythical mode found an easier transition in the figures of the Gospel and in Gandhi and Buddha"

http://www.geocities.org/kavitayan/palakeel.html.

Every language group and local culture in the Indian subcontinent has offered something to the larger India. In the context of Kerala, aside from its local achievements and high literacy, its exemplary harmony among Christians, Muslims, and Hindus, classical Kerala also contributed illustrious mathematicians like Narayana Pandit, Paramesvara, Chitrabanu, and Jyesthadeva. Most of all, the greatest Vedantic scholar-philosopher-saint Adi Shankara hailed from Kerala. He has had a more far-reaching impact on the development and preservation of Hindu metaphysics, philosophy, and spirituality than almost any other Indian thinker. It has been said that were it not for this intellectual and spiritual giant, India could well have become entirely Buddhist at one point in its history.

In Malayalee culture there is an artistic creation that combines dance and music, lyrical poetry and mime. This is the famous Kathakali dance drama which is said to have had its origins in the seventeenth century. The characters wear colored masks where green with red streaks, yellow, black, etc. indicate their nature: good or evil, chaste or profane, etc. (Pandeya, 1999).

Ahom, Asamia, and such

It was almost sixty years ago that I first heard of Shillong to where my sister's husband had been transferred. I believe at that time Shillong was the capital of Assam. To me, there seemed to be something exotic about Assam whose very name sounded different from Orissa, Maharashtra, Bengal, or Gujarat.

Once, flying from Delhi to Calcutta, I chanced to sit near a woman with whom I struck up a conversation. I discovered that she was from Assam. I told her I had once been to Assam. She corrected me by pointing out that old Assam had been chopped up into more states than I have kept tract of. Today Shillong is the capital of the state of Meghalaya. I liked the poetic name. A temple is called *Devalaya* in Sanskrit: Abode of God; and the mountain range in North India is called *Himalaya*: Abode of Snow. The state in which Shillong is now called *Meghalaya*: Abode of Clouds: *Domus nebulae*.

The woman sitting near me said she was a Khasi. She spoke the Khasi language which is said to be a dialect of the Mon-khmer family of languages. Not many mainstream Hindus may have even heard that this is one of the languages spoken in India. Her religion was Niam Khasi. I had never heard of this before.

The Khasi lady told me that Meghalaya is a beautiful state, with hills and waterfalls. Shillong has many parks, and a museum of the tribal people, she informed me. I also discovered that it has one of the largest golf courses in the world. Later, I read about a monument there in honor of some fallen soldiers who had served the British cause in World War I. There they have a quote from Horace in Latin, *Dulce et decorum est pro patria mori*: Sweet and appropriate to die for one's fatherland. I wondered for whose fatherland the Khasis died.

I had learned in my geography class that Cherrapunji, where it rains practically all through the year, had more rainfall than anywhere else. I understand that things have changed even there, and that the nearby town of Mawsynram now has claim to that fame. Much of the tea that people drink all over the world comes from the hills of Assam.

At our table at a wedding dinner I once met a gentleman with the name Lachit Bailung. My usual curiosity prompted me to ask where he was from. He described himself as one with an Ahom lineage, which made me feel ignorant again, since I had never heard that term before. He came from a priestly class of people who were astrologers, he explained. I learned during that evening more about Assam than I would ever have on my own initiative. Ahoms, he said, were the original people of the region now called Assam (Gogoi, 1991). They ruled the region from the thirteenth to the eighteenth centuries. The Ahom language has its own script. Some letters of Ahom roughly resemble, quite coincidentally, some letters of lower case cursive Latin. Thus, for example, we have, m: *kha*, w: *ya*, v: *pa*. Apparently, this language, belonging to the Tibeto-Chinese Tai family, is no longer spoken as widely.

Before they embraced Sanskritic worldviews, the Ahom people had their own cosmology, which differed considerably from what mainstream Hindus are familiar with. Their name for the Supreme Being was Pha who manifested himself as a huge crab floating up-turned on the waters. He produced a female counterpart, not unlike Eve from Adam's rib, from whom emerged four eggs, and so on. India has given rise to more theories of cosmogenesis than the Vedic.

Modern Assamese is called Asamiya by the people who speak the language (Medhi, 1988). Like Odiya, it was also regarded during the nineteenth century as no more than a dialect of Bengali. It too had a hard time asserting its independence and integrity as a language from the more dominant Bengali whose script it uses with only slight modifications. Even granting that there are many words in common between Bengali and Assamese, this is no different than the commonalty between Marathi and Hindi, or Tamil and Kannada. On the other hand, the word for fire is *aagun* in Bengali, but *zui* in Assamese. There are also syntactic rules and words that are quite different (Kakati, 2007) from Bengali.

At one time, some Bengali scholars went in large numbers to Assam, not unlike highly trained Indians who in our own times go to Dubai and places like that. These were usually Brahmins, and they were given high positions in the service of the kings. Assamese with names like Chankakoti are in fact descendents of the early Bengali upper class settlers in Assam. Though they speak Assamese, many of them still have deep attachment for the Bengali language and culture of their ancestors.

For a brief period in the first part of the nineteenth century, the region of Assam was annexed by the Burmese, but thanks to the British, it reverted back to mainland India. At about the same time, American Baptist missionaries began publishing an evangelical monthly called *Arunodai* in the language, which turned out to be a boon for the rebirth of the Assamese language.

But during a good part of the nineteenth century, Assamese did not come in for the kind of Western secular impact that launched Bengali and Marathi into the modern world. One had to wait till its closing decades for this to begin. Chandrakumar Agarwalla, Laksminath Bezbarua and others, trained in the liberal educational institutions of Calcutta, wrote short stories, poetry, novels and essays in Assamese. They spoke to their own people on modern themes, and opened up possibilities for literary expressions such as previous generations had not done or seen.

Of those who thus enriched Assamese literature, Kamalakanta Bhattacharya is regarded as one of the most important. He was a nationalist poet who inspired the people to think in terms of freedom from alien yoke. Poetry was the favorite mode for many Assamese writers. Some continued with traditional religious themes, while others turned to love and philosophical reflection for their verses. Many gifted poets contributed to the enrichment of Assamese literature, and today this language has taken its rightful place among the major Indian languages.

Urdu: a language that spills over to another country

The ship which I took from Bombay to Genoa on my way to Paris in 1955 first docked in Karachi. "How ironic," I scribbled in my journal that night, "that Sindh, the region which had given India her name, now harbors Pakistan's capital, and the Indus river flows in Pakistan!" The power of religions to uproot cultures and affect the course of history is tremendous.

We were allowed to disembark in Karachi, and we walked to the Menora Head which was reeking with the sounds and smells of the harbor. We took a short bus tour of the city. The streets, the buildings, the people, all reminded me of the region around Chitpur Road in Calcutta. In matters of food, social customs, language and musical interests, I observed more in common between the people of Karachi and those of, say, Lucknow, than between the people of Lucknow and those of, say, Tirunelveli.

I heard Urdu everywhere, and the signs on the roads were inscribed in Urdu too. It was there that I felt an urge to learn this alphabet which seemed so different from anything I was familiar with then. It struck me as beautiful also, with all its curves, dots, squiggles, and occasional vertical lines.

On board the ship I befriended a student by the name of Ahmed B. who was from Karachi, and was going to London to do his Ph.D. in history. He introduced me to the Urdu alphabet which differs from Arabic and Persian only slightly. Contrary to my fears it was not that difficult to get acquainted with its basic patterns and symbols, though I still have problems knowing the correct vowel sounds when I try to read Urdu or Arabic. In the 1960s, while I served as a UNESCO educational expert in Algiers, teaching in the physics department of the university at Maison Carrée (El Harrach), I managed to learn some Arabic from a graduate assistant.

Urdu is unique in that it evolved from the fusion of speakers from two religions: Hindus and Muslims. More exactly, it developed from the encounter of Hindu and Muslim soldiers. Once it consisted largely of Hindi words, its syntax was Hindi, and it was written in the Devanagiri script. Genghis Khan's impact cast Urdu into the Iranian orbit, adopting a modified Arabic (*nastaliq*) script. Farsi became the fuel for the evolution of Urdu. Students in Mogul India began to study Persian as earnestly as modern Indians study English in our own times. This was true in the Muslim-dominated south as well.

Urdu is culturally rich. It has been described as a *Kohinoor*: Persian for Mountain-peak of Light. In an interesting sort of way, Hindustani may be seen as a language with two extreme versions: one with mostly words of Sanskrit derivation, which is Hindi; and another with mostly words of Persian-Arabic derivation, which is Urdu. Millions of people regard Hindustani as their first language.

There are more than 150 million Urdu speakers and more than 300 Urdu newspapers in India today.

My newly acquired friend Ahmed knew many *ghazals*. He explained to me what a ghazal is. Couplets in Urdu are known as *shers* (shayrs). The prosodic meter in an Urdu verse is called its *beher*. Both lines in a *sher* should have the same *beher*. If the two lines in a *sher* rhyme, the rhyming word is known as its *radif*. There is something else called the *kaafiyaa* which refers to the rhyming pattern in the words preceding the *radif* in the second line. A collection of *shers* with the same *beher*, *radif*, and *kaafiyaa*, is what one calls a *ghazal*. Urdu is famous for its many beautiful *ghazals* (Kanda, 2004). Urdu words should enrich anyone with a good knowledge of Hindi.

Once I had a Hindi teacher at school who was also very good at Urdu. His name was Rama Dorai Iyengar. He taught me to appreciate Urdu, and suggested I keep a parallel list of words, one Sanskrit derived and the other Urdu derived: like pustak and kitáb, ásán and sulab, khándán and parivár, mard and manush, etc. It soon became clear to me how Hindustani, like Tamil, is so rich in vocabulary.

Every language has its great poets; often one of them stands above all others like Goethe for German, Shakespeare for English, Tiruvalluvar for Tamil, Kalidasa for Sanskrit, Rabindranath Tagore for Bengali, and so on. For Urdu there is Mirza Ghalib, who began composing *ghazals* when he was barely ten. His original name was Mirza Asad Ullah Khan. In his youth he was entangled in romances with pretty women, he used to drink himself into debt, he indulged in gambling and was once thrown in prison. In his life he saw Mogul rule collapse, and British sovereignty rise. But his poetry never relented, and his works in Persian and Urdu have immortalized him. Sufi poet that he was, he transcended the hackneyed visions of heaven as spelled out in holy books, and was bold enough to write:

> In paradise it is true that I shall drink at dawn the pure wine mentioned in the Qur'an but where in

paradise are the long walks with intoxicated friends in the night, or the drunken crowds shouting merrily? Where shall I find there the intoxication of Monsoon clouds? Where there is no autumn, how can spring exist? If the beautiful houris are always there, where will be the sadness of separation and the joy of union? Where shall we find there a girl who flees away when we would kiss her? (Dalrymple, 2007).

Muhammad Iqbal (1877 – 1938) was a prolific writer in Urdu. His love of Islam was kindled while he was a student in Cambridge where he learned from English books about the glory days of the Islamic Arab world (Munnawar, 2004). In his bitterness at its humiliation by the West, he wrote, almost presciently: "Your (Western) civilization will kill itself with its own dagger." In a famous ghazal composed in 1907, he prophesied:

> At last the silent tongue of Hijaz has announced to the ardent ear the tiding that the covenant which had been given to the desert-dwellers is going to be renewed vigorously:
>
> The lion who had emerged from the desert and had toppled the Roman Empire is, as I am told by the angels, about to get up again (from his slumbers).
>
> You the dwellers of the West, should know that the world of God is not a shop (of yours).
>
> Your imagined pure gold is about to lose standard value (as fixed by you).

Your civilization will commit suicide with its own daggers. A nest built on a frail bough cannot be durable.

The caravan of feeble ants will take the rose petal for a boat. And in spite of all blasts of waves, it shall cross the river.

I will take out my worn-out caravan in the pitch darkness of night. My sighs will emit sparks and my breath will produce flames.

Powerful words, and understandable reaction to the overthrow by the West of Islamic empires all over the world during the past three centuries. This inspiring call for the cultural destruction of the West has been taken up by many twenty-first century Islamist groups. Unfortunately, in the process they are wreaking more death and destruction in their own countries and to their own people than the degree of havoc they would like to perpetrate in the Non-Islamic world.

Moreover, in his well-deserved condemnation of the imperialist West, the poet either forgot or chose to ignore the rape and rampage, the looting and destruction that imperialist Muslim invaders had perpetrated in their glory days in the Middle Ages in many parts of the world, including in India. He also seems to have ignored the fruits of Western science, technology, medicine, trade, and enlightenment that were brought to countries that at one time wallowed in relative scientific darkness.

Iqbal probably wished for the death of Hindu India also, and succeeded in this goal. He was the man who planted the seeds for a separate Islamic nation in the Indian subcontinent. In 1930 he wrote ominously:

"I would like to see the Punjab, North-West Frontier Provinces, Sind and Baluchistan into a single State. Self-

Government within the British Empire or without the British Empire. The formation of the consolidated North-West Indian Muslim State appears to be the final destiny of the Muslims, at least of the North-West India." Blaming only the British for India's mutilation sounds somewhat one-sided when we read this dream of Iqbal which did come to pass. Sometimes poets can be as influential as politicians in charting the course of history. Whether those influences are for the good or for the bad depends on who benefits and who suffers from the changes they ignite.

There are universities in India where Urdu is the principal language, but the language is propagated and made universal by movies from Bollywood. With the colorful costumes which have their origins in the Islamic world, these movies are extremely popular in the Middle East. Practically all Muslims in north India and in Hyderabad regard Urdu as their language because of its Islamic roots. But many Hindus in U.P. and Punjab use Urdu because they were brought up in that language.

Can you think of a nation whose national language is mother tongue to less than twenty percent of its citizens? Pakistan is such a nation, where 48% of the people speak Punjabi which is written in the Urdu script they call *Shahmukhi* to contrast it with *Gurmukhi*; and less that 10% speak Urdu as their mother tongue. Other languages of the people include Pashto, Sindhi, Balochi, etc. Yet, though it is mother tongue to less than 8% of the people. Urdu is the national language, and is compulsory in schools in that country.

English and its role

I remember being introduced to B-A-T *bat* and C-A-T *cat* by my sister any long years ago. One day I read G-O as jo which made her laugh. This little incident happened because of a momentous debate that took place in Calcutta on February 2, 1835, in which a thirty-five year old Englishman argued for introducing English as the medium of instruction in British-occupied India. The debate was about whether a substantial sum for opening new schools in India should be spent for education through Arabic and Sanskrit media, or through English. Thomas Babington Macaulay—scholar, historian, liberal, and very British—argued with great passion that the Indian people would benefit more in the long run if they were initiated into English and to European thought and science than if they were trained in the languages and worldviews of Arabic and Sanskrit literatures. He was convinced that English would usher Indians into the modern world sooner and more effectively than any other language. Also, the British could create "a class who may be interpreters between us and the millions whom we govern, a class of persons Indian in blood and colour, but English in taste, in opinions, words and intellect" (Clive and Pinney, 1972). Of course, he wasn't thinking about Call-centers and out-sourcing jobs from America when he argued for his cause, although these too have come to pass.

Macaulay's opponents argued that with the awakening that would come from English and modern science, Indians would become intellectually so strong that the British could no longer have their hold on India. To this Macaulay replied famously, "It would be ... far better for us that the people of India were well governed and independent of us, than ill governed and subject to us; that they were ruled by their own kings, but wearing our broadcloth, and working with our cutlery, than that they were performing their salams to English collectors and English magistrates, but were too ignorant to value, or too poor to buy, English manufactures" (Young, 1935). Not many critics of Macaulay, some of whom surreptitiously circulate spurious malicious quotes from him on the Internet, are aware of or care to refer to these words.

Macaulay won the debate. The die was cast. English became the medium of instruction in Indian schools. Within a generation a new class of Indians was formed. They were English in words and intellect, as Macaulay had predicted, but contrary to his hopes and expectations, not all were English in opinion and taste, unless one means by that, awakened to the new thought currents of a Europe that was itself struggling to cast off its past superstitions, narrowness, religious bigotry, and church domination. Many English-educated Indians became very patriotic. Versed in English and alerted to the notions of freedom, equality, and liberty that were becoming the refrains in an enlightened Europe, they led a movement that overthrew British rule from India. All that is history which has flowed down the river of time.

Never before or since in all of history had the convictions and eloquence of a single man affected the course of the culture and history of a whole nation in so dramatic and irreversible a way as Macaulay had done. English is now an integral part of India's mind. The language has brought together the educated classes from every region, such as India had never seen before.

In 2004 The Jawaharlal Nehru University bestowed on me the Raja Rao Award at a ceremony in the hall of the Bahai Temple in New Delhi. On that occasion I gave an acceptance speech in Hindi. The Chancellor Dr. Karan Singh began his remarks by saying that while he appreciated my speaking in the Bharatiya bhasha Hindi, he would like to remind me that English was no longer a foreign language in India. It was another Indian language. But he added that he had come prepared to say a few words in English, but now after listening to this Tamilian speak in Hindi, he too was obliged to do so.

The Sanskritic mode of earlier times was largely for the upper castes. Mogul-Persian influence was reserved for the select cream of society. On the other hand, the vast majority spoke and thought in their local languages, as they still do, and seldom communicated with people from other regions. There was nothing unusual or bad in this. It was much like the current situation in Europe. But in nineteenth century Europe, including Russia, French was the lingua franca of the elite. So it became with English in modern India.

It would be wrong to hold that English was indispensable for India to be unified as a political entity. Nor can one say that Indians needed English to be ushered into the modern world. Russians, Poles, Koreans and Japanese, to name a few, have all been modernized without English being imposed on them. What may be said positively about English is that many Indians have reaped valuable fruits from their familiarity with English for one important reason. Aside from the fact that English is enormously rich in its literary treasures of great quality, no matter what subject you take—whether cultural, historical, scientific, philosophical, informational, or whatever—you are likely to find a book or article on it in English such as in few other languages. French and German may be the only competitors of English in this regard.

Just as modern civilization is dependent on the computer, India has become dependent on English for its survival as a modern nation. As of now, she cannot have her universities, IITs, banks and communication systems without English. This intellectual and cultural dependence of a free people on a foreign language is what makes many patriotic Indians understandably uncomfortable. Hindus rightly complain about conversion to Christianity. But the fact remains that most enlightened movers and leaders in India are converts to the English language.

On the positive side, English-speaking Indians find it easier to get jobs in the world market, they are able to have pan-India meetings, they feel a oneness as citizens of the same country, and they participate more easily in international discussions. Quite a few of them have also contributed to modern English/American literature.

There is no question but that English has played an important role in the rejuvenation of India. It is equally true that a knowledge of English serves people well in opening their minds to new perspectives. Indeed India has its own varieties of English. As long as Indians employ English as a useful and enriching instrument, like a knife or a musical instrument, for its beneficial rather than culture-destructive potential, it can serve them well.

Yet, English education has also done some serious harm. It has created a huge chasm between the English-knowing population and the rest. Many regard themselves as superior, exactly as those from the West tend to do when they compare themselves to those from the non-West. When Indians are so mesmerized by English that they lose touch with their own culture, and are unable to appreciate its finer elements, then they become what one derisively calls Macaulayites. A Macaulayite is not just one who is "Indian in blood and color, but English in taste, in opinions, words and intellect," but rather an English knowing Indian who is ignorant of the richness of his own traditions and culture, who mindlessly adores whatever comes from the West, and sometimes even has contempt for whatever is culturally indigenous.

In other words, a valid reason for regretting the introduction of English into the Indian educational system is that Anglo-indoctrination created a whole class of Hindus who lost touch with their own roots, between whom and the vast majority of their compatriots who have not been exposed to English and related thought modes, there is even today a gaping intellectual divide. This is the predicament of English-educated citizens of other former British colonies as well. On the one hand, they want to kick out lock, stock, and barrel the British (and the French and the Dutch, and the Portuguese, etc.) and everything these exploiting colonizers have left behind. The massive body of literature (all in English) that argues about, condemns, bashes, abuses, and verbally spits upon the West in books, articles, and Internet postings is growing in magnitude in our own times. On the other hand, most of those who think this way are more at ease in the world of discourse with fellow English-educated West-haters than with millions of their own Non-English-educated compatriots. Many of them are cozily installed in England, Europe, Canada, the United States, or Australia, educating their children in Western tongues.

For my part, though I detest the British of the colonial era from the bottom of my heart for all the terrible things they did to my forebears, I am glad their intervention saved me from having to pay obeisance to a descendant of Bahadhur Shah Zaffar or even of Shivaji, as my most exalted monarch, whether Mogul or Maratha. I am very grateful too for parliamentary democracy and the penal code in India. I know I am not speaking for many of today's Indians, but perhaps I am also speaking for at least some of them, when I say I am glad my worldviews have been molded by the thinkers of the European Enlightenment. I feel more fulfilled because I have derived aesthetic delights not only from Kamban and Kalidasa but also from Shakespeare and Shelley, not only from Khajurao and Mahabalipuram but also from Rubens and the Sistine Chapel. My mind has also been immeasurably enriched by the physics of Galileo and Newton, and by the equations of Einstein and Schrödinger.

We certainly did not need humiliating British colonialism for all this. The British did not have in mind my aesthetic, scientific or intellectual thrills when they inflicted their grammar and vocabulary on India. But I have personally benefited immensely and immeasurably from Macaulay's victory in the 1835 debate. If his motives were malicious, so much the worse for him. The saying is that the road to hell is paved with good intensions. In my case, the road to (my) heaven was paved with (his) bad intentions.

I have had enough of this carping on now-dead alien demons, and pronouncing passionate curses on Western devils. Verbal mud-slinging is not going to change the past in any way. Secondly, while the British plundered us economically for more than a century, we have been beneficiaries of the fruits of modern (Western) science, technology, and medicine in many ways. That, as I see it, is the only realistic *quid pro quo* we can hope to have.

This does not mean that India must not keep watchful eyes on similar machinations whether by Western mischief-makers or by India's (currently no less dangerous) neighbors across her borders. So I make no apologies for taking whatever is best from the East as well as from the West. I relish ecstatic bhajan songs and listening to the suprabadham in the morning as much as reading about the standard model in physics and playing with Riemann tensors. If some Indians describe this as falling at the feet of alien oppressors, intellectual enslavement or worse, I plead guilty and trust my accusers will confine their commitments to Tantric studies, Vedic physics, planetary astrology and the like in pristine Sanskrit, and eschew Western languages, ideas and inventions like the plague.

Concluding thoughts

As in many other matters, India is blessed in her linguistic legacies as well. It is home to the language which first formulated the science of grammar and to linguistic families that enrich one another and have been enriched by alien streams; it is the fount of long epics and birth-place of tall tales, mystical poems with sophisticated prosody; It is the country where plays classical and modern, may be seen in a dozen different languages. Fortunately for all, the linguistic buffet that India offers is truly sumptuous, and the offerings continue to grow.

III

Epic of the Ideal Hero: The Ramayana

(The Ramayana) is a single work, harmoniously constructed, and written, for the most part, in a language which bears witness to a high literary and aesthetic culture.

- Paul Masson-Oursel et al.
(Ancient India and Indian Civilization)

I vaguely recall hearing from my grandmother the story of Rama breaking a most extraordinary bow, and thereby winning the hand of fair princess Sita. My older brother and sister were also listening. The story did not mean much to me then, as I was as yet too young to know what winning the hand of a fair princess meant. But I was fascinated by the narration in my own ignorant way.

When I was a little older I used to attend expositions of the Ramayana, presented every year by a scholar-musician-raconteur who was a master in that characteristically Indian art form—reminiscent of ancient Greek rhapsodists—in which a religious classic is narrated with reverence and erudition, accompanied by devotional music, and spiced with commonsensical wisdom and humorous commentaries on human folly. *Kathá-kálakshepam*, it is called in Tamil, which literally means spending time by listening to (religious) stories.

I am glad I wasn't mature enough to ask my grandmother why a bow had to be broken for Rama to win Sita, for that would have spoiled all the charm and thrill of the episode. I am happy too for not having blurted out other such irrelevancies to the learned man who was re-telling the epic to an audience that was experiencing the joys that come from listening to a familiar and moving story. Nevertheless, questions used to pop up in my mind every time I encountered a Ramayana episode.

Great narratives—especially of the religious kind—have to be read or listened to while grazing in the realm of ideas and ideals, for their truth lies not in factuality but in the meaning, message, and inspiration they impart. So it has been with me all through the years. The Rama and Krishna I read about in the epics and Puranas are not the same that I pay homage to in a temple. The epic heroes are supreme symbols of the culture. Their words and deeds may be analyzed and admired, even criticized and castigated here and there in academic discourses, but more importantly they are icons of traditions which have invested them with sanctity through generations of reverence and worship. The images in the temples to which we sing kirtans and bhajans may be only religiously and denominationally sacred, but what they stand for is of universal significance. Taken as characters in an epic of literary worth Rama and Sita are transnational of universal interest, like Agamemnon, Hamlet and Faust. They carry the weight and wisdom of centuries and have imparted indelible cultural imprints on an entire civilization.

Their names are imbued with a mysterious connotation in the hearts and minds of those who are part of the tradition.

The Ramayana is the saga of the divine personage Rama and his consort Sita. The two have become ideals of truthfulness and chastity in the Hindu world. Very few names in history have provoked the love and respect that Rama and Sita have been able to do in the hearts and minds of millions of Hindus.

The Ramayana has nourished the Hindu spirit and India's culture for many centuries now. Yet, we have no idea of when or how the magnificent epic seeped into our collective psyche and became an intrinsic part of it. Even after centuries of scholarship, no one has a definitive answer. The traditional view is that the work is several thousand years old. Rama's reign is said to have been during the treta yuga which, per traditional Hindu reckoning, was at least a million years ago. If we take the findings of modern archaeology and geology seriously, this contention will have to be moderated.

There seems to be some literary evidence to suggest that even before the actual composition of the masterpiece, certain more ancient ballads treating the story of a Rama and a Sita were popular in northern India. It has been suggested that it was perhaps from these that a great poet took his germinal ideas. Specifically, some Buddhist Jataka tales speak of a brother and sister called Rama and Sita (Winternitz, I. 384). Sita's name is also mentioned as a furrow in some Vedic hymns (IV: 57), while there is mention of a King Janaka (Sita's father in the epic) in the Brihadáranyaka (IV) Upanishad.

A related question is the historicity of Rama and the other characters. Bluntly put, is the Ramayana literature or history? This may be a matter of enormous interest from the perspective of history and comparative literature; but it is also an extremely sensitive question from the point of view of a dynamic living religion, let alone current politics. Dispassionate scholars may explore the genesis of what they regard as one of the most marvelous creations of the human spirit with great reverence and admiration for the work. The eminent scholar Dr. Suniti Kumar Chatterjee wrote in a Bengali newspaper article (*Ananda Bazaar Patrika*, Calcutta, Jan 17, 1976) that "Ramayana is not a historical fact of any age; it is from beginning to end a fiction. ...... No scholar of Indian history thinks that Rama, the hero of Ramayana was a historical person who can be relegated to a particular period of time." He was severely criticized by orthodoxy to which this sounded blasphemous. But it was also feared, perhaps rightly, that questioning the historicity of a divine hero could shake the stability of ancient customs, practices, and worship modes.

We may recall that when scholars in the Western tradition began to examine the historicity of Jesus Christ in the eighteenth century, there was uproar from the religious establishment. In some traditions, there would be more than uproar. It is a blessing for Hindus that there is no authority in our system who is invested with the power to issue a death warrant on a Hindu for entertaining an unorthodox view. No authority can even excommunicate a person in the Hindu world. In our own times spokespersons for ancient traditions take to the Internet to abuse skeptical thinkers with a variety of adjectives. We may contrast this with the fate of the Egyptian scholar Nasr Hamid Abu-Zayd for publishing his view that the Holy Qur'an is essentially a literary and religious work, largely mythical. He was denied promotion at his university in Cairo, declared a *murtad* (heretic), and stripped of his Muslim-status. This made his marriage to his Muslim wife invalid, so he was asked to divorce her. When he left with his wife to a Western country, a fatwa (death warrant) was put on him (The Guardian, 20 October 1999).

As long as minds are free to think and wherever they are allowed to express their thoughts, challenges to religious dogmas and further explorations will continue. And as long as minds that are slavishly fettered to mindless religious bigotry, and the latter holds political power in a nation, free thinkers will have to remain silent and terrified, or flee to lands where freedom reigns.

While it is true that historical inquiries into the claims of religions could have negative impacts on some aspects of religions, they also enrich the culture by deepening understanding of a culture's past.

On the author of the Ramayana

I once asked a teacher in my school who had authored the Ramayana.

"Valmiki," he replied unhesitatingly.

"And who was Valmiki?" I asked further.

"He was the author of the Ramayana," the teacher said with a smile.

"When and where did he live?" I persisted.

"Why do you want to know that?" he replied, somewhat testily. "When you eat a *rasagulla*, do you ask who made it, or do you just enjoy it?" Everyone in class laughed aloud. I felt embarrassed. Though I thought the teacher had replied to me with another question (not unusual when one doesn't have a good answer) I was unhappy that my curiosity was not quenched.

Gradually I came to realize that this is an intrinsic feature of the Hindu world: the authors of some of the most sublime and long-lasting works and the originators of some of the most powerful ideas that have influenced the culture have slid into the nebulous past, unrecognizable as men and women who once lived, leaving their mantras and messages resound for themselves.

Nevertheless, I continued to wonder many times about who was the master poet who wrote the saga of Sri Ramachandra in Sanskrit. When did he live and where? What were his other interests? How old was he when he composed the work? What was his family like? Who was his guru? How did he manage to put down thousands of poetic lines long before the invention of paper and pen? How did the first listeners and readers of the epic react to the work? How was this powerful narrative in meters conveyed to distant places in ancient times?

Unfortunately, very little of historical reliability is known on any of these matters. Among the lost treasures of humanity's heritage are details on the lives and doings of the creative minds of the ancient world. We know next to nothing about the geniuses who first contrived the wheel and the shovel. Our knowledge of the architects of the Pyramids and the Stonehenge, of the authors of the Vedas and the epics of India: all this is a gaping void in humanity's hazy memory of the distant past. It is as if veil has come down between us and the lives of those giants. We don't have a glimpse of them as mortals in flesh and blood. Instead we have fables and fantasies on them, often told with a straight face.

But we do have lore that preserves tales about those once-real people. Thus, the Ramayana is attributed to a sage poet called Valmiki. His is surely the most prestigious name in all of Sanskrit literature. We honor him as *Ādikavi*: the first of poets. What little we know about his life is gathered from the Ramayana itself, and from assorted writings and references, from a blend of fact and fancy with the same teasing indifference to physical possibilities as any puranic legend.

As per the Balakanda, a bird had been cruelly killed by the arrow of the hunter Valmiki. Seeing this, he expressed his dismay, and said, "May this utterance (with its prosodic measure) issuing from my sorrow become the Shloka mode and none other!"

(*shokártasya pravritto me shloko bhavatu nányathá.*) This has become the legendary etymology for the word shloka which is actually one of the five standard meters in Sanskrit prosody. It is often used in aphorisms.

In the opening canto of the Bala Kanda we are told of how the sage Narada revealed to Valmiki the entire epic in answer to a query, and how the Creator (Brahma) Himself appeared before the poet and induced him to compose the work as magnificent poetry.

In the Ayodhya Kanda we meet Valmiki in a hermitage which Rama and Sita visit along with Lakshmana. In the Uttara Kanda we read that it was in Valmiki's hermitage that Sita spent her years after being renounced by Rama on the suspicion that Ravana had violated her. Lava and Kusha, the twin sons of Rama and Sita, are said to have been under Valmiki's care and guidance in their boyhood years.

True or symbolic, there is also a story to the effect that this noble author of the Saga of Rama was once a highway robber who plundered innocent travelers to add riches to his family. This story occurs in the Adhyatma Ramayana (which is part of the Brahmánda Purana, and expounds the spiritual significance of the Ramayana). Here we read that the great Valmiki confessed to Rama: "I was born in a family of a Brahmin, but kept myself in the company of thieves and hunters. I lived their life. My wife was a Shudra woman and I had many children from her. I knew of no other profession and was therefore turned into a way-layer and a bandit" (Munilal, 2001).

One of his victims once asked the future poet if his kith and kin would share the penalties of his sins. When the robber put this question to his wife and children, they frankly told him they would take a share of his loots, but certainly not the bitter berries of his sins. Having thus learned the lesson that we alone are responsible for our actions, even if their benefits may be used by others, the robber went to the sages for counsel. In a variant of this story, it was Nárada who instructed the robber to mend his ways. The legend goes on to say that the robber-turned-sage went into a meditative posture for many years at the end of which his whole body was covered up by a huge anthill. Other sages now came to the scene and named him Valmiki, which is Sanskrit for ant-hill. Incredible, but fascinating, as most of our puranic stories are. But this could also be the concoction of a punster, playing on the word Valmiki, somewhat like the joke that Mr. Bush's family were once bushmen.

Emperor Dasharatha

Aside from the usual history, we have in the cultures of the world a *sacred history* whose elements are etched in the framework of the culture. The personages and episodes in our sacred history are at the root of many aspects of Hindu thought and observances. It is difficult to know the origins of these stories, but it could be that they sprang from personages and events of ordinary history and took on creative lives of their own.

According to sacred history, there once was a great king by the name of Raghu. Like other great kings he made many conquests. In Kalidasa's *Raghuvamsam* we read that King Raghu subdued the Persians (Parasikas) and the Ionian Geeks (Yavanas) (Anantapadmanabhan, 1973). Emperor Raghu had a son named Aja, which means one who was not born. Aja's son was the emperor Dasharatha who, as everyone in the Hindu world knows, was the father of the hero of the Ramayana.

Dasharatha's glory is described with poetic flair by Kamban. Rendering this into English would be like making a clay duplicate of a Michelangelo's David. Fully aware of this, let me try to spell out some of what Kamban says (I.4-12): "The king of that great city (Ayodhya) was king of kings (*am má nagarukku arasan arasarkku arasan*). The qualities of a good ruler are wisdom, compassion, serenity, strength, unblemished heroism, generosity, meting out justice, and fairness. Dasharatha had these qualities twice in measure as any other king. His love for his subjects was like that of a mother for her child. He guided, led, and took his people along the righteous path. He cured their ailments too. He traversed the ocean of the indigent by answering to their needs, the ocean of knowledge by vast reading, the ocean of enemies by felling them with his sword, the ocean of pleasures by wisely enjoying them. This glorious king held sway over turbulent rivers, birds, beasts, and even the minds of women of questionable morals. From the heights of his well-guarded capital whose hills resembled palaces with precious stones, the world seemed to the king like his own capital. His spear was often blunted by use against enemies, and his golden anklets suffered wear and tear as they often rubbed against the crowns of the kings he subdued..."

The genius of Indian poets for creating hyperbolic imagery is among India's great treasures. Few poets elsewhere have come anywhere near the Hindus in this regard. The phrase oriental hyperbole is sometimes used to characterize such descriptions. But then, there are hyperboles of this kind in the Bible also.

Dasharatha's love for Rama was extraordinary, bordering on what some would call abnormal attachment. He could not live without Rama whom he literally adored. If Freud had read the Ramayana he might have described excessive love to one's own son as *Dasharatha complex*.

Once during a hunting excursion, the great marksman Dasharatha shot a fateful arrow in the direction of a gurgling sound, imagining it was from a wild elephant at a water hole. But the arrow pierced a young ascetic who was drawing water from a well for his aging blind parents. "Which fool did this to me!" he wondered aloud, and upon seeing Dasharatha, said, "Be not tormented by the thought that you have killed a Brahmin, for I was born of a Vaishya father and Shudra mother." (Apologists notwithstanding, caste hierarchy is found in many episodes in Hindu sacred writings.) The remorseful king duly carried the water to the blind parents. When he told them what had happened, the father cursed the king that some day he too would die of *putrashoka*: pain from the loss of one's son. After uttering these words, the dejected father promptly died. This was one of two major events in Dasharatha's life which were to serve as a springboard for the saga of Rama.

Next, during a battle an axle of his chariot lost grip on the wheel. Queen Kaikeyi who was with him then used her own hand as the axle. Deeply moved by her devotion and service, the king promised to give her any two boons whenever she would ask. Years later, Kaikeyi chose to ask for the coronation of her son Bharata and for fourteen years of exile of Rama.

Dasharatha's end came as per the imprecation of the old man in the forest. He writhed in pain and fell unconscious at the sight of Rama leaving for the forest, watching the dust rise and fall on the road as Rama walked away. The next few days were sheer agony. Six nights after Rama's departure, alone in his chamber with queen Kaushalya, he recalled to her in great detail the incident with the young man with blind parents, saying, "One reaps the fruits of one's actions, good or evil. If one cuts a mango grove and plants straws, what fruits can he expect?" After recounting the whole story, King Dasharatha exclaimed "Oh Raghava who relieves me from my suffering, who is so precious to your father! Oh Kaushalya, I cannot see anymore! Oh austere Sumitra! Oh cruel Kaikeyi, enemy and disgrace to family!" After uttering these words, he left his physical frame.

Dasharatha was blessed with four wonderful sons as a result of an elaborate sacrifice. He had the joy of seeing them grow till they were adolescents, he was happy to see them married. Not long after that, events became unhappy in his life. It was a great anguish for Dasaratha when Rama left, but this turned out to be for the benefit of humankind.

Bharata of Kekaya: His dream and his character

When I started reading the Ramayana in four different languages, I discovered that the standard abridged versions skip many interesting sections.

India's ancient geography is lost: Places like Mohenjo-Daro and Harappa are described as the seats of ancient Pakistani civilization. Sindh, which gave India her modern name, is no longer in India. Kashmir, which is to remind us of Rishi Kashyapa, has been the scene of religious conflicts for decades. Of many other places there are hardly any relics.

The Kekaya kingdom in the North-West of India was between Gandhára and the River Beas. The Puranas say that Kekayans were half Sanskritic. They once had a king called Ashvapati. His daughter (Kaikeyí) so fascinated Dasaratha that (long before the maid Manthara's instigation) he promised his kingdom to her son, if she would be given in marriage to him.

Kaikeyí's son Bharata was a remarkably righteous person who, like practically everyone in the epic, had enormous respect and reverence for Rama, his elder brother.

Bharata was at his uncle's residence in Girivraja when he was summoned to Ayodhya. He did not know that Rama and Lakshmana had gone into exile, and that king Dasaratha had died. When the messengers arrived, a cheerless Bharata was narrating to his companions a foreboding dream that had tormented him the previous night. In the dream he saw a dejected Dasharatha plunge from a mountain peak into a quagmire of cow-dung where he was swimming, drinking oil from the hollow of his palms and laughing intermittently. The king was smearing his body with sesame oil. Bharata also witnessed the oceans dry up, and the moon fall on earth, and the world thrust into darkness. He saw the tusk of the king's elephant shattered, and raging fires suddenly extinguished. Young women, of dark and reddish brown complexion, clad in black, attacked the king, and took over his seat. Then, with red flowers and painted in sandal paste, the great king departed southwards in a donkey-driven chariot. An ugly demonic woman who mocked the king was dragging him. Such had been the scenes in Bharata's horrible dream which presaged or simulcast in symbolic images what the great king was going through. We are reminded of the Latin poet Ovid's words: *Somnia me terrent, veros imitantia casus*: Dreams frighten me that imitate a real fall. Now, fully awake, Bharata was asked to return immediately to Ayodhya.

Upon his return, Bharata heard what had actually happened, and he realized the significance of his nightmare. He became furious. He gave a severe tongue-lashing to his mother Kaikeyi, calling her sinful, greedy, contemptible, and more.

Describing this emotional tempest, the poet introduces two animal-similes in one sentence by saying: "Having thus spoken, the very enraged Bharata hissed like a serpent, and fell down unconscious like an elephant pierced by a javelin."

Kaikeyí had misread Bharata, and so had Kaushalyá, Rama's mother. The former had imagined that Bharata would accept the crown greedily and gleefully. However, learning that Lakshmana too had left with Rama, Bharata began to curse him in the strongest terms, wishing him the consequences of many awful kinds of sins for going away with Rama, instead of urging him not to leave the kingdom and abandon his royal prerogative.

Bharata saw his mother Kaikeyí's maid servant Manthara bedecked in the jewels that Kaikeyí had given her, and wearing ostentatious robes, looking, says the poet, like a female monkey bound with a number of strings. When a guard handed Manthara to Shatrughna the latter seized the poor woman with rage and dragged her on the floor. Tulsi Das describes the scene starkly: "Her hump was smashed, her head split, her teeth were broken, and there was a stream of blood from her mouth." Associating deformity with evil was part of the ancient worldview. Bharata calmed Shatrughna's anger by saying that women did not deserve to die at the hands of men, and that Rama would be much upset if he knew they mistreated the wretched woman (Tulsidas, I.161). Respecting women was among the ancient dharmic principles that were, in a Shakespearean phrase, more honored in the breach than in the observance.

Bharata ordered engineers to build broad roads to where Rama and Lakshmana were, so he could march there with his army to persuade or force Rama to return to Ayodhya. Lakshmana mistook Bharata's advance, thinking he had sinister intentions. Rama calmed Lakshmana down. Actually Bharata had come to insist upon Rama to return to Ayodhya and be crowned king. Upon Rama's adamant refusal to return, Bharata went back reluctantly, placed Rama's sandals on the throne under a parasol. The Rama-Bharata encounter is reckoned as one of the most moving episodes in the epic. Bharata ruled the land for fourteen years from outside the capital, in Nandigrama, living modestly, without any royal splendor.

In the Uttara Kanda we read about a terrible battle which lasted for seven nights in which three million Gandharvas are said to have perished in an instant: another clear instance of oriental hyperbole. One has to take the figure of three million as poetic exaggeration, unless nuclear weapons were involved.

At the end of that war, Bharata's sons Taksha and Pushkara were installed to rule over those regions. Such was Bharata, another hero of the epic. He was strong, yet unassuming, and meant only the best for his beloved brother. Valmiki reminds us through him that many good people are sometimes misunderstood even by their own kith and kin.

Urmila (Úrmilá)

In a Hindi course I took at school we had to read a short story by Maithili Sharan Gupt, the great Hindi poet and writer who spoke with pride and understanding of the glory that was Ind. While talking about this great writer, our teacher said that he had written a version of the Ramayana called *Saket*, (another name for Ayodhya) in which Lakshmana's wife Urmila is the central figure. He also told us that Rabindranath Tagore listed Urmila among the forgotten heroines of Indian literature. *Kabbey Upekshita:* Neglected in great literature, is regarded as one of Tagore's masterpieces.

Some years later, I looked into the three major versions of the epic (Valmiki, Kamban, Tulsi Das) and discovered how true this was in all these versions of the Ramayana. The most glaring episode is when Lakshmana fervently pleads with Rama to take him along in the fourteen-year exile to the forest. Rama tries to persuade Lakshmana to stay in Ayodhya to serve Kaushalya and Sumitra (their mothers), with no mention of Urmila. But Lakshmana absolutely wants to accompany Rama. What is sorely missing is that he does not so much as inform Urmila of his decision, or take leave of her, let alone consult with her on the matter.

During a chance conversation with a Telugu scholar, I discovered that there is an ancient song in Telugu that is entitled *Urmila Devi Nidra* (Divine Urmila's Sleep). I believe this is the source of a story to the effect that Urmila was an artist who was painting when her husband Lakshmana walked into her chamber, calling aloud her name. Somewhat concerned, she stood up hastily, and in the process, spilled the paint from the pot. She explained to Lakshmana that she was painting a picture of Rama on the day of his coronation, and was planning to send it to her father Janaka.

Lakshmana explained that because of Kaikeyí, the coronation had been cancelled, and he went on to say that he was going away with Rama to the forest for fourteen years. According to this story, Urmila was happy for her husband since he had this wonderful opportunity to serve Rama and Sita. She even asked Lakshmana to go right away, without wasting time with her. She added something that would seem strange to many. She asked Lakshmana never to think of her as this would be a distraction from his focus on service to Rama and Sita which, after all, was the primary motivation for his going with them. She didn't want to accompany him so as not to take away his attention from Rama.

We may note two things here. First, this is an entirely new creative episode by a later-day poet, for such an incident is not reported in Valmiki's original. Secondly, this author has beautifully constructed a story in which we see Urmila as a selfless and extraordinary wife. At the same time, one may also interpret Urmila's reaction as arising from deep disappointment, not to say resentment, at Lakshmana's devotion to Rama and Sita at her expense. She knows that it would be of no avail asking Lakshmana to stay home or to take her along, for his devotion to Rama was way beyond his attachment to her or to anyone else in the world. By letting him go without her, she is accepting with wisdom what would happen anyway: What is unavoidable is to be accepted.

The Telugu transcreator of the Ramayana also introduced a scene in the last book in which Urmila, along with the wives of the other two brothers, protests Rama's treatment of Sita. The women even demand that, if that was how he would treat Sita, he should kill them all (Nagar, 2001).

In our own times, the Malayalee playwright Srikantan Nair wrote a play entitled *Kanchana Sita* in which, during the fourteen years when her husband was separated from her, Urmila undertook serious studies of the shástras (canonical texts) under the guidance of learned scholars. Furthermore, she engaged Rama in a debate when the hero banished his wife. When the hero tried to justify it on the basis that he had to submit to the will of the people who suspected Sita's chastity during her stay in Ravana's prison, Urmila wondered how Rama managed to ignore the will of the people and went on his exile, inspired by his own will and judgment (Sreekantan and Joseph, 2005). Rama does not say, *touché*!

Whether Valmiki so intended or not, the story of Urmila is a sad one. A young bride, beautiful and devoted to her fine and handsome husband, she was forced to spend the better part of her youthful years in celibacy and solitude, with no communication with her beloved. Some have said, we do not know on what basis or authority, that during those years Lakshmana kept in touch with Urmila, by means of *pranic* energy: some sort of magical cell-phone, one would imagine. Apologetics knows no constraints.

I am inclined to think that Valmiki introduced Urmila and her plight precisely to provoke thoughtful people to reflect on how it was/is not uncommon for men—especially the idealistic ones—to plunge into the pursuit of their grand goals at the expense and to the neglect of their wives who often bear it with equanimity. Neglect of women and wives is ancient in human culture. That writers brought this out explicitly or implicitly shows that there have been keen observers and thinkers in the Hindu world, as elsewhere, who were/are appalled by some of the shameful practices in society of which people are totally ignorant. Unless and until this realization affects the attitudes and actions of people, there will always be Urmilas everywhere in the world.

Shurpanakha (Shúrpanakhá)

Once when I was traveling by train from Calcutta to Bombay and the train stopped at the town of Násik (or Náshik), a gentleman got out and made a worshipful gesture on the platform. Back in the compartment he said he always paid his reverence to the place where Rama, Lakshmana, and Sita had stayed during much of their exile years. It was from here that Ravana kidnapped Sita, he explained. It is said that the forest of Dandaka was once part of Ravana's colony in India, with its own governor. Many rakshasas (tribal people) lived there happily. Today the city has several temples, of which the Kalaram Temple is the most famous. The Godavari River passes through the city, offering a pilgrimage spot for the Kumbh Mela.

The gentleman on the train also told me triumphantly that it was in the Tapovan in that town that Lakshmana cut off Shurpanakha's nose, which is how the place got its name. *Násika* means nose.

Shurpanakha is a tragic figure in the Ramayana. She was no paragon of beauty. She was a rakshasi, a giantess of horrendous proportions and ugly features. Her nails were like a winnowing basket (which is the etymological meaning of her name). Valmiki describes her as having a large belly, deformed eyes, coppery hair, a frightful voice, hard-hearted and aged, vile and repulsive, and deformed to boot. In the same sentence where this description is given the poet refers to Rama as having a charming face, a slender waist, large eyes, beautiful locks of hair, pleasant aspect, sweet voice, youthful, righteous and amiable (III.17). It is as if the poet is saying that the entire epic is about the confrontation of the bad and the ugly with the good and the beautiful.

When Shurpanakha saw Rama, her infatuation for him was ablaze. She wondered why such a man was clad in ascetic garb and what brought him to the forest where ogres and beasts dwelt. Rama calmly told her about his exile, and asked her who she was, albeit with a touch of sarcasm for he described her as possessing charming limbs.

Shurpanakha told Rama about herself and her five brothers, and confessed her passion for him—the second instance of love at first sight in the epic, for this happened between Rama and Sita also— She asked Rama to become her husband, while also deriding fair Sita whom she called ugly and unworthy of him. Recognizing perhaps that she was making a fool of herself, Rama tried to have some fun at her expense. He pointed to Lakshmana who, he informed, was without a wife. "Take my brother as your husband, large-eyed beauty," he teased her. When she came to Lakhsmana, he too decided to have some fun. Humbling himself as a slave at the service of his brother, he re-directed the ogress to Rama.

The infatuated Shurpanakha now rushed back to Rama, and attempted to attack poor Sita who was merely observing the comical scene. Rama thwarted the attempt to assault his beloved and advised Lakshmana not to jest with cruel and unworthy persons, forgetting, it would seem, that he himself had done just that. But, of course, this was okay for a hero.

Furthermore, Rama asked Lakshmana to mutilate the ugly, vile, fat woman (*virúpá, asatím, mahá udarím*). The angry Lakshmana obeyed right away, and cut off the ears and nose of the unfortunate Shurpanakha. Bereft of nose and ears, bleeding profusely and writhing in pain, the ogress fled into the woods to complain to her brothers Khara and Dhushana.

The Tamil poet Kamban says that Lakshmana also cut off her nipples (*mulaik-kankal-* literally, eyes of the breasts) too (Kamban: III.5.94). Kamban's description of Shurpanakha as a result of this mauling is very moving: She pressed a cloth over her bleeding nose, heaved like a hot furnace. She beat the ground with her hands, she held and looked at the pathetic condition of her breasts. She was sweating as she ran with her strong legs, and then collapsed from much bleeding.

In her extreme rage Shurpanakha wanted Ravana to punish Rama, but she recognized Rama's supreme strength. So she advised him to go in disguise to ravish Sita. But in the end, when Ravana set out to fight Rama face to face, she begged him not to dare, for she was sure that would be Ravana's end. Shurpanakha was obviously quite intelligent.

I never liked the nose-cutting episode. There is something needlessly savage in this inhuman treatment of a woman by the two noble brothers. Not long ago I read a tasteless re-telling of this incident by someone who had clearly not read the original, and thought he was writing a humorous piece. In contrast, Sharmila Biswas produced a more sensitive and enlightened treatment of the story in an Odissi dance drama, raising such questions as: How could Rama and Lakshmana—said to be incarnations of Vishnu—mutilate a woman? Most male interpreters and cultural patriots simply say that Shurpanakha was evil and so deserved the treatment, and that it was because of the merciful nature of Rama and Lakshmana that they only cut off her nose and ears, instead of killing her right away, forgetting how Tadaka had been treated earlier.

Practically all the great literatures (and histories) of the ancient world were authored by men, many of whose view of women did not always include the respect which at least some in our own times are trying to cultivate. What this means is that while it may be unfair to judge past generations by the standards of present values, it would be dark-age-minded to offer apologetic explanations for such behavior which amounts to justifying it.

Nose-cutting and other forms of mutilation were not uncommon modes of punishment in many ancient societies. Vestige of such practices still remain in some languages. In Tamil one sometimes warns a child to behave, or else one would cut off the nose (*múkkai aruppén*). Similar practices have been reported in some present-day Islamic countries, as enjoined by sharia laws.

Whether symbolic or not, Shurpanakha and Manthara, the two personages who are ultimately responsible for the downfall of Ravana, were both women. Manthara managed to send Rama to the forest by instigating Kaikeyi, which she did by arousing her jealousy; Shurpanakha sent Ravana to the same forest by arousing his lust. Even from behind the scenes, women can and do accomplish much of significance in history. Unfortunately, in the Ramayana, both women were evil. Yet, but for them, there would have been no Ramayana to tell, no glorious return to Ayodhya to celebrate.

Rakshasa (Rákshasá) Ravana (Rávaná)

When I first heard about ten-headed Ravana I told my grandmother this was impossible. She simply said he was a rakshasa, as if that was proof enough for the possibility. This was not unlike saying that leaves are green because they contain chlorophyll when this word simply means green-leaf in Greek. Then my grandmother went on to explain that rakshasas were abnormal beings, huge and with magical powers. In fact, in some South Asian languages, the word rakshasa simply means a giant, often an unpleasant or evil one at that.

There is hardly a mythology without beings stupendously larger than humans. Titans (Greek), Gig antes (Roman), Bustle (Norse), Afghan (Celtic), and Rakshasas (Sanskrit) are various species of mythological giants. Giants were good, bad, or both in ancient tales. Later writers like Jonathan Swift in *Gulliver's Travels* and Rabelais in *Gargantua-Pantagruel* created their own mythical giants.

Once I recognized this, it was easier to accept the idea. The key to understanding or appreciating any mythology or belief-system is to agree with its basic premises or postulates, and then proceed. One does this all the time in mathematics and logic.

Ravana, perhaps the best known rakshasa, was a mixture of some fine qualities and many horrific ones. We get a glimpse of his stature in a number of contexts. For example, when furious Shurpanakha showed up noseless, this mighty rakshasa was in the penthouse of his seven-storied palace, clad in heavenly attire, adorned with garland, dazzling with jewels studded with stones that glittered like stars, and surrounded by ministers.

After ten thousand years of austerities, he had obtained from Brahma a boon by which no god or demon, no bird, serpent, beast or monster could kill him, nor vanquish him in combat. Endowed with such power he wrought untold havoc, killed pitilessly whoever dared to raise a head against him. His body had scars from battles with demons and deities, from which he always emerged victorious with his awesome decacephalous body.

Enraged by the sight of his nose-chopped-sister, and aroused by the tantalizing description of Sita she gave him, Ravana schemed to bring Sita within his grasp. With his unquenchable appetite for women, he had ravished Rambha when she was married to his brother Kubera, and had kidnapped a Naga queen. Before the abduction of Rama's wife, he bragged to her about his great prowess. Boasting that he had seized the aerial chariot from Kubera, he said that even the gods fled from him in fright. The winds were afraid of him, the sun cooled off in his presence, while leaves on trees and flowing waters stood still when they saw him. He vaunted about his great capital where buildings were of gold, the city gates were bejeweled, where, amidst horses, elephants and chariots, one heard the sound of soothing music.

Ravana claimed, unlike Archimedes, that he could lift up the earth without a lever, with his own bare hands; that he could drink the oceans dry, kill even Death, and torment the sun. So stupendous were his powers.

But he committed the most heinous crime when he took Sita away. This was the most unpardonable sin of all. He had gotten away with similar offenses before. But this time, all his might came to naught. His crime spelled humiliating disaster and death.

The climactic sections of Yuddha Kanda (War Book) is replete with notes on ancient (epic) warfare where mantras and magical missiles breathe life into archery of the highest caliber. The battle is between Rama and Ravana, one representing Good and the other embodying Evil. The scenes remind us of what we sometimes see in modern science fiction movies. It is remarkable that a poet spelled out so many gory details about war millennia ago.

The battle was tough. At one point, in Kamban's version, Rama said: "Though arrows numbering more than grains of sand have struck Ravana's eyes, and arrows sharper than the thoughts of scholars have gone into his wounds, he is still alive!" After a long combat during which many, many men and monkeys died, and the sky grew dark, as if by clouds, because of the arrows that flew every which way, Ravana was finally felled down by a fatal arrow from Rama's bow. It was the end of a long life that had lasted 30 million days (*mukkódi nál*) (VI.35.196). Kamban says that Rama saw Ravana's wound on his back, and felt ashamed that he had shot a fleeing man, which he took as a dishonor upon himself (VI.35.205-206). In these lines the poet shows that Ravana was a coward and Rama a man truly noble.

Ravana was reminded of all his evil deeds when he confronted Rama. It has been said that "The destruction of the entire Rakshasa army made clear to him that Brahma's boon was expressly inapplicable in his encounter with Rama and that another curse brought on him the Vanaras, that Vedavati was almost born as Sita and her curse that if he ever touched an unwilling woman, he would be destroyed (Sitaramiah, 1982, 97).

Ravana is remembered as a vicious monarch who ruled Lanka and ravished Sita. But his grieving brother Vibhishana reminded us in his eulogy that he was generous in gifts to mendicants, enjoyed pleasures, and maintained his dependents. He gave riches to friends and avenged his enemies. He practiced austerities, mastered the Vedas, and was a master of rituals. He was also known for his deep devotion to Lord Shiva.

Ravana reminds us of the ancient truth that power corrupts. Francis Bacon wrote: "It is a strange desire, to seek power and to lose liberty: or to seek power over others, and to lose power over man's self" (Eliot, 1937, 28). How true this was of Ravana! Power corrupts men by making them arrogant and ruthless, and also by enabling them to subdue the weak and the defenseless. Every conqueror from Alexander and Attila to Genghis Khan and Ibrahim Lodi, was a Ravana in his own way. Often power also prompts men to seek fulfillment of their baser desires.

Most traditional writers portray woman as temptress. In the Ravana-Sita episode it is man who tries to seduce a chaste woman. The Ravana story tells us that lust, left loose, results in the downfall of even the most powerful. We have seen this all too often in humanity's long history.

Sometimes I have wondered: Sita was saved because of who she was. But what about the thousands of others who were harvested for Ravana's pleasure? Nothing happened to Ravana for all those derelictions. Do we always need a great victim to bring down a powerful oppressor and establish justice in the world?

Hanuman (Hanumán)

In many ancient cultures, animals have been held sacred (Cooper, 1992). So it is in the Hindu world also. Thus, we pay homage to the figure of a monkey, long tail, flattened cheek and all. We call him: Hanuman (One with large jaws).

The year was 1937. My grandfather, who had once been Head Master of the Hindu High School in Tirunelveli, passed away. In the tradition, if the ashes of a departed person are strewn in the sacred waters of the Ganga, the entry into the emancipated state is facilitated, if not accelerated. This becomes especially so when this is done at one of the sacred ghats of the prime pilgrimage center of Varanasi (Benares).

So the family took a trip to that very ancient sacred city which is known to have been part of the Khosala kingdom already in 650 BCE. Emperor Ashoka's famous columns were erected at Saranath near this great city. I still remember the fast moving scenery of the countryside I saw through the window of the train: fields of grain and huts, bodies of water and grazing cattle, men at a distance doing their ablutions, and more.

After the night's ride and crossing the River Sone we reached our destination. In Varanasi, Ganga's long and curved bank is paved with stones, punctuated by sections with large steps to the water level. These are the ghats, every one of which is consecrated to a deity or a mythological figure.

What has all this to do with the Ramayana? Well, we spent our days there at Hanuman Ghat. Countless monkeys roamed freely near the Durga Temple which we visited. These simian ancestors of Homo sapiens moved among the pilgrims with a supreme sense of security, though (and perhaps for this very reason) many people carried batons to keep the creatures at a respectable distance. It was good to see such happy harmony between man and beast: after all, we are all here to share the bounties of nature. But it also exposes people to diseases peculiar to other creatures.

We paid our homage to the gods at the Kashi Vishvanath golden temple and made a pilgrimage walk along the Panchkosi Road. If the holy man who escorted us was telling the truth, we had in the process rid ourselves of practically all our sins to date. When I think of that visit, many images come to mind: muddy roads, damp and narrow alleys, ornate temples, and cosmopolitan crowds. I see holy men smeared in ash and clad in meager strips of cloth sitting in cool contemplation, while other god-fearing men are standing in the sacred flow with their wives and children, producing pious sounds before clenching their noses with two fingers prior to making a redeeming plunge into the waters. Ubiquitous mendicants are appealing to people's charitable instincts. Barbers are doing brisk business on the riverbank because, in the tradition, shaving one's head before entering a temple is one way of paying homage to the deity.

There was in all of this a magic and a mystery that will elude those not of the tradition. Most of all the respectful interaction with the monkeys is related to the venerable Hanuman who is a major personage in the Ramayana.

Hanuman plays a central role in the Ramayana. He is chief of an army of monkeys which fight on Rama's side in the war with Ravana. In spite of his simian appearance Hanuman is superhuman rather than subhuman. He is erudite and wise, virile and virtuous, strong in physique, keen in intelligence, and possessing magical powers. He can expand a hundredfold and contract likewise. His tail can become frighteningly long if he chooses, or a tough long stretch that weighs a ton or more. He is an extraordinary personage who commands respect and admiration.

His mother was Añjali: daughter of the monkey chief Kuñjara. So he is called Áñjaneya. Once Añjali was seduced by Váyu, the Wind-God or God of Cosmic Breath, who entered her with his mind. Thus was Hanuman conceived, and so he is called Pávanaputra: Son of the Wind God.

I remember listening as a lad with rapt attention to Hanuman's exploits. It all sounded so exciting when I first heard these as a lad. When but a child he thought the sun was some fruit, and leaped to the sky to grab it, reaching a height of 24,000 miles. Indra sent a thunderbolt, and Pavanaputra fell on top of a mountain. His left jaw smashed and swelled. That is how he acquired his name and form.

Hanuman is revered because of his unswerving devotion to Rama. From the moment he saw Rama, he became his instant and intense devotee. Hanuman represents pure bhakti in a framework of learning and wisdom, showing that these are not incompatible qualities. Even scholars can be pious, even thinkers can be devotional.

Hanuman's sighting of Sita in captivity and bringing news about Rama to her are among the most moving episodes in the epic. In another episode, Ravana's minions set fire to Hanuman's tail and took him round Lanka for the inhabitants to jeer. But Hanuman grew to immense proportions. Protected by a prayer from Sita to Agni to keep him safe and cool, he went on a rampage that destroyed the beautiful capital of Ravana.

In the course of the climactic war, Lakshmana was wounded by a javelin which Ravana hurled. He lay bleeding on the ground and Rama was saddened since he thought that Lakshmana was dying. Instructed to go to Mount Mahodaya to fetch four specific medicinal herbs for Lakshmana, Hanuman flew to that mountain. Unsure about the prescribed herbs, he sliced off a chunk of the entire mountain, and carried it back to the battlefield with his amazing capacity! Yes, he took a leap across the sea from Mount Mahodaya to Sri Lanka. The force of his take-off caused flowers from trees to fall on him who had himself become large as a mountain. Trees were uprooted; they flew behind him like relatives accompanying a traveler up to a distance, then they fell on the surging sea. Hanuman's body glittered like a hill where fire-flies were swarming. He flew with his tail curled, his arms stretched out. His gigantic shadow was eight miles long and two hundred wide. He encountered obstacles, but eventually reached Lanka on top of Mount Lamba. Valmiki devotes a long chapter describing Hanuman's subcontinental flight.

Tulsi Das wrote a hymn in forty verses, *Hanuman Chalisa*, addressed to this hero. The poet extols Hanuman's prowess, mentions how even gods sing his praise, describes his valiant deeds, refers to his humility when he met Sita, and calls him an incarnation of Lord Shiva. He hails him as the ocean of wisdom and virtue (*gyán-guna-ságar*), and invokes him as Rama's messenger wielding incomparable strength (*Rámdút atulit bal dhamâ*). But Hanuman is equally an intermediary between the devotee and Rama. Hanuman Chalisa is a powerful element in Hindi-Hindu culture. Few Hindi-speaking Hindus have not listened to or recited it. I am still moved when I recite it in a temple.

This reverence for a simiamorphic divinity may seem weird to one not of the Hindu world. But for those brought up in the tradition, there is more to Hanuman than his ape-like visage. Cultural upbringing infuses a sensitivity to sounds and symbols with which outsiders can't resonate. The magic in Hindu deities can be appreciated only by those who are part of the culture. Hanuman is a monkey vis-à-vis Rama the human. One interpretation is that Man is to the Divine, as Monkey is to Man: imperfect in appearance, but committed to serving God which consists, above all, in rectifying what is morally wrong.

The crux of the episode is that when Hanuman heard of Sita's abduction, he determined to find her for Rama, and nothing would deflect him from this determination. In other words, when one witnesses injustice, one should decide right away to correct it, and never flinch from the commitment. Furthermore, when one resolves to right a wrong, one is filled with extraordinary powers to accomplish what one sets out to do. Such strength comes to those who fight for what is ethically right (Nagar, 1995).

A note on Barbri masjid and Ram Setu

My own interest in the Ramayana—as indeed in all aspects of Hinduism and of Indic traditions more generally, has been primarily cultural, historical, and to an extent emotional too; but never to the point of being a breast-beating Hindu, and never with even a touch of xenophobic fervor when it comes to

Non-Hindus in India. This is the result of my upbringing. My father, a devout Hindu who practiced with traditional devotion, had respect for all religions: a precious gift which most Hindus generally have had for many centuries.

At the same time I have always recognized and reluctantly accepted it as a sad part of India's long history that at various phases she has been invaded, conquered, oppressed, and exploited by foreign intruders from Greece, Iran, Afghanistan, Portugal, France, and Great Britain. Hindus have also been converted in large numbers to Islam and Christianity. Like most Hindus I have come to regard this as an unfortunate legacy of the past with far-reaching consequences, both positive and negative. It is doubtful that this transformation of India into a multi-religious and multi-cultural nation can be reversed. If anything there are ominous signs that this enrichment as well as corruption of the original culture of the people will continue even more.

The long range effect of Islamic invasions of India has been the splitting of the subcontinent into three major chunks: India, Pakistan, and Bangladesh. The long range effect of British intrusion into India has been the imposition of English on Indian intellectuals and the establishment of a unified parliamentary democracy. The penetration of Islam into India has enriched Indian music, architecture, cuisine, poetry, and literature in immeasurable ways, and that of the British drained India of considerable wealth and caused a virtual caste hierarchy between Anglophonic and only-vernacular-speaking Indians.

Now, back to the Ramayana. The Valmiki text and others declare that Dasharatha ruled Ayodhya where Rama and his brothers were born. As a result that city became a sacred city in the minds of Hindus at some time in history. For whatever reason the invader Babur had a large and impressive mosque built in Ayodhya: more exactly, a grand and beautiful mosque in Ayodhya came to be called after him, the now famous *Babri Masjid*. There are many who believe that this mosque replaced a Rama temple there.

Be that as it may, it has been said that for many centuries, Hindus and Muslims prayed together at this place, and even took the water there to be sacred: a not inconceivable possibility within the Hindu cultural framework. But in the turmoil that emerged with the formation of Pakistan as a separate Islamic state, Hindu nationalist sentiments were provoked to the point of demanding that the mosque in Ayodhya be re-transformed into a temple. While churches, synagogues, and temples have been converted into mosques in many parts of the world, the reverse has seldom occurred, nor is likely to occur in the foreseeable future.

The Mezquita in Córdoba is a glaring exception to this rule. Though it too was built on what was once a modest church of St. Vincent, its reconstruction as a magnificent mosque of unparalleled beauty is a triumph and wonder of Muslim aesthetic creativity which deserves the respect and admiration of every lover of architecture. On both occasions that I visited the place I simply marveled at its grandeur and felt it was even more awe-inspiring than the Taj Mahal. Thanks to its re-transformation into a Christian place of worship, countless Non-Muslims are able to visit and admire it today. I recall standing there for a while and praying for peace between Christians and Muslims.

In any event, I was saddened to read about the riots and rancor in the 1990s which ensued from the efforts of some Hindus to re-take the Barbri Masjid into their fold. Who could have thought that the grand epic would someday be the cause of inter-religious conflicts. It was ironic that whereas Muslims in Spain are agitating to re-convert the Mezquita into a mosque where they can pray, a similar demand by Hindus in India is opposed and resisted by Muslims in India. Such is the asymmetry in religious tolerance today all over the world.

Another unrelated furor arose some years later. It related to the passage in the epic wherein Rama's army of monkeys brought stones and sand, and constructed a bridge (*Ram Setu*) between the southern tip of India and Sri Lanka to enable the army to cross over and rescue Sita from the clutches of Ravana. When I first read about this, I was fascinated by the concept of a civil engineering feat accomplished by the army corps of engineers under Rama's command. I was impressed, not by what they had done, which skeptics might doubt, but by the rich imagination of the poet who pictured such a trans-strait bridge.

It is well known that there exists a rocky ridge formed by corals in an area which the British, in their customary Eurocentric framework, dubbed Adam's Bridge. The Encyclopedia Britannica describes it as "a chain of sand banks between the islands of Mannar near north-western cost, lying between the Gulf of Mannar on the south-west and Pak Strait on north-east".

In the 1990s the National Aeronautical Space Agency of the U.S. announced that photographs from their space shuttle revealed a strip of uplifted patch between India and Sri Lanka. This was immediately touted by the press in India and in NRI Internet messages as scientific confirmation of the Ram Setu alluded to in the epic. The scientific bodies in India confirmed its existence, but declared that it could never have been an artificial construction. It was a purely geophysical occurrence such as happens in many regions of the globe. This gave rise to a bitter controversy between the Indian scientific establishment and the Hindu cousins of American Creationists. Once again, all the grand glory of the uplifting epic was drawn down to the mire of literalist interpretations of epic poetry. The claim that conflicts between science and religion can never arise in the Hindu world is clearly not valid. Such conflicts are inevitable in every religious tradition where scientifically ill-informed traditional enthusiasts insist on giving literal interpretations to ancient texts, and cannot regard sacred writings as the work of inspired poets and keen philosophers.

In the Ashoka grove

The Ramayana is a religious work, for sure. But it is also rich in history and geography, in poetry and philosophy. Valmiki was as much a nature poet as a keen observer of human nature. His opus is rich in meticulous descriptions of birds and beasts, plants and trees, rivers and streams and more.

Consider, for example, some of his descriptions of the botanical garden in Lanka. Hanuman sneaked into that garden in his quest for Sita. He discovered it to be abundant in trees like Bhavya, Champaka, Uddalaka, Nagakesara, and most of all, Ashoka (*Saraca indica*). This tree is sacred for Jains since Mahavira attained enlightenment under it; for Buddhists since Buddha was born under it; and for Hindus because Sita was found by Hanuman under an Ashoka tree. Ravana's orchard in Sri Lanka had mango trees galore. Herds of deer looking golden and silvery were sauntering amidst the arbors. The ruddy thickets looked like the rising sun. The plants were in full bloom, countless crimson fruits were hanging from the branches of mango trees.

When Hanuman stealthily stepped in the grove, he jolted the sleeping birds. He heard lots of cuckoos. The creatures were in heat, the poet says. The breeze caused by the flapping of the wings of the birds made flowers fall on Hanuman. Thus covered, he looked like a multi-hued floral mountain. The trees, thinking he was spring embodied, shed their blossoms and leaves, and looked like gamblers who had lost all in a game, including their clothing.

The giant stride of Hanuman with his long whipping tail battered some trees, making the grove look like a young woman with disheveled hair with her tilak removed. Her red lips, accentuated by shining teeth, had faded away.

Then Hanuman came upon a magnificent ground with sheets of gold and silver studded with gems. He saw pretty ponds with crystal bottoms with various contours, with sparkling water, and with steps adorned with precious stones. They were surrounded by sands of pearls and corals. Tall golden trees were standing around the ponds.

Valmiki reminds us in this way that Ravana was not a wild savage, but a super-rich potentate with sophisticated tastes who had grand mansions erected, magnificent groves planted, and beautiful ponds carved out, all for his royal pleasure. We also realize how in the midst of such material abundance there can occur fatal moral decay.

Hanuman spent the whole night in that garden. At dawn he heard the chanting of Vedas by Brahmin rakshasas. If you thought some Brahmins behave like rakshasas (in the moral sense), this passage tells us that some rakshasas were Brahmins. Hymns lauding Ravana were sung to wake up the king whose attire was chaotic for he was tossed by passion for Sita. Now he wore adorning ornaments and walked to the Ashoka grove which was replete with fruits, flowers, plants, trees, birds, deer and lotus ponds. A bevy of lovely rakshasis followed him. Some carried torches with golden handles. Others bore water jugs, yet others circular cushions. The pitchers they brought were studded with gems and filled with wine. One woman was holding a canopy in the shape of a swan. She shone like the full moon. The rakshasis were transpiring as a result of their exertions. So their jewelry got displaced, the sandal paste on their bodies rubbed off, their hair was messed up, and their faces were moist. The flowers they wore had shriveled. Some of the women were intoxicated, but all were eager to see Sita.

Hanuman could hear their tinkling bangles and anklets. He spotted Ravana from his hiding place, his face illumined by torches, his body smeared with fragrant oils. The rakshasa king was full of lust, looking like Kama (Cupid) without his bow. He adjusted his garments which were white as foam from churned milk. Thus did Ravana ready himself to see Sita. Then he approached her. She is described here as one with charming limbs and well-formed breasts, with tresses black like the corners of her eyes.

When Sita saw Ravana, she sat and wept, hiding her abdomen behind her thighs and her breasts with her arms. She looked miserable in her pain. She was left there like a bark on a beach. Her limbs were covered with dirt from the ground, she looked like a lotus stalk mired in mud. She was charming and yet not charming. Her thoughts were with Rama as she wept. The poet goes on to say that Sita seemed like fame that had dimmed, faith that had been held in contempt, understanding grown feeble; she looked like shattered hope and doomed prospects, like an order disobeyed, worship intruded upon, full moon in eclipse; like an army whose soldiers had been killed, like sunlight obscured. She was like an altar desecrated, flame extinguished, a flock of birds scared away. All this reads like observant poetry, not history.

Such a volley of similes it is hard to find elsewhere in literature. The poet refers to sunset and seasons, to moon and mountains, to creepers and creatures all through his work. He reveals enormous knowledge of nature and of geography. Valmiki must have traveled much and meticulously observed the sceneries. His lines couldn't have come from imagination alone.

Kumbhakarna

The giant Kumbhakarna was Ravana's brother. He too did years of austerities to obtain extraordinary powers. But before he was to receive a boon, the gods begged Brahma not to grant him anything because he had devoured nymphs, rishis and others, and might gobble up all the three worlds with his prowess. Whereupon Brahma summoned Sarasvati to cast a spell on the rakshasa. When Kumbhakarna was about to ask for *nityatvam* (permanence or immortality), Sarasvati twisted his tongue, so he asked for *nidratvam* (somnolence) instead. Brahma granted this. So Kumbhakarna became the sleeping giant of Hindu lore. But out of pity, he let him be awake one day every six months. This is an example of wordplay which Hindu writers reveled in, but which is not always recognized as such..

The Tamil poet Kamban gives a hair-raising description of this astonishing personage (VI:15). The giant slept on a stupendous bed in a hall seven yojanas (56 miles?) wide. He looked like the embodiment of sin. Breeze from his garden, bearing the fragrance of heavenly karpaga trees refreshed him. Celestial nymphs were caressing his limbs. Water was gently sprinkled on his face from moonstones in the pillars of the hall. The giant breathed so heavily that had Hanuman not been careful, he would have been sucked into those nostrils. Compared to him Brobdingnagians were miniature Liliputs.

When Ravana's troops were almost routed out, he ordered Kumbhakarna to be woken up, for the giant was a great fighter who possessed the ability to defeat anybody. The ways by which they tried to wake up Kumbhakarna are incredibly humorous. They took perfumes, garlands, and vast quantities of food to Kumbhakarna's bedroom. The food consisted of antelopes, bullocks and pigs, and huge pots of blood to drink. They smeared his body with sandal paste, burnt incense in the hall, made loud noises, blew conches, and shouted. Kamban says that myriad horses (*áyiram parigaL*) galloped on Kumbhakarna's body. Valmiki says a thousand elephants (*váraNán sahasram*) ran up and down his body. Finally, when the giant woke up, all the worlds shook. His head touched the sky, his eyes were grander than the sea. He gulped 600 cartloads of rice, countless pots of liquor, and 1200 buffaloes. He gobbled elephants, even steel weapons! The gluttony of François Rabelais' Gargantua seems pale and paltry compared to the outrageously omnivoracious of Kumbhakarna. It is hard to believe that there still are some Hindu scholars who take the Ramayana literally.

When the half-drunk glutton went to Ravana's palace and heard about his brother's misdeed, he reprimanded him with a sermon on how to behave, and with much wisdom too. Ravana, with a touch of repentance, declared there was no point looking back, and appealed for Kumbhakarna's fraternal love. Friends console us when we are in trouble, he said, but kinsmen come to our rescue when we have morally strayed.

Recognizing Ravana's predicament, Kumbhakarna resolved to destroy Rama with his awesome might. He spoke with extreme confidence that he would route out the enemy's army, and promised to bring Rama's head to Ravana. Then, ignoring the counsel of those who tried to dissuade him, Kumbhakarna marched to the battlefield and took hold of the most fearsome arms made of iron, adorned with garlands, generating flames.

The battle between Kumbhakarna and the monkey horde fighting for Rama, narrated in a lengthy chapter (LXVII) of Valmiki's Yuddhakanda, is one of the most brutal and bloody scenes in any narrative, historical or fictional. Beatings, gushing blood, maiming and mutilation: the sheer violence is stunning. The excessive violence in today's entertainment world is mild in comparison. The only mitigating factor is that it all sounds too fantastic. When Hanuman's chest was struck by Kumbhakarna's weapon, blood oozed from his mouth and he shrieked so loud that it sounded like cosmic thunder at the end of the world! Kumbhakarna's body was covered by monkeys galore, but he gobbled up many of them. The parties hurled mountain chunks at each other. Kumbhakarna's nose and ears were cut, then his arms and feet, and Rama finally decapitated the monstrous rakshasa. His body plunged into the sea, killing crocodiles and other creatures.

Thus ended the life of the tragi-comic Kumbhakarna who lived for but a day during the entire Ramayana. The poet Shelley spoke of death and his brother sleep. Here the real brother woke him up from sleep and sent him to death. Kumbhakarna, the symbol of sleep and sloth in the Hindu framework, was also wise and loyal to his brother. Tulsi Das says that he exclaimed to Ravana: "Fool, you carried away the Mother of the Universe, and still hope to live well!" (VI:62). Kumbhakarna has added color and excitement to the epic.

Like Kumbhakarna, we all wake up periodically from our sleep in eternity: which is one way of considering our periodic births on the planet. During our day that is life, we too can be wise and give good counsel. We too can be mindlessly consuming. Sometimes, by misplaced loyalty we too can wreak havoc and perish.

Jabali (Jábáli)

Ravana is physically strong but morally weak. There is another personage in the epic who is rationally bright but ethically misguided. He was a rishi, an illustrious Brahmin too, descended from Kashyapa. He was a counselor to Dasharatha. His name was Jabali (Valmiki, 1992, II:108,109).

When Rama embarked on his exile, Jabali was one of many who tried to dissuade him from the heroic sacrifice. He described Rama's decision as not worthy of a wise man, arguing that every person must live just for his own self. In truth, he said, none is a friend, and one can't gain something through someone else. We are born alone in this world and we will die alone. It is mindless to be attached to father and mother. Just as we stay for a while at a resting place when we are on a journey, our family is but a temporary place of shelter. With such logic Jabali tried to influence Rama into thinking that he ought not to follow that arduous path of exile with potential for pain and suffering. He belittled the role of the father as no more than having been the passing guardian of the sperm from which one is born. Now that Dasharatha was no more, Rama was undergoing all the hardship for nothing, said the sage.

Jabali went on to denigrate funerary rites (*shraddha*) by which food is offered to the spirits of the departed. He called this a waste: how could dead people eat? If one could feed those who are far away, one should be able to feed one's traveling friends too. Jabali said that those who instruct us to give religious gifts, perform sacrificial rites, and renounce wealth were clever schemers who try to draw us to charity for their own benefit.

Jabali also propounded the materialistic philosophy by which the tangible world is everything, there is nothing beyond what tickles the senses. He advised Rama to forget promises and principles, and return to the kingdom that was legitimately his.

Rama, the embodiment of virtue and righteousness, was appalled that one who had served as his father's minister uttered such words. He rejected Jabali, calling his ideas unwholesome, sinful, unclean and worse. He would follow the righteous path, not only because that was the right thing to do, but also because if he abandoned truth and returned, he would become a terrible role model for the people. "Truth alone is the eternal royal path," he declared, an ideal that is as valid today as whenever it was spoken. It is in statements like this that the core wisdom of Indic seers may be found.

Rama went on to elaborate on righteous conduct to the confused Jabali, reminding us of Krishna's preaching to Arjuna in the Gita; except that, unlike Krishna (who spoke from his own divine wisdom), Rama kept saying what Vedic rishis and other sages had told so, reminding us that the Rama of Valmiki is noble, but still only human.

When the Ramayana was composed, there were unbelievers (*nástikas*) in India, as there have always been in any dynamic civilization. That a rishi would make a cynical remark about the shraddha ceremony may sound strange. Perhaps the poet wanted to bring to our attention the fact that such views were entertained even by some intellectuals of the upper caste. The episode also hints that unbelievers lived in fear of the establishment, and quickly recanted if those in power were upset. Thus, upon seeing Rama's reaction, Jabali promptly said, "Normally I don't champion the ideas of unbelievers. I do it only if I think it would serve a purpose." The purpose was to bring Rama back to Ayodhya. Since that didn't work, he became a believer in dharmic morality again. In fact, Vasishtha came to his colleague's defense right away, assuring Rama that Jabali was only pretending to be an unbeliever in his desire to bring Rama back home.

As in all great works, there are several conflicts in the Ramayana: The initial conversation between Manthara and Kaikeyi is a conflict between jealousy and generosity. The Kaikeyi-Dasharatha conflict is between self-centered heartlessness and paternal love. The Rama-Ravana conflict is between nobility and depravity, between supreme good and supreme evil. And the Jabali-Rama conflict is between materialistic atheism and idealistic righteousness. All these reveal that human life is multi-faceted and wrought with perennial conflicts. Through the poet's exaggerations we see the deeper roots of superficial confrontations. If these situations had been presented in a milder manner, we might not be able to see their full implications. By painting them in all their gory extremes the poet helps us understand where meanness, jealousy, lust, self-centeredness, ignoring of righteousness, and the like can lead us to.

We may note in passing that in this reply of Rama, as stated in Valmiki, there is an intriguing statement: "It is well known that one who follows the Buddha should be punished as one would punish a thief; an unbeliever is equal to Buddha" [*yathá hi corah sa tathá hi buddhastathagatam nástikamantra viddhi*] (109:33). A reference to Buddha (600 B.C.E) by Rama who is said to have lived in another yuga, raises serious questions about the date of composition of the Ramayana, if not of Rama himself.

In any case, Jabali's story shows that India is a complex civilization with many streams of thought even in that distant age.

Lakshmana

Respect for older brother is part of the Hindu tradition. But Lakshmana's devotion to Rama was unusual and extraordinary. To him his elder brother was more important than mother or father, more important even than wife. His entire life was dedicated to the companionship, defense, service, and adoration of Rama. Using a phrase from the Latin poet Horace, Rama and Lakshmana were *par nobile fratrum*: a noble pair of brothers.

When sage Vishvamitra took Rama on a mission to rid the forest of miscreants who were intruding in his sacrifices,

Lakshmana followed without being even asked. Though Vishvamitra often addressed only Rama, as when he endowed him with potent mantras and celestial weapons, to all intents and purposes he was talking to both the brothers. When Rama married Sita, Lakshmana married her sister Urmila. A persistent inseparable bond between the two runs all through the epic, as it still is in pictorial representations of Rama and Sita. The two were like twin brothers, though from different mothers.

When Kaikeyi obstructed Rama's coronation, Lakshmana grew more agitated than anyone in Ayodhya. He was enraged that his father had succumbed to Kaikeyi's demands. He accused emperor Dasharatha of lust and senility when he conceded to Kaikeyi. He urged Rama to take over the reins of power forthwith, before people heard about the king's order. In his uncontrollable anger he declared that if the city of Ayodhya dared to oppose Rama, he (Lakshmana) would depopulate the whole city with his piercing shafts. He went so far as to say that if Dasharatha acted like a foe, he should be taken prisoner and gotten rid of. "I will kill my old and miserable father who, because of his infatuation with Kaikeyi, is re-living his childhood." Kamban says, Lakshmana exclaimed that Kaikeyi wanted to give the delicious meat (the throne) fit for a lion's cub to a puppy dog (Bharata). Lakshmana's reactions were ugly transformations of intense love for brother into rage at whoever might have caused the offense against his brother. Kamban says that Rama exclaimed: "How can you use the same tongue that recites the scriptures to speak thus?"

Lakshmana was invariably quick to anger whenever he felt that Rama's interests were at stake. When he spotted Bharata with his army (coming to beg Rama to return), he jumped to the conclusion that Bharata's intentions were sinister. He declared to Rama that he would kill the entire army along with Bharata, and then kill Kaikeyi also.

Lakshmana was always concerned about Rama's safety. When Maricha, disguised as a beautiful magical deer passed by in the forest and captivated Sita's heart, Lakshmana warned Rama that it was a demon in disguise, a scheme to lure Rama away. But, to please his beloved Sita, Rama set out to capture it, saying that he (Lakshmana) and Sita would sit on its skin of golden hue. When Maricha yelled the names of Sita and Lakshmana before being killed, Sita was frightened, but Lakshmana did not budge because he had full confidence in his brother's capacity to defend himself. Now Sita turned mean and hurtful, calling Lakshmana an enemy of his brother, and said he wanted to see Rama perish for ulterior motives. Even then, and even when she called him ignoble, heartless, and a disgrace to his lineage, Lakshmana said he would not answer her because she was a Goddess to him. Finally, he left in search of Rama only because Sita attributed to him unethical motives. When Rama discovered that Lakshmana had left Sita alone, he castigated him, says Valmiki. In Kamban's version, Rama did not blame his brother.

In the war, we are reminded of Virgil's line in the *Aeneid* (IX. 182): "*His amor unus erat pariterque in bella ruebant*: Between them was mutual love, and side by side they were wont to rush into battle." That was how Rama and Lakshmana went to Sri Lanka. There, Lakshmana fought valiantly, and after a fierce exchange of insults and deadly arrows, he decapitated Ravana's son Indrajit.

After Rama's coronation, Lakshmana walked to the banks of the Sarayu river and performed a yoga, whereupon Indra appeared and teleported him to the celestial world where all rejoiced at the return of this fourth part of Vishnu.

Though the epic is called Rama's saga, Lakshmana is an inseparable part of it. Critics may chastise Lakshmana for ignoring his wife, for being too subservient to Sita, and for being too short-tempered. But it was never for a selfish reason, it was always for his brother. His love for Rama and deep loyalty to the hero symbolize true friendship at the worldly level, and also faith and bhakti at the religious level. In the Hindu vision, God is friend and companion too: *tvameva bandhu ca sakha tvameva.* At one point in the Kamba Ramayanam, Lakshmana calls Rama his father, leader, and mother [*nal tandaiyum nee; tani náyakan nee; vayitril petráyum nee*] (Kamban, II:5.132). He could have added brother and said in Sanskrit: "*tvameva máta ca pitá tvameva, tvameva netá ca bhrátá tvameva.*" His affection for Rama was so deep and his loyalty so steadfast that another name for Lakshmana was *Ramánuja*: Rama's brother.

In Greek mythology the step-brothers Castor and Pollux had the same mother, but different fathers (like the Pandava brothers). Rama and Lakshmana had the same father but different mothers. Like Rama and Lakshmana, Castor and Pollux also married two sisters. They too were inseparable brothers, and were transported to the skies where they shine as the stars in the constellation Gemini. Sometimes I imagine Rama and Lakshmana in that twin star system. Mythopoesy can be beautiful. Hindu astronomers could name them Rama and Lakshmana. The Romans built a temple for the twin brothers who had fought and defeated the Latins.

Dasharatha's daughter and Rama's brother-in-law

I once asked a devout reader of Rama-charitamanasa who was Rama's sister. He said that Rama did not have any sister. I pointed out to him that one of Dasharatha's ministers tells the king: "It is Rishyashringa, your son-in-law (*jámátá*), who will ultimately help you get your sons" (Valmiki: I.9.19). Dasharatha's son-in-law? Yes, indeed, the Sanskrit dramatist Bhavabhuti also says in his *Uttara Rama Charita* that Dasharatha had a daughter by the name of Shanta; he does not specify the queen-mother (Belvalkar, 2004). Shanta was adopted by King Romapada, ruler of Anga. She was given in marriage to Rishyashringa, son of Vibhandaka.

The Rishyashringa story, as narrated in Balakanda, is very interesting. This young man was raised in a forest amidst a population of deer. Hence his name which means *one with the horns of a deer*. He spent most of his youth serving his ascetic father.

The kingdom of Anga was once afflicted by draught. Romapada's ministers said this was due to Rishyashringa's powerful abstinence. A belief of the time was that if too austere celibacy was practiced in a realm, there would be drought and infertility in the land. This reflects the great importance placed on men with intense spiritual discipline for the good of a country. When the plight of a nation turns out to be unhappy, it becomes all the more important for people of character and spiritual strength to come to the fore. Men and women of goodwill generate around them thoughts and feelings of an essentially positive and life-giving nature, and this is valuable for society at large.

So the ministers suggested that if Rishyashringa could be persuaded to marry, that would bring rain. But they were afraid to make this proposal to Vibhandaka since he might get upset. The question arose: How to entice the austere youth to feminine charms?

They schemed and sent a bevy of damsels to the forest where Rishyashringa lived. When the youthful ascetic was alone, the young women sang and danced in their colorful attire, attracting the curiosity and interest of the youth who was fascinated and excited by their presence. The next day, when he returned to the place, the beautiful women had little difficulty in slowly alluring him to king Romapada's palace where he was received with great respect. Then he was induced to marry Dasharatha's daughter Shanta. When this happened it began to rain in torrents.

It was Rishyashringa, Dasharatha's son-in-law, who conducted the renowned sacrifice from which arose the potions that eventually led to the birth of Rama and his three brothers. The whole story is told in great length in the first book of the Ramayana.

The episode suggests that even the firmest ascetic can be bent by the allure of a female. No matter how continent one has been, and how many years of penance one has accumulated to one's credit, vows of abstinence can be broken if there is strong enough temptation. The plea "Lead us not unto temptation!" in the (Christian) Lord's Prayer is based on this wisdom and fact of experience. Irrespective of how elevated our principle, as long as we are in a well functioning physical frame, our thoughts, actions, and reactions are governed by our nervous system. Shakespeare, in one of his sonnets (Sonnet 94), describes persons of very strong will and self-discipline, whom we would call rishis, in these terms:

> They that have power to hurt and will do none,
> That do not do the thing they most do show,
> Who, moving others, are themselves as stone,
> Unmoved, cold, and to temptation slow,
> They rightly do inherit heaven's graces
> And husband nature's riches from expense;
> They are the lords and owners of their faces,
> Others but stewards of their excellence.

The bard does not say they *resist* all temptations, but that they are *slow to react* to them. The expedition of many voluptuous maidens is to suggest that the greater the self-discipline of a person, the stronger will have to be the distracting force needed to deviate from the vows of celibacy. Those with little character can be more easily corrupted than those of stronger moral strength. But no one is totally protected in this matter. That plunge, in George Meredith's phrase, "from ascetic rocks to sensuous whirlpools" is not such an arduous one. Circumstances rather than intentions often provoke people in this matter. We overestimate our will-power in exposing ourselves to certain situations.

Milton, in his narration of the story of *Samson Agonistes* (lines 210-11) wrote, "Wisest men have erred, and by bad women been deceived." However, in the Rishyashringa episode it is not the idea of woman ruining a man's life that is brought out. Here after yielding to marital life Rishyashringa is much enriched personally, and he brings enrichment to the whole country.

The story also makes us think of an important ethical principle: Depending on the context, the same act (in this case Rishyashringa's celibacy or the breaking of it) could bring about either bad or good (draught or rain). A Tantrik formula says: "By the same acts that cause some men to roast in horrible hell for hundreds of eons, the yogi is liberated." Is it proper to kill a human being? Of course not, we would say. But what about a situation when you have to protect others from a murderer whom you see massacring people? Is aborting an unborn child right? Of course not. But what if the fetus is known to be seriously mentally deformed or the mother's life would be endangered during birth?

A description of the cold season

India is rich in flora and fauna. It has mountains and valleys, plains and meadows, beautiful lakes, long rivers, and ponds galore, fertile grounds and parched deserts too. It has seasons hot and cold, and in between; it is treated to rains, draughts, floods and storms also. Its physical features are like its people: impressive in variety, colorful in shades, and ranging from extreme to extreme.

So when a poet like Valmiki presents to the reader his grand epic he does not speak only of heroes and villains, conflicts and confrontations. He describes the land and its beauty and changes in sceneries. Sometimes he does this while narrating the story. Sometimes he leaves it to one of the characters to speak. So it is that early one morning when Rama walks to the banks of the river Godavari to take his bath, Lakshmana and Sita follow him, and at that time Lakshmana describes to Rama the winter scene.

A good portion of a whole sarga in the Aranya Kanda is devoted to a description of the cold month in the southern regions: both its good and ill effects (Valmiki, III.16). I will try to recast its essential contents, without translating the lines literally:

"The season which you like has come, Rama. It is a blessing to the year, indeed it is like a jewel. There is dryness in the air. The land is abundant in crops, the water is generally pleasant, and so is fire. The good ones who have performed their religious rites are cleansed of their sins. The peasants have reaped their harvests, and cows give greater quantities of milk. As the sun moves away to Yama's quarters (the south), the northern regions have lost their charm, looking like a woman without her auspicious mark. Snow is winter's treasure for the Himalayas which now deserve the name more than ever.

"It is nice to take a stroll at noon; it is a delight to be touched by sunshine. The sun is pleasant while shade and water aren't so. Since it is not so hot, the fog gets thick. Sometimes the cold is bitter in the wind. There is frost in the blighted woodlands. We can no longer sleep in the open at night. The Pushya constellation (Cancer) is up there. But the frost makes the night look dusty, and the nights get colder and longer too. The moon has lost her pleasantness to the sun, and with its orb rendered ruddy by the snow, it looks soiled as if by exhalation. It does not shine in all its glory even on a full-moon night, obscured as it is by frost, just as Sita, when tanned by the sun, looks unattractive. Already cold by nature, the westerly wind, saturated by snow, is bitter cold in the morning. With their abundant crops of barley and wheat, the land looks attractive early in the morning when birds like herons and cranes make their sounds. The golden paddy crops slightly bend over, looking charming and much like date flowers. Its rays weakened by fog and frost, even at high noon the sun looks like the moon.

"The sun's radiance is felt but slightly in the forenoon. But it is pleasant at noon. The sun is reddish and somewhat pale, casting its charm everywhere. The fields are beautiful too, and the grass is moist with dew. Even the wild elephant, though very thirsty, pulls back its tusk from the water sometimes: the water is that cold. Birds near water dare not put their beaks into it, just as the meek don't get into a fight though they may be near one. Trees without blossom seem to have gone to sleep, covered as they are with dew drops and a darkness born of heavy fog. Streams are barely visible, though we can hear the shrieks of cranes nearby. Due to the frost caused by the cold and mild sunshine, water on the tops of mountains taste good. Lotus beds have lost their charm for their flowers have decayed and even their filaments have withered away."

Valmiki's description of how the scorching summer sun is transformed into a soft and soothing touch in wintertime is as true today in many parts of India as when those lines were written. But what is intriguing is the reference to snow in the region of the Godavari which is in South India. Could it be that there has been a climate change since the era of the Ramayana?

Or was our poet extrapolating from what he had observed in the hilly regions of the north, I wonder.

The poetic mind sees the world in ways that others do not, and it gives expression to what it sees in aesthetically pleasing ways. Other poets in other climes and in other tongues have reflected on winter too. Some seem to echo Valmiki's reflections. Recall, for example, what Alexander Pope wrote :

> But see, Orion sheds unwholesome dews;
> Arise, the pines a noxious shade diffuse;
> Sharp Boreas blows, and nature feels decay.
> Time conquers all, and we must time obey.
> (*Ode to Winter*, l. 85).

There is more in the Ramayana than jealousy, exile, lust, heroics, and war. One may be reverential to the Rama principle in temples and songs. The epic's religious dimension touches the soul of the devout, and that is good. But if we lose sight of its literary aspects, it would be like focusing on the rituals of a wedding and skipping the feast. There is also so much about India's past we can learn from the Ramayana.

Mandodari

Ravana had a great many concubines. Mandodari was his principal wife. She was a rakshasi: often translated as ogress. But she had none of the negative qualities which one usually associates with ogresses. Even giantess would be a misnomer, for the epic describes Mandodari as a beautiful woman. Kamban informs us that her father was the celestial architect Máyan who made Lanka magnificent, inspired by suggestions from Brahma.

Mandodari is said to have been very attractive. When Hanuman saw her in Ravana's palace, her decacephalous husband was fast asleep. At his feet were women-musicians, wearing huge ear-rings and gorgeous jewelry of gold, diamonds and gems. They too were sleeping, exhausted and inebriated from too much dancing and drinking. Valmiki says they had lovely breasts and graceful limbs, and they were hugging musical instruments.

In that chamber there was also a sumptuous couch on which richly ornamented Mandodari of exquisite beauty was sleeping. For a moment Hanuman thought she must be Sita, and in the joy of his imagined discovery he clapped his hands and kissed his tail, jumped and climbed the pillars, says Valmiki. In Kamban's version, Hanuman spotted Mandodari whose face was as beautiful as the moon, in a mansion all her own. In Kamban's customary hyperbole, celestial nymphs were massaging her feet which resembled the quiver of the god of love. (Kamban, V.2.195 et seq.) Her body was emanating a magical light. Seeing her in such comfort in that magnificent palace, Hanuman was deeply pained. "The whole purpose of my life is shattered," he told himself. "If this be Sita," he went on in despair, "then I too must die along with the fair name and reputation of Rama, and so must Lanka and the entire rakshasa horde." But he soon realized his error and left Mandodari's palace at once.

Mandodari was another victim of Ravana's infatuation, for he lost interest in her and longed for another woman. This was humiliation enough. Then Hanuman slew her son Akshakumara on the battlefield. This was even more terrible. Mandodari wailed at Ravana's feet, beating her body in intense grief, her disheveled hair was touching the soil.

Her lamentation when the other son Indrajit died in battle was just as sad and pathetic. She walked around the corpse, as if treading on fire, and fell on his body like a peacock that had been shot down, and swooned. After a while she came to herself and cried: "As a child you grew like the waxing moon. You subdued the powerful ones with you archery. Now I see your head-less body. I am losing my mind. I can't think of living any longer. Oh my sweet and handsome child! When you were but an infant crawling with anklets, you caught two lions, teased them, and played with them. Once you held the moon in your hand, spotted the dark patch on it, and said it was a hare. Oh, how I wish I could re-live that scene! I am terrified because Lanka's king may die tomorrow, having imbibed the poisoned nectar Sita."

Here we may recall the lamentation in Shakespeare's lines: "O lord, my boy, my fair son! My life, my joy, my food, my all the world!" (King John, III.4).

When Ravana fell down and died, Mandodari's anguish was intense, and her wailing more painful. Both Kamban and Valmiki devote many stanzas to that tragic scene. Mandodari wondered if Rama's arrows which covered Ravana's entire body, were probing his heart to see if Sita was imprisoned there. She recalled her husband's greatness and his invincibility, and said she always believed no man could ever bring defeat to him. She referred to the fate that had planted lust for Sita in Ravana's heart, which was to lead him to death. At last, says Kamban, she stood up from the corpse which she had embraced, called out Ravana's name aloud, fell down, and heaved her final breath.

Though a rakshasi, Mandodari was a good woman, and like many other Indian heroines she suffered much, had been abused, and was devoted to a husband who ignored her. She went through the agony of seeing both her sons die, and she witnessed the gory end of her dear and misguided husband too. None of the other heroines were subjected to such mental torture.

Mandodari is therefore reckoned among the five great women of Indic lore who are held in very high regard. It is good that she belonged to the tribal class of ancient India, for that was the rakshasa class. Maybe Valmiki painted her and Ravana's good brother Vibhishana in positive terms to remind us that it would be wrong to judge all rakshasas by Ravana's behavior. The denigration of a group on the basis of the misbehavior of some, or on the unpleasant impression created by a few is one of the major blunders that people commit. It is the attitude by which a race or nation is characterized as consisting of only evil or inferior people. This is an ailment from which many suffer all over the world even in this day and age. We call it racism. Perhaps through Mandodari and Vibhishana the poet is reminding us that group denigration or hatred is blind to facts, and morally wrong. This may be one of the hidden messages in the Ramayana. We extract messages from our own reading and reflection.

Agastya

Agastya is another rishi of eminence in Hindu sacred history who appears in the Ramayana. Rama, Sita, and Lakshmana visited his hermitage too during their exile years. He received them with great affection and respect.

Agastya's genesis in puranic mythology has the usual element of incredible imagery and eerie fantasy. It is said that the sage emerged from a jar into which the Vedic gods Mitra and Varuna had shed their seeds upon being aroused by the sight of the celestial nymph Urvashi. There must surely be some symbolism here, but it is not easy to fathom what it is.

The impression one gets from the Ramayana passages is that the whole Dandaka forest region was infested with rakshasas who rudely intruded into the yajñas (rituals, sacrifices) performed by sages and ascetics of the Vedic tradition, and that this was a major problem for the practitioners. In Kamba Ramayanam, Rama tells the rishis explicitly that if the rakshasas do not promise to desist from their mischievous behavior, his arrows will pursue and kill them. He foresees a day when those rishis would see decapitated rakshasas dancing. Thus, his resolution to rid the region of the trouble-making rakshasas had been formulated even before Ravana's ravishing of Sita. This sounds very much like how civilized governments feel these days about terrorists who kill people indiscriminately.

Kamban also tells us that the extraordinary sage Agastya had once gulped the waters of the ocean to expose the evil asuras who were hiding in the bottom of the sea. He thus acquired the epithet of *Samudra chulaka*: Ocean-imbiber.

The Vindhya Mountains in the middle of the Indian subcontinent are not as tall as the Himalayan range. A puranic explanation for this geological asymmetry is that once, on his way to the south from his northern abode, Agastya commanded the mountains to prostrate before him so that he could cross over with ease. He instructed them to so remain until his return. The heights of the obeying mountains were thus reduced. But the rishi did not return, leaving the Vindhyas shorter forever. There are variants of this legend (Uttara Ramayana).

Valmiki also tells us about how the rakshasa Vatapi (Vátápi) once tried to play a trick on Agastya, disguising himself as a ram which the rishi would hunt and eat. Vatapi was scheming to regain his original form once in the stomach of the rishi, and explode him to smithereens. Agastya found out about this, and ate up the whole ram. When Vatapi's brother instructed him to cut to pieces Agastya's entrails, the rishi calmly retorted, "Vatapi has been fully digested!"

Agastya is also mentioned in the Mahabharata. In the Vána Parva, we read the story in which he happened to see his ancestors hanging topsy-turvy in a dismal pit. He wanted to help them out of that uncomfortable plight. But they told him he could accomplish this only if he fathered a son. The sage was not even married. And no ordinary woman was attractive enough to inspire him to matrimony. So he collected the finest features from nature. Another text elaborates on this by saying that he took the deer's eyes, the leopard's grace, the flower's fragrance, the swan's swiftness, the palm leaf's suppleness, and so on. From these he formed his own ideal female. Lopamudra (literally, loss-form), was her name, since her beauty resulted from loss to other creatures. She grew up in a royal palace. Agastya finally married her and begot a son. In this way, he rescued his ancestors. Lopamudra's name is appended to one some Vedic hymns.

Agastya is held in high esteem in the Tamil speaking world, as Parashurama is in the Kerala country. Tamil tradition says that this master of the Vedas learned Tamil grammar from Lord Shiva, and brought it to the people of the south. He is said to have retired into the Podiyil Hills of the south (Pillai, 1985).

Legends abound on this dwarfish rishi. He is called the founder of the Tamil language. These stories originate in early Tamil literature. Examination of the relevant writings suggests that the assertion that he was the one who brought the Tamil language and grammar to the Dravidian people, though fascinating, is rather improbable from historical considerations. His name gets to be popular in the Tamil world only after the seventh century CE. What seems probable is that there was an erudite Sanskrit scholar who, at one time, moved to the South where he mastered and propagated the richness of Tamil: not unlike a good Indian professor in an American university today who may be teaching English to American students. Agastya's is not the only name that is a memorable mix of fact and fantasy in the Hindu tradition. Whatever the truth of the matter, Akattiyar (as he is called in chaste Tamil) is perhaps the only great (known) scholar in the classical Indic tradition who was deeply learned in both Sanskrit and Tamil. In this sense, he could well be taken as a symbol for a Pan-Indic cultural heritage. While there have been many Tamils who have excelled in Sanskrit, there are not as many scholars from the North who have shown such great scholarship in Tamil. For this reason he has always been my hero.

Agastya occupies a position of eminence in the pantheon of Kampuchea and Java. The star Canopus (in Argo Navis) is named after Menelaus (Rama's parallel in Greek mythology). Hindu astronomers called this star Agastya.

Sita

Just as the physical world consists ultimately of matter and energy, there is in the divine world of Hindu vision *deva* and *devi*. One cannot be there without the other. Among the many male-female pairs that adorn and enrich Hindu lore, legend, and lofty pantheon, perhaps the most revered is the Rama-Sita principle.

Leaving for a moment the Sita who is venerated with her consort in temples, let us reflect on her as the epic heroine. Sita was of divine origin, born neither of father nor of mother, but of Mother Earth. Her name means a furrow for it was in a furrow on plowed ground that she was discovered by king Janaka. She represents the element Earth.

As a woman, Sita was exquisitely beautiful. Amidst the innumerable charming women who strew flowers on her path, she looked like the queen of lightning in a dazzle of countless lightning flashes. Her piercing eyes could kill even the Lord of Death. She was the personification of whatever is best in femininity. Ornaments and necklaces became true adornment for women only after Sita began to wear them. Such is Kamban's description of Sita.

Kamban goes on to say that the moment Sita saw Rama on the streets of Ayodhya as he was walking with Vishvamitra and Lakshmana, Rama's gaze reciprocated hers. Their mutual piercing looks were intertwined and the two became one. When Rama went out of sight, Sita became restless, like a rutting elephant gone berserk, says the poet, and she wilted like a flower. Tear drops fell on her breasts like rainfall on mountain tops. The warmth of her sighs dried the sweat on her forehead. The poet describes Sita's pre-marital love for Rama in such poetic terms (Kamban, I: 10.35 *et seq.*).

Sita was a woman of very strong will. We see this again and again in numerous episodes. When her maid, dancing with delirious joy, broke the news that the bow had been broken, Sita was sure the feat had been accomplished by Rama's strong hands, but she told herself that if it wasn't so, she would put an end to her life.

Another instance of Sita's iron will: When Rama suggested that she ought to stay in Ayodhya while he went in exile, she grew furious. She answered him back in strong terms, saying his words weren't worthy of a brave prince. In this context she even called him a woman in a man's frame. She would march ahead to clear his path. However, even while claiming her right to act her will, she conforms to the traditional Hindu wife's ideal, declaring that to be protected under one's husband's feet was preferable to living in a palace pent-house.

Who can forget her adamant determination to get the deer that had caught her fancy, her irritation when Rama hesitated to go fetch it for her, and her intemperate words when Lakshmana did not leap to see if his brother was safe? Her unswerving resistance to Ravana's inducements to win her for his own pleasure shows wifely chastity and feminine resistance to moral corruption that are of the highest order.

Then there is the episode wherein Rama questions if Sita's purity had been violated. The war had been undertaken, not for her sake, but to vindicate his own goodness and to erase the calumny on his dynasty. Rama asks her with uncharacteristic heartlessness to go away to any of his brothers or to the vanaras or to Ravana's brother Vibhishana. Rama acts here very much like a normal, not to say ordinary, jealous male who could not accept the fact that his beloved wife had been under the control of a vicious and lustful man.

Sita sobbed with sadness, but after wiping her tears, she told Rama calmly that such unkind words were unbecoming of a person of his stature. She re-affirmed her character, pleaded her innocence, and explained her helplessness under Ravana's control. Then she proclaimed that if he, Rama, trusted her not, then there was nothing more for her to live for. She asked Lakshmana to set up a fire to merge into. Rama, who had acted on the principle of *yathá prajá, tathá rájá*, (as the people think, so must the king) corrected himself after Agni (the fire-ordeal) vindicated her. This was not the high point of Rama's greatness.

Sita is the only one in the epic who rebukes and advices Rama. Once she preached to him listing three *adharmic* behavior: untruth, adultery, and needless cruelty; and added he was unwittingly slipping into the third of these when he went hunting for the raskhasas.

Sita is never weak: She is strong in spirit and character, even when in pain. But her goal is to serve her husband. She is patient and accepting of things except when it concerns her integrity and her love of Rama. She evokes our admiration when she refuses to take no for an answer, even from Rama; our respect when she speaks out against injustice; and our awe when she decides to end her life in self-immolation upon being repudiated by the only one she loved.

Sita epitomizes traditional woman: strong-willed, resolute, outspoken, and aggrieved, yet devoted to the service of man. If pride and aggressiveness characterize males, psychological submissiveness has generally constrained even the bravest of women. Hasn't this been the plight of women in many cultures: to endure hardships with an inner strength and occasional protests, but often in despair? Fortunately, things are changing.

Rama of the Ramayana

Valmiki's Ramayana begins with questions posed by the poet to sage Nárada: "Is there anyone who merits to be called a perfectly virtuous man, anyone who fully understands the power of ethical comportment? Who is there that fully comprehends the value of selfless service, who always speaks the truth, and is firm in his resolutions? Who has such power and majesty, and has also mastered himself and subdued anger? " (Valmiki: I.1 *et seq.*).

To these questions, the sage Nárada answered: "Yes, there is one with all these noble qualities. He is a prince of the Ikshváku dynasty. His name is Rama. He has complete self-control, he is with glory, is resolute, and free from attachments. He is intelligent and wise, eloquent and illustrious, a powerful destroyer of foes. His shoulders are broad, his arms powerful, his chin is sturdy, and his neck graceful. His chest is broad, his collar strong, and he wields a mighty bow. With a handsome face and well-shaped forehead, he has a charming gait too. He has a soft complexion and big endearing eyes. He keeps his word, he cares for his people. He protects all that is good. He defends dharma. He is versed in the Vedas and in science, and in archery too. His knowledge is deep, his memory sharp, and his wit is quick. He is revered and respected everywhere. He is pious, noble, and of keen mind. The righteous always seek him just as rivers long for the boundless sea. His knowledge is deep as the ocean. In sheer firmness, he is like the stupendous Himalayas. When in anger, he may burst forth like cosmic fire (*kálágni*). Yet, he is patient as Mother Earth..."

What can one add to this portrayal of the epic hero? We can only sing the glories of this Ramachandra. Rama becomes relevant because we can't imagine an intangible faceless God out there somewhere in regions beyond reach. We need a divinity that can be visualized, in name and in image, conceptual or real, to elevate our spirits to lofty levels, to give meaning to existence, to concretize our ideals. If such an *avataric* divinity deviates ever so slightly from perfection, he comes even closer to us, for he is like one of us. That is why, I feel, the Rama of Valmiki slips here and there: stubborn in his obedience to father at the cost of pain and anguish to countless people, indiscriminately exterminating all rakshasas, harsh to Sita when tossed by jealousy. Rama is human now and again.

Rama always adheres to Truth. By this we mean that he is committed to all that is good and noble, to fairness and justice, that he is always upright, honest, and sincere. Rama's devotion to his father is equaled only by his father's love for him. But even more powerful is his devotion to dharma. When Lakshmana begged him not to accede to Kaikeyi, Rama reminded him that "dharma is primary. My father's command is paramount because it rests on dharma (*dharmohi paramoloke dharma satyam pratishtitam; dharma samkshitamapyetat pitur vacanam uttaman*)" (Valmiki, II.21.41). He asks Lakshmana to reassure Kaikeyi that her wishes will be fulfilled. He refuses to blame anyone, says it was all so ordained. When others get emotional, angry and annoyed, Rama remains calm, patient, and with equanimity.

But when Sita disappears, Rama loses all his composure and ability to bear a burden, and blames poor Lakshmana for the predicament. The sargas (III: 58-60) that Valmiki devotes to Rama's plight in this context are perhaps the most poignant of all. Nowhere else is Rama more human than here. He wails and he raves. He talks aloud to his beloved, imagining she is hiding behind the boughs of an Ashoka tree, saying he can see her thighs behind a plantain tree, and begging her to return because the hut is desolate without her. He is shamed by the thought that people might say he was without the power or the caring to prevent Sita's abduction. He does not know how he would confront Sita's father. He asks Lakshmana to go proclaim in Ayodhya that Sita was dead and that he too would die soon. He calls himself the greatest sinner: Why else would he lose his kingdom and his father, be separated from family, have to leave his mother? Now, with Sita gone, all those sorrows were back again. Kamban says that Rama's shock was like that of a soul which had briefly left the body, only to find out upon its return that the body was not there (Kamban, III: 10.71-71). Or, as that of a man who had buried his immense treasures underground, only to find out that it had all been stolen.

Rama is surely one of the best known and most revered of all epic heroes in history. More people have uttered and written his name more often than that of any other. Few have been worshiped with such devotion over so many centuries. No other name in all human cultures is invoked as a greeting mode (Ram, Ram). Yet, scholars are still arguing about whether this personage whose saga was presented by the sage-poet Valmiki even walked on earthly soil.

Rama is divinity incarnate on the religious plane; on the mythological plane, he is a symbol of goodness that subdues evil. He is an extraordinary role model on the ethical plane. His adherence to truth is exceptional. His respect for parents surpasses any ideal. His refusal to throw blame on others is exemplary. His skill in archery and power over miscreants is awesome. The name of this Lord of the Raghu dynasty, Raja Ram, who protects those who have fallen, is forever associated with that of his beloved Sita in the moving Hindu hymn of unknown authorship that resonates in every Hindu heart:

> Raghupati Rághava Rája Rám, patíta pávana Sitá Rám.

The ideals formulated in a culture serve to enhance its image and self-image,

Shri Rama Charit Manasa (Shrí Rámacaritmánasa)

I was drawn to Shri Rama Charita Manasa of Tulsi Das (Saint Tulasi Dasa) by some of my Hindi and Punjabi friends who invited me to participate in their *Akhand Ramayan* sessions: uninterrupted relay-reading of the holy book from cover to cover in 24 plus hours, interspersed with bhajans dedicated to Rama and Hanuman, culminating in *árati*, all followed by a sumptuous, shared meal. I recognized that in the course of the rhythmic chanting—which could strike a stranger as a drone—the readers, while immersed in the recitation, sometimes seeming to be in a hurry to complete the task, are not always conscious of the meanings of the words and phrases of the sixteenth century Hindi.

I have derived some spiritual enrichment in the process. Once, I read the work in the quiet of my study, in an edition with modern Hindi translations of the verses (Pande, 1974). Later I discovered an English version of this classic. (Growse. 1978: Most of my quotes below are from this work.) I was struck by the fact that this Ramayana is quite different from Kamban's and Valmiki's versions.

Kamban is exceedingly modest in his prelude, and asks scholars to forgive him for daring to write the work. Tulsi Das is modest too, but he is quite harsh on the (imaginary) critics of his opus, describing them as people who, without cause, delight in vexing the righteous, for whom a neighbor's loss is gain; who rejoice in another's ruin and weep over his prosperity," and so on (Tulsidas, I.4). Like Marc Antony who displayed magnificent eloquence even while declaring himself to be no orator, Tulsidas reveals his great gift of poetry even as he says he is no poet: "Though no poet, nor clever, nor accomplished, though unskilled in every art and science; though all the elegant devices of letters and rhetoric, the countless variations of meter, the infinite divisions of sentiment and style, and all the defects of excellences of verses, and the gift to distinguish between them are unknown to me, I declare and record it on a fair white sheet." When I read passages like this, the spiritual aspects of the work recede from my plane of appreciation, for I am filled with admiration for the poetic genius the writer.

But in the same chaupat, the poet warns us that "Those who have taste for poetry but no love for Rama's feet will find pleasure in jeering at my verses.... To those who are truly devoted to the Lord's feet, but whose understanding is poor, the tale will seem insipid enough when they hear it, but to the true and devoted worshipers of Hari and Hara the story of Raghubir will be sweet as honey."

The poet is also exceedingly pious. He says that at the thought of Rama's grand mystery, he trembles. He begs readers to bear with him as he sings Rama's glory. All through, we can feel his intense devotion to the Lord. He adores Rama as one from whom all the light of fire, the sun and the moon emanates. Rama is the vital breath of the Vedas, the source of all that is good. Rama is God, not just prince of Avadh. "Though he is without attributes or form, though unlimited and unchangeable, out of love for his devotees he has incarnated." When the poet says that Avadh's virtues are sung in the Vedas, we may take the term to mean time-honored values and tradition, for the Vedas do not mention Avadh, let alone the Rama of Ramayana.

Like Kamban, Tulsi Das starts with a description of River Sarju. Rama's story is told as if Shambu (Shiva) is narrating it to Uma. This work too is interspersed with nuggets of wisdom. It extols the spiritual glories of Varanasi, emphasizes the importance of loving devotion (bhakti), and stresses the value of unquestioning surrender to God.

In Dostoyevsky's *The Brothers Karamazov* there is the famous quote to the effect that if there was no god then everything would be permitted. Tulsi Das expressed a similar idea when he wrote that if lust reigned unrestrained, all rule of law, religious vows, responsibilities, self-discipline, rites and rituals, pursuit of knowledge, philosophy, virtue, prayer, and asceticism will flee.

Tulsi Das evokes Rama's greatness with exclamations like: "A hundred thousand Seshas can't describe the power and glory of Rama. His one shaft can evaporate a hundred oceans." But he also reflects the (racist) mind-set of his times when he says that even a chandala, a shavara, an idiotic alien, an outcaste, and the like can be purified by repeating Raghubira's name. Among the characteristics of the horrible things in Kaliyuga, he says, men would be subject to women and Shudras would be wearing the sacred thread.

Leaving aside the social constraints imposed on the poet by the age, the essential message of Tulsidas's masterpiece is that there is but one God, that the Divine took on flesh and blood to save humanity from its intrinsically sinful nature, and that the Ramayana can redeem us. He proclaims that love should be shown even to very lowly creatures. Mahatma Gandhi transcribed a stanza from Tulsi Das, which I have heard read from the Unitarian hymn book: "This and this alone is true religion: To serve thy brethren. This is sin above all other sins: to harm thy brethren."

Not surprisingly, Tulsidas's book has been called the Bible of Northern India. However, unlike the Bible, this is the work of a single gifted poet who ranks among the most illustrious bards of India, and among the most influential poets of the world. His words exude boundless love for the Divine in a specific form.

The Ram-Charit-Manas is not a re-telling of the ancient epic. Rather, it is an inspired narration of the deeds of God-on-Earth, uttered with consummate piety, made magnificent by feelings of crystal purity. The stanzas touch us, not as meters constructed by a calculating mind, but as heart-felt outpourings brimming with love for Rama.

As with other great poets, Tulsi Das reads but poorly in translation. The magic of his work is lost in another language. The frequent mention of Raghurai's lotus feet (*kamala pad*) may sound confusingly repetitious to those unfamiliar with the framework. Unlike Valmiki's and Kamban's, Tulsidas's work is not for literary analysis. It is for the devotee seeking spiritual connection. It has been as powerful as the holy book of any tradition, and more so than the Bhagavad Gita or the Upanishads, for it touches the soul of those who recite it with reverence, and has been incorporated into a worship mode. It has soothed more hearts than any other version of the Ramayana. The saintly, the scholarly, the peasant, the professor, the wretched, and the rich of the Hindi-Hindu world have heard and experienced Tulsidas's Manasa. Few poets have written so much out of pure love of God, nor raised so many millions to pious spiritual experience.

Reflections on Ramrajya

Many cultures and writers have imagined the ideal country where everything is perfect. In *The Republic*, Plato presents his view of an ideal state: here, celibate philosopher kings rule. There are artisans, auxiliaries, and philosopher-kings, with specific natures and capacities. In this ideal society every citizen should follow a profession in which he is more apt (*svadharma*, as Krishna would say), while the head of state should commit himself to justice.

Plutarch who fantasized about humanity's mystic past idealized Sparta as a perfect country where celibacy was a crime. In that famous city-state (sixth to third century BCE) people lived frugally—a virtue we moderns would do well to cultivate—but they also had the nasty habit of summarily disposing off their unhealthy babies by throwing them into a pit. They are said to have gained supreme control over their emotions and mistreated their lower castes (serfs) inhumanly (Talbert, 1988).

Sir Thomas More's *Utopia* (sixteenth century) is an ideal country where there is no private property or luxury, urbanites and peasants alternate roles, everyone participates in harvesting, houses are never locked, and everything belongs to everybody. This imaginary island was supposed to have been somewhere in the Atlantic Ocean (Turner, 2003). Sadly, the man who imagined such an ideal country was beheaded because he refused to recognize King Henry VIII as the Supreme Head of the Church of England.

In an Arthurian legend we read about the town of Camelot where peace and love and all that is good and great reigned supreme under King Arthur (Ashley, 2005). Francis Bacon's *New Atlantis* is enriched by countless scientific inventions, and its emissaries were called Merchants of Light.

During the era of India's fight for independence from the British, Gandhiji inspired the people to lofty ideals by invoking an image of Rama's realm where only justice and peace would prevail, where every citizen would help every other, where men and women would labor as equals in a caste-less mode for the good of all. He was not speaking of a past age though he invoked it in name, but of a future one for India. Gandhi did not believe in the historicity of the Ramayana, but he had the wisdom to recognize that its value lay, not in whether Rama brought petrified Ahalya to life by the touch of his foot, whether Hanuman leaped across the waters, or whether *pushpaka vimana* was an ancient airplane, but in its message: an ideal hero's commitment to truth, justice, honor and compassion; and the need for vigilance when there are ill-wishing forces around. Gandhi called his ideal government *Ramrajya*.

Just as catholic (with a lower case c) means broad-minded and universal and not just that which pertains to the Church at the Vatican, Ramrajya is not just for the Hindu world. The enlightened vision implicit in this concept is what makes it interesting. The term is sometimes exploited by politicians for whipping up religious fervor and nationalist passion. Sometimes it is condemned by those who interpret this vision as too narrow and religion-laden for a secular India because Rama's name is tagged on to it. It is unfortunate that in the name of secularism, some Indians have to apologize for or are prohibited from using one of the names of its historically rooted culture.

A healthier approach would be to regard Ramrajya as the idealist's dream of what any nation could become. It is the portrait of a government we may never see in our imperfect world, but one which all the peoples of the world can aspire to: Camelot, Utopia, Ramrajya, call it what you will. All this is more than poetry: They stand for hope, an uplifting dream to fantasize about. Who knows, some day it may even come to pass! Some years ago, inspired by this vision of the Ramayana I read, I wrote the following:

> It has been said by Valmiki sage
> That when the great Rama ruled,
> No disease was there, nor early death,
> No person was unschooled.
>
> No man did die in a fruitful phase,
> Leaving behind a wife.
> Nor mothers wailed the loss of babes
> That died in early life.
>
> No thieves there were, nor cheats nor crooks,
> All did whate'er they should.
> All loved and cared for those who lived
> In their neighborhood.
>
> Plants and trees did richly grow,
> Yielding lots of fruits and grains.
> The earth itself enriched the land
> With breeze and regular rains.
>
> No lightning, thunder, or blazing fire
> Did bring to hearts alarm,
> No gale or hail or quakes of earth
> That to people caused harm.
>
> With valleys green and flowing streams
> All Nature smiled so well.
> Men toiled hard and produced goods,
> Traders things did sell.

> There was law and order, justice fair
> In this ancient realm:
> That was the kingdom which had the great
> Rama at its helm.

It is not enough to think of just technological and economic progress. There is much promise that India will do very well in that arena in the decades to come. But one shouldn't forget social justice, equal opportunities, help for the disabled, respect for all, and other enlightened values implicit in Ram Rajya. Consciousness raising in these matters was the greatest achievement of the twentieth century.

Cruelty and corruption, exploitation and injustice, conflicts and confrontations abound in our world. People of goodwill are making efforts to forge a better future for all. In the Ramayana, the poet reveals the human potential through a narrative of the distant past. When we read about Dasharatha's word of honor, Sita's unswerving love for Rama, Lakshmana's loyalty to his brother, and Rama's commitment to dharma, we are deeply moved. In that experience we feel we are citizens of Ramrajya, for in that land so distant in time and memory everyone experienced love and admiration for Rama who symbolizes all that is noble. When we imagine a land where there is freedom, fairness, justice and jubilation, no corruption, cruelty, or injustice, we may conjure up Ramrajya in our minds. This is a metaphor for the good and the great elements in any nation. Names and symbols give meaning and pride to a people's culture and history.

Each of us is ruler of a realm: our internal world and the one in which we interact with others. If in thought, word, and deed, we live up the highest ethical principles, that would be our own Ramrajya. If all did this, what a global Ramrajya that would be!

Ramayana Beyond Valmiki

Many years ago, during a brief stay in Bangkok, I visited the famous *Wat Phra Kaeo*: Temple of the Emerald Buddha: a magnificent structure dating back to the eighteenth century. There I was surprised to see murals which seemed to depict scenes from the Ramayana. Then I went to a temple not far from there, where there is the Reclining Buddha. Here again I saw marble panels with scenes from the Ramayana in bas-reliefs. I haven't seen anything like that even in India. These were based on the *Ramakien*, of which I had never heard before: this is the Thai version of the Ramayana (Thongthep, 1993). It has been a part of Thailand's cultural history for many centuries. I learned that the Thai capital was once called Ayutthaya, and that many Thai kings bore the name of Rama. Dance drama versions and puppet shows of Ramakien are still popular in Thailand.

A version of Ramakien was written by King Rama I who ruled the land from 1782 to 1809. Theodora Bofman has written a poetic analysis of the work (Bofman, 1984). In the Thai epic, King Tosarot of Ayutthaya has three wives who, as a result of special rituals, give birth to Phra Ram, Phra Prot, Phra Lak and Phra Satarud. They are all incarnations of Phra Narai. Phra Isual had a gate-keeper by the name of Nontuk (Nandi). Nontuk incarnates as the ten-headed Tosakanth, king of Longka. Tosanath's wife Monto gives birth to Sida. His astrologer predicts that she would destroy the demon race. So the infant is put in a jar which is left in the ocean. She is discovered by King Chanok of Mithila. Phra Ram once ridiculed Queen Kaiyaket. So, years later, she reminds king Tosarot of his pledge to her, and asks for a fourteen year exile of Phra Ram. There are adventures here. Tosakanth's sister Samanakha tries to seduce Ram, Lak cuts off her ear, Sida is abducted, a race of monkeys led by Pali, Sukreep and Hanuman come to the aid of Phra Ram and there is a climactic war.

I found this version interesting in its own way, but it lacked (for me) the moral majesty of Valmiki. But remarkably, its impact on Thai culture—which is now Buddhist - seems to have been considerable. Like other permeations of the Rama story in South East Asia, it has served to propagate the name of Rama beyond the shores of India.

Temple carvings in Kampuchea going back to the tenth century have the Rama theme. Characters of the Ramayana are deified there. In the Khmer version, *Reamker*, the hero is called Preah Ream, and his wife is Neang Seda. Ravana is known as Reap. Bali has a Ramayana Monkey Chant. In Java there is a Ramayana in the Kawa language, and so on. As a book title proclaims, *ramakathá lokeshu pracharishyati* (Iyengar, 2003; Jacob, 2002).

The Rama story has traveled to several other distant lands and climes, as far as Siberia and Mongolia. It has undergone regional metamorphoses, no doubt. In one, Hanuman is the child of Rama and Sita, and he is fond of women. Even after Muslim conquests and conversions, the spirit of Rama flourished for long in the culture of many peoples. As if all this is not enough, there are department stores called Ramayana, and a Thai restaurant in The Hague has the name *Ramakien*. Valmiki must be smiling, if not roaring with laughter.

Within India too, the saga of Ramayana is impressive. Whereas Valmiki has been translated several times into English, there is perhaps no verbatim translation of his work in any Indian language. Whether it is *Madhava Kandali* in Assamese or *Krittivasa* in Bengali, whether *Narahari* in Kannada or *Ezuttacchan* in Malayalam, the great poets of India's vernaculars have trans-created rather than translated the original masterpiece, realizing that the message of the epic is more important than details of the specific episodes, and that translations of a master-poet can never transmit the grandeur in the original. There are also other Ramayanas in Sanskrit, besides Valmiki's, such as the *Adbhuta*, the *Adhyatma* and the *Bhushundi Ramayanas*. In one Jain version, Lakshmana is punished because he breached the rule of ahimsa when he killed Ravana.

Versions of the Ramayana have also been published in Persian and Arabic. Most European languages have some version or other of the Ramayana. Gaspare Gorresio was one of the first to bring out a complete translation of Valmiki in several volumes in Italian, already in the 1840s. In 1864 Hippolyte Fauche brought out a French translation of the epic. More recently an abridged version, *Le Ramayana*, was published by Charles Le Brun. A Spanish *El Ramayana* has been published in Mexico, and Claudia Schmölders has written *Das Ramayana* in German. In the political rancor against the colonizing West, many modern Hindus tend to forget the commitment of a number of European scholars to bring to their own peoples the richness of Indic literature and culture.

Few names in history have spread so far and wide as Rama's. As with Christ and Buddha, Rama's name has inspired great painting, poetry, music and places of worship. But unlike Buddha and Christ, Rama's existence is clouded in the mist of mythic history, in a timeless realm, as it were, making the Rama Principle historically eternal. It is on this intangible that I sometimes meditate.

IV

The Longest Epic: The Mahabharata

What is found here, may be found elsewhere. What is not found here, will not be found elsewhere.

-Adi Parva of the Mahabharata

The epic

Once at school I won a prize in a Tamil elocution competition. It was a leather-bound copy of C. Rajagopalachariar's *Vyásar Virundu*: *Vyasa's Feast*: a simplified narration of stories from the Mahabharata. Besides being a lawyer, C. Rajagopalachariar was a scholar of Sanskrit and Tamil literature, and author who was deeply enriched by tradition. He was an astute and enlightened politician who became the last Governor-General of India. I remember listening to him with the utmost admiration when he came to deliver a speech at the National High School in Calcutta in early 1948.

Every child that grows up in a Hindu home in India has heard episodes from the great epic of Mahabharata, so I was not unfamiliar with the theme of the book. But this book gave me an opportunity to read the stories in Tamil, written by one of the foremost scholars and thinkers of the India of my boyhood days. I found C.R.'s Tamil to be chaste, simple, elegant and unpretentious.

The Mahabharata is a magnificent composition, incredibly long and impressively colorful. It consists of over a hundred thousand couplets, and is acknowledged to be the most elaborate epic poem in any language. It is an epic with a hundred side stories, each interesting in itself and often suggestive of an ideal or a moral principle. The work has been translated into English. Tradition tells us that the work was authored by Rishi Vyasa. According to the Vishnu Purana (III.3) Vyasa is looked upon as an incarnation of Vishnu who classified the Vedas. Indeed, he is said to have done this twenty-eight times (Wilson, 2006).

As with the Ramayana, many devout Hindus regard the Mahabharata as being more historical than mythological. By the close of the nineteenth century, thanks to the work initiated by Heinrich Schliemann, archaeological remains of Homeric Troy were unearthed. Likewise the work of S. R. Rao and others at Dwaraka have brought back the remains of some episodes of the Mahabharata. Some years ago there was a television program in India according to which more than 35 sites pertaining to the Mahabharata have been put into evidence. This was quite revealing. Other inquirers, based on astronomical data, have estimated the years of the Kurukshetra War, arriving at a wide range of dates: all quite early, compared to the traditional view by which it all occurred in another yuga: i.e. millions of years ago.

Scholars are not unanimous as to the historicity of all the episodes in the epic, some of which—like the churning of the ocean to obtain ambrosia—are clearly mythical. But the central story may have considerable factual bearing. It may well be that the majestic narrative, centered around some historical royal rivalries, grew over the centuries, enriched by the talents and imagination of more than just one poetic genius, amply fertilized by many imaginative minds. The name Vyasa means arranger or editor. The epic, some contend, assumed its present form only in the second century CE.

In brief, the story line of the Mahabharata is as follows:

It happened in the course of the long dynastic history of Hastinapura that the blind prince Dhritarashtra became heir to the throne. Recognizing his physical disability, Dhritarashtra allowed his younger brother Pandu to become king. Dhritarashtra himself had a hundred sons through his wife Gandhari. They came to be called Kauravas, after an ancestor named Kuru. Pandu's two wives, Kunti and Madri, bore him five sons, and these were known as the Pandavas.

In due course, Pandu decided to abdicate the throne and retire to a quieter life. Soon, however, Pandu died. Now Dhritarashtra became king of Hastinapura. His sons were brought back to the kingdom for care and education. The blind king received them warmly and treated them as his own. As the children in the royal palace grew and developed, the Pandavas turned out to be more capable and talented than the Kauravas. Because of this, the king appointed Yudhishthira, the eldest of them, to succeed him. This did not please his own sons, the Kauravas. Thus began a long rivalry between the cousins, which is the central theme of the epic.

Dhritarashtra, sensing the unhappiness of his sons, suggested to the Pandavas to move to a different city. Duryodhana, the first of the Kaurava brothers, was not entirely satisfied even with this. Fearing that eventually the Pandavas might come back to claim the throne, he plotted to exterminate them, by first installing them in a highly flammable structure, and then arranging to set fire to it. But the Pandavas managed to escape the arson, and settled in a nearby forest, disguised as pious Brahmins.

During their sylvan sojourn, the Pandavas heard of the *svayamvara* of princess Draupadi of the Panchala kingdom. A svayamvara is a public ceremony in which a princess chooses her consort on the basis of his proven accomplishments in a contest. The Pandavas decided to take part in the competition. Arjuna, the third of the Pandava brothers, made a tremendous impact at the sport by his extraordinary skill in archery, and won fair Draupadi's hand in marriage. She became wife to all five brothers.

When it became known that the Pandavas were alive and well, Dhritarashtra invited them to his capital, and bequeathed to them a part of his vast kingdom. The Pandavas thus became rulers of a country, with its capital at Indraprastha. Yudhishthira was chief of state, and his reign was a model of justice and good sense. The Pandava kingdom shone by its righteous glory. This made the Kauravas seethe with envy. They tempted the Pandavas into what seemed like an innocuous gambling game. By fair and foul means, the Kauravas made the Pandavas lose miserably. The stakes grew higher and higher each time, until the Pandavas lost their wife Draupadi, their properties and eventually their entire kingdom. Furthermore, they had to live in exile for a full twelve years and pass another year unrecognized before they could retrieve their possessions. During this long period the Pandavas went through many adventures.

Then came a time when the Pandavas felt that enough was enough. With strong allies, they met the Kauravas on the battlefield of Kurukshetra. It was in this climactic encounter that Lord Krishna, charioteer of Arjuna, revealed to the perplexed hero some fundamental truths about the human condition and the hereafter in the form of the Bhagavad Gita.

That great war raged for eighteen successive days, causing much death and destruction. The Kaurava brothers were all killed, their armies were routed, and the Pandavas, as victors, came to Hastinapura. When Yudhishthira eventually reached heaven where he was warmly received, his dog was not admitted. He refused to enter paradise under these conditions, whereupon it was revealed that it was Dharma—the Lord of Justice—who had been in canine disguise all through. But years in heaven still kept Yudhishthira sad, because his brothers and Draupadi were suffering elsewhere for their earthly misdeeds. He therefore joined them there, shared in the painful punishments of hell to rid themselves of the fruits of sins. Finally they all moved into heaven, there to live happily forever.

Even with many modifications, which the Mahabharata must surely have undergone from generation to generation, the basic line of the story remains the same. In its myriad digressive anecdotes, spiced with reflexive dialogues and discussions the grand epic paints many facets of ancient life and mores, it portrays the value system of the freshly forming Vedic society, and above all, it reiterates in countless ways the perennial principles of truth and justice, of righteousness and law. More than any other single work in humanity's heritage, the Mahabharata, while reflecting a rich and dynamic culture, has also served to fashion and perpetuate it. If it was history, never has historical narrative influenced the course of the future as this work has. If it was imaginative writing, never has fiction so transformed society and civilization as this work.

The composition of the epic and its symbolism as history

On Brahma's suggestion, Vyasa invoked Ganesha to whom he dictated the entire work, requesting him to be the scribe. Ganesha agreed on condition the story would be narrated without interruption. Vyasa agreed, but with the proviso that Ganesha should fully understand the significance of all that was going to be told (Ganguli, I.4). I was fascinated by this: I thought this was an interesting way of saying that the story was going be long, but also with deeper meanings than what might seem upon first hearing or reading.

I was struck by the statement that Vyasa had conceived of a great story which he wanted to put down to words. This seems to imply, contrary to tradition, that this was a creative work, rather than a historical record of events that once transpired. Who knows?

The Mahabharata may be regarded as the story of Bharat (India). It is as if the epic foresaw the patterns of future history. The author describes it as one in which "Devas, Devarshis, and immaculate Brahmarshis of good deeds, have been spoken of; and likewise Yakshas and great Uragas." What else is history if not the narration of the deeds of the good and the great, as well as of the evil and the ignoble, and their impacts on human events?

The Mahabharata tells of the conflicts between two families, symbolizing the eternal confrontation between good and evil. All human history is sprinkled with conflicts: between kingdoms, among dominions within and beyond continents, each trying to expand its borders and boundaries by encroaching into the territories of others.

But there is more than self-aggrandizement in wars and conflicts. There are also confrontations between ideas and ideals. One side is righteous and the other not, though each side invariably believes itself to be the moral one. Indeed, every theological sect, ancient and modern, which has claimed to have a hold on ultimate truth, has found itself in opposition to some others. Philosophers have propounded mutually opposing interpretations of scriptures, generating controversies among scholars and god-men, resulting in cults and sects. There have been—and there continue to be—conflicts between secularism and theology, between philosophies of fighting wars and working for development, between political ideologies, etc. Conflict is the perennial theme in life as in literature. The Mahabharata illustrates this in myriad contexts.

In the first section of the first chapter of the Mahabharata it is stated that when the four Vedas and the great epic were placed on the two trays of a scale it was the epic that tipped the balance to its side. We may interpret this to mean that when we try to understand the culture of a people, we find their history to be more revealing than their religion. For life consists, not in what one believes, but in what one does with it. Then again, religion is embedded in history: it is only a subset of history.

The Mahabharata has been translated in its entirety into English. In fact, one can find more than one version of translation. Many important sections from it have found expression in other languages too. We may note in passing that not many classical masterpieces of other languages have been translated into Sanskrit, and until recently, into any Indian language. I have sometimes wondered if this could reflect a mindset which believes it has little to learn from other cultures: one that still persists with the associated reluctance to acknowledge anything positive that one's own culture might have absorbed from others.

Be that as it may, few other works in all of human heritage encompass such a wide spectrum of the human condition as the Mahabharata does. Raw passions and desires are here, as well as spiritual pursuits. There are references to duties of the householder and also to rules of engagement in war. We read about games and gambling, archery and disguise, politics and diplomacy, rivalry and cooperation, and much more. Then there are excursions into fanciful tales and some sermonizing too. Most of all, there is the refrain of adherence to truth and righteousness. Indeed, the central message of the epic is that it is not victory in war or material possessions that should be the end and aim in life, but something loftier. To be able to renounce the most precious possession or achievement is what distinguishes the evolved human from one who is still at a very base level. But there is also the refrain that evil should not be allowed to persist, much less to dominate. Compassion is a virtue, but should not be extended to those who overtly violate the moral order and usurp and dominate: a lesson that is as important today as when the epic was composed. The mindless, vicious, and destructive determination to impose one's own religion and truth on the rest of the world is very much alive and active to this day.

The Mahabharata is unique in that it embodies much wealth of thought and culture. It has had a tremendous impact on the history and culture of the Indian people. It is not a sacred book like the Bible or the Qur'an, but it has had no less an impact on civilization. Its values and worldviews have penetrated the mind and spirit of the Hindu world. Its hero Krishna has become divinity in places of worship. With the other epic (Ramayana) the Mahabharata is in many ways the backbone of Indic culture.

Inspiration from Romesh Chunder Dutt

During my years in college I used to browse in secondhand book stalls of which there were (are) many in Calcutta. One day I happened to see a worn-out copy of a book by Romesh Chunder Dutt (Dutt, 1929) in a store on College Street. It was dedicated to "The Right Hon. Professor F. Max Müller." I bought the book and read the note on the author by S. K. Ratcliff. After graduation from Presidency College in Calcutta, Dutt went to England, much against the will of his family, and he entered the Indian Civil Service in 1869. He served the government of the Raj for twenty-five years, and retired. In the meanwhile, he wrote plays and poems in his native Bengali and even dared to publish a Bengali translation of the Vedas. This infuriated the orthodoxy, for in those days, not unlike in some other traditions, it was blasphemy to render the Vedas into another language. I wonder how many Hindus would be reading the Vedas today with any understanding of their meanings sans translations, and whether Anglo-Hindus who profusely condemn everything Western would allow this restriction to continue.

Dutt also authored in English *The Economic History of India* and *India in the Victorian Age*. It was after his retirement, and in England, that he composed his verse-form selections from the Mahabharata (1898) and the Ramayana (1899).

Dutt's Mahabharata starts with a description of *The Tournament*, with a brief summary of the story. The prose introduction begins thus: "The scene of the Epic is the ancient kingdom of the Kurus which flourished along the upper course of the Ganges; and the historical fact on which the Epic is based is a great war which took place between the Kurus and a neighboring tribe, the Panchalas, in the thirteenth or fourteenth century before Christ." Then comes the rhymed narration:

Wrathful sons of Dhritarashtra, born of Kuru's royal race,
Righteous sons of noble Pandu, god-
born men of godlike grace,

Skill in arms attained these princes
from a Brahman warrior bold,
Drona, priest and proud preceptor,
peerless chief of days of old!
Out spake Drona to the monarch in Hastina's royal hall,
Spake to Bhíshma and to Kripa, spake
to lords and courtiers all:
"Mark the gallant princes, monarch,
trained in arms and warlike art,
Let them prove their skill and valor, rein
the steed and throw the dart."

I was so fascinated by Dutt's versification that I decided to try to condense the story of the Mahabharata in a few stanzas myself: Not an easy task, given that it has more than ten thousand couplets. But this was my youthful attempt at this:

In Hastinapura's dynasty long
Blind Dhritarashtra came along.
His queen Gandhari, it has been said,
Bore him sons numbering hundred.
Since Dhritarashtra was without his sight,
To brother Pandu he gave the royal right.
Pandu's wives Madri and Kunti
Had sons who numbered two plus three.
The blind king's sons were the Kauravs
Pandu's five were the Pandavs.
The epic's thread has to do
With conflicts 'tween these families two.
Evil Kauravs usurped the kingdom
From Pandavs who were with virtues and wisdom.
Kauravs wouldn't the kingdom yield,

The two thus met on the battle-field.
This was the great Kurukshetra war
Where Krishna was the major star.
It was here that Krishna famously gave
The Bhagavad Gita to Arjun brave.

Ganguli's Translation

Years later, I bought Kisari Mohan Ganguli's complete translation of the epic in twelve volumes. I had never realized there was so much in this extraordinary epic. When I began reading it, I started making brief comments on passages from various chapters. The first one, from the first book (Adi Parva) was this: "When the universe was without light and brightness, plunged in utter darkness, there arose a mighty egg: the primal cause of all Creation, the inexhaustible seed of all beings. This Mahádivya was formed at the beginning of the Yuga in which, we are told, there was Brahma, the eternal One, the magnificent and inconceivable Principle that is omnipresent, the imperceptible and subtle cause which includes both entity and non-entity."

Compare this with the Big Bang of modern cosmology. Georges Lemaître, a proponent of this theory called this the *Primeval Atom* or the *Cosmic Egg*, which sounds much like *Brahmanda* (Brahma's Egg) of Puranic imagery. Ancient insights can sometimes be astoundingly similar to modern findings.

Or again, "Time createth all things and Time destroyeth all creatures. It is Time that burneth all creatures and it is Time that extinguished Fire" (Mahabharata, I:14). Ovid wrote *Tempus edax rerum*: Time devours all things (*Metamosphoses*, xv. L. 234). The idea that time extinguishes fire reminds us of the prediction that eventually our sun will turn to a black dwarf, as will most other stars in the firmament.

As aside: Vedic Creation Hymn

One creation hymn in the Rig Veda is known as *Násadíya Súkta*. It has been rendered into English in many ways, but it is hard to capture the majesty of the original in translation. My English version of it:

>Not even nothing existed then
>No air yet, and no heaven.
>Who encased and kept it where?
>Was water in the darkness there?
>>Neither deathlessness nor decay
>>No, nor the rhythm of night and day:
>>The self-existent, with breath sans air:
>>That, and that alone was there.
>Darkness was in darkness found
>Like light-less water all around.
>One emerged, with nothing on
>It was from heat that this was born.
>>In it did Desire, its way did find:
>>The primordial seed born of mind.
>>Sages do know deep in the heart:
>>What exists is kin to what does not.
>Across the void the cord was thrown,
>The place of everything was known.
>Seed-sowers and powers now came by,
>Impulse below and force on high.
>>Who really knows, and who can swear,
>>How creation arose, when or where!
>>Even gods came after creation's day,
>>Who really knows, who can truly say
>When and how did creation start?

Did He do it? Or did He not?
Only He up there knows, maybe;
Or perhaps, not even He.

On the historicity of the Mahabharata

Many years ago a friend of mine came back after a visit to Kurukshetra, on his way to Chandigar. He told me he had taken a dip in the lake where Brahma had created Man, and had stood at the place where Krishna had revealed the wisdom of the Gita to Arjuna. It was a thrilling experience, he said. I was excited just listening to him.

As in other traditions, for long centuries many Hindus take the names and episodes of the Mahabharata (and the Ramayana) to be literally true. Many still do. The question of its historicity did not occur to most Hindus in the past, and it did not occur to me when I first heard my friend.

But it all began to change for me with the emergence of the so-called scientific-historical mode of seeing things and inquiring about origins. To thinkers who adopt this framework, it is a matter of intellectual honesty to explore the authenticity of names and incidents on the basis of discoverable facts and extant relics, and to date documents on linguistic data, references to contemporaneous events, and the like.

For more than two centuries now, history, critical analysis of texts, epigraphy, archeology, and such have combined forces to determine the historicity of the narratives in the Judeo-Christian Bible, as also of the Mahabharata (Raghavan, 1969). The most honest answer one can give on the basis of what scholars proclaim is that nobody really knows. But every non-expert has a firm opinion on the matter. It is easy to be sure about matters we have not fully explored or understood, but have heard from respected authorities.

So at one extreme, there are people who say that the Kurukshetra War occurred sometime between 5000 and 3000 B.C.E. If it is true that the Vedas themselves date back to at most 2000 B.C.E., as most scholarly probes seem to suggest, then it is difficult to imagine how the Mahabharata, which mentions the Vedas, could have been a thousand or more years older. One author has identified the following precise dates:

> 26 September 3067 BCE : Krishna departs for Hastinapur
> 28 September 3067 BCE : Krishna arrives at Hastinapur
> 8 October 3067 BCE : Krishna departs from Hastinapur and speaks to Karna about the war
> 22 November 3067 BCE : start of the Mahabharata War
> 13 January 3066 BCE : the winter solstice (not the customary 22 December date !)
> 17 January 3066 BCE : Bhisma's death on the eighth day of the bright fortnight of Magha month.

At the other extreme, we have scholars who declare that the entire Mahabharata should be given no more historical validity than Homer's *Iliad*: a narrative which is perhaps based on some historical events, but by no means a historical account of events that actually transpired. They regard the work as lofty poetic creation, not unlike similar, though much shorter, epics in other major cultural traditions. They find literature, entertainment, and profound messages in epics, but little hint of reliable history. As to the existence of places with the names mentioned in the epic, they contend that just because there is a Venice or a Verona, it does not follow there was a Shylock or a Juliet.

In between are people who hold that some incidents in the epic are indeed based on actual events, such as a feud between clans and a belligerent encounter between them. But they also maintain that with the slow march of time, much fantasy has grown around names and places. We know of a more ancient and shorter version of the epic which was popular at one time. It grew in size from additions and manipulations in later centuries. Some have even pointed out that in an earlier version the Kauravas were the good guys. It is true that archeology has unearthed relics of a submerged Dwaraka, which confirms that it was there at an ancient time, but it is difficult to conclude from this anything reliable regarding the date of the Kurukshetra war.

What makes the issue of historicity of the Mahabharata difficult for many is that the epic centers around one of the most important personages of temple Hinduism: Lord Krishna. This means that if factual validity of the epic is questioned or denied, then the associated Puranas and temples must also be reckoned as constructions inspired by fantasy. This would be a fatal blow to centuries of meaningful art, devotional music, esoteric poetry, temples, sacred shrines, and modes of worship. Krishna, the associated festivals, and the Gita have been among the vital elements of the Hindu tradition. We would all be culturally impoverished and spiritually pained if it is established that all these were based on mere myths.

Perhaps many of the things we take to be real are not reliably so, but it is extremely useful, even indispensable, to interpret them as such. For example, the solid substantial world we see around us results essentially from the way that our brains interpret sensory inputs. There is no objective color in the world, but the photons that impinge on the retina are transformed into various colors by the rods and cones in the eyes. The noise and music we hear are essentially pressure waves of various audible frequencies. Music itself has no *objective* existence: it is essentially a subjective experience.

At the cultural level too, certain abstractions are transformed into belief-modes that carry enormous meaning and weight. They embody values and worldviews of great import. They enrich and enhance our collective psyche and sanity. Probability clouds of hadrons and leptons create the tangible world of perceived reality, so necessary for our life as creatures on earth. Likewise, the visions and images of what one calls myths, whether true at the core or not in an objective sense, sustain our cultural lives. They have to be taken as real in certain contexts in so far as they are culturally fulfilling and spiritually meaningful, at least until we replace them by other no less effective and enriching myths.

Thoughts on Krishna

I remember the joyous ways in which we used to celebrate *janmáshtami*: the birthday of Krishna, a most universally revered member of the Hindu pantheon. It is baby Krishna who is commemorated on this day. One draws on the floor tiny footprints of Krishna, using water whitened with chalk powder, picturing his coming home to the altar where he is worshiped with leaf, flower, fruit and water (*patram, pushpam, phalam, toyam*). The divine Krishna in temples, whether as icon or in painting, is a handsome youth of dark or azure hue, wearing a crown, garlanded and in golden robes, with a flute at his lips. Often there is a cow or a calf in the background to remind us of his legendary fondness for milk and butter, and his lineage of cowherds. The Bhagavata Purana, composed many centuries after the Mahabharata, introduces episodes not in the original epic. The Krishna of the Puranas is full of frolic and boyish pranks, that of the Mahabharata is a politician, man of wisdom, and divinity incarnate. I did not realize until I became acquainted with Harivamsa that this book has had a far greater impact on worship, poetry, and pictures of Krishna in the Hindu psyche than the Mahabharata. Oh, the power of poetry again!

Krishna is regarded as the eighth incarnation of the Divine. His name means dark or black. In this context we may recall what Graves observed: "(Christ) is uniformly represented as being black. And to make this the more certain, a red tinge is given to the lips; and the only text in the Christian Bible, quoted by orthodox Christians as describing his complexion, represents it as black. 'I am black, but comely, Oh ye daughters of Jerusalem' (Solomon 1.5), is often cited as referring to Christ" (Graves, 2001).

Krishna's color has prompted some New-Age Africans to claim Krishna as the Black Christ of India. John G. Jackson (1996) has elaborated on this. Some Hindus, in their all-embracing mood, have seen more than a coincidence of sounds in the names of Krishna and Christ. There are also religionists, both Hindus and Christians, who vehemently reject such conjectures. All this is understandable in our age of internet-scholarship where anyone and everyone can post anything and everything and set theories ablaze.

The fact of the matter is, leaving soothing cultural claims aside, the last name for Jesus is derived from the Greek term *ho Christós* (ὁ Χριστὸς) meaning *one who has been rubbed with oil, i.e. anointed.* This is how one referred to the messiah (of the Jews) in Greek. In fact, the word Christ occurs in the Greek version of the Book of Daniel (9.25) of the Old Testament exactly in this meaning. This was, historically speaking, before the birth of Jesus.

On the other hand, we read in the Mahabharata that the reason for Krishna's dark complexion is that Vishnu plucked a black hair from his own body and let it enter the womb of Krishna's mother Devaki when he was conceived. Incidentally, elsewhere in the Mahabharata where the origin of various names for Krishna is explained we read that "he is called Krishna because he unites in himself what are implied by the two words *Krishi* which signifies what exists and *na* which signifies eternal peace" (Udyoga Parva, 70). Some of the other names for Krishna mentioned here include Keshava, Vásudeva, Vishnu, Mádhava, Madhusudana, Sattvata, Pundarikaksha, Janardana, Hrishikesa, Mahavahu, Adhakshaja, Purushottama, Govinda, and Ananta.

According to the Bhagavata Purana, King Ugrasena was a great king of Mathura. It happened that on one occasion while his queen was lost in a forest, a demonic being, allured by her beauty, took on the form of Ugrasena and made love to her. The result of this encounter was the birth of a cruel and vicious offspring by the name of Kansa who grew up only to taunt and torture children, and to abuse the real Ugrasena. Eventually, Kansa kicked the monarch off his throne, and made himself lord of the land. He forbade prayers and instituted such tyranny that the earth shook in agony. It was to redress the world from this oppression that Vishnu descended as Krishna.

As a child, Krishna already showed superhuman powers. When the female monster Putana with venomous nipples stealthily came one night to feed him with her fatal milk, Krishna grabbed her heinous breasts with merciless vehemence and flung her in the air. The ogress screamed in excruciating pain, and fell to the ground in pitiable pieces. There are other episodes in the Purana which also tell of evil spirits and naughty forces, often coming in disguise as crane or serpent or whatever, to attack the invincible Krishna. Again and again, Krishna annihilates evil-doers with his divine powers. These stories were thrillers in ages past, but they continue to have cultural significance in our own times.

Other Krishna episodes relate to his exploits with the *gopis*: milkmaids and wives of cowherds. When he played his magic flute, the women would throng around him and dance with joy. Each one of them would want to hold his hand. To satisfy them all, he would transform himself into a thousand Krishnas. Sometimes he would steal their garments when they were wading in water, and hide them up on a tree. Elsewhere we read that Krishna had sixteen thousand wives.

One may wonder how a god could indulge in pranks that would strike some as licentious. The paradox is usually cleared up by explaining that these incidents are symbolic of a spiritual truth: of god's perennial interest in strayed souls. The women are symbolic of the individual souls while their mortal husbands represent the physical bodies. What is suggested is that the Supreme Soul is beckoning us all the time, for merger with it is far more blissful than the ephemeral titillations that physical bodies offer.

Unlike Shiva and Vishnu, Krishna is not an abstract divinity. Such a personage could well have once trodden the soil of India in flesh and blood, though passages to the effect that he had thousands of wives and sons, as stated in the Bhagavata Purana, probably have some esoteric meaning not all that obvious to lay readers. Whether Krishna was a historical figure or not is totally irrelevant in the context of tradition and festivities, but need not be so in a book.

Krishna has been the focal point of Hindu culture for many post-Vedic centuries now. He is what the hero is to history: to be remembered and revered; what the library is to the scholar: a vast storehouse of knowledge; what nature is to the poet: an inspiration for song and dance; what colorful toys are to children:

an instrument for mirth and merriment; what the beloved is to the lover: the instigator of intense joy; what insight is to the inquirer: a flash of enlightenment. Rarely, if ever, has so much been combined in a single name to serve such diverse needs. A more consummate blend of the human and the divine is hard to find elsewhere in fact or in fantasy. Such indeed has been the marvel of Krishna. Since time immemorial, generation after generation, his name has been venerated and sung, and his form celebrated throughout the length and breadth of India. He is an epic hero, an infant god, and also a majestic symbol of cosmic consciousness.

Arjuna

The Mahabharata paints countless significant characters, and has one great hero: Krishna. Of the many other men and women who enrich its pages, is there anyone who can be ranked as second to Krishna in grandeur and glory? If there are candidates for this, Arjuna would surely be among the top few. He was the third of the Pandavas, the boon-son through Kunti of the Vedic God Indra. The epic says that when Arjuna was born, celestials came forth to sing, dance and rejoice in the skies. The names of some forty large-eyed celestial damsels, decked with all ornaments who sang and danced are listed. They included Anuchana, Anavadya, Gunamukhya, Gunavara, Adrika, Soma, Asita, Suvahu, Supriya, Umlocha, Urvashi, and more. The heavens proclaimed that the child would bring glory to humanity. It was as if a prophet was born. A voice from heaven proclaimed that the child would be as powerful as Shiva and invincible too, that he would conquer many kingdoms and subjugate evil (Adi Parva:123).

Arjuna was known by many names. Also called Partha, at one point he was challenged to enumerate the ten names of

Partha. He listed them as Arjuna, Phalhuna, Jishnu, Kiritin, Svetavahana, Vibhatsu, Vijaya, Krishna, Savyasachin, and Dhanajaya (Virata Parva: 44).

Arjuna was valiant and virile, handsome and charming, and endowed with keen intelligence too. He is the best known and the most admired of the Pandava brothers. He mastered archery and was renowned for his exceptional skill in that martial art. More Indian boys have been named after this hero than all the other Pandava brothers combined. You can meet a Yudhishtir, a Bhim or a Sehdev or a Nakula, but not as often an Arjun.

Arjuna acquired many weapons and extraordinary powers in wielding them. Agni, the Vedic Fire God, gave him the magical bow known as *Gandíva* (Adi Parva 220-24). Once, while he was in the Himalayan forests to practice penance in order to obtain a celestial weapon, Indra appeared in the guise of an ascetic and told him there was no need for weapons. This was a place for peaceful ascetics who were devoted to austerities without anger or joy. There was no need for a bow, for there was no dispute or conflict. After recognizing Indra, Arjuna replied by insisting he wanted nothing less than learning about all the weapons, and he said, "I don't desire regions of bliss, nor objects of enjoyment, nor the state of a heavenly being…I am not seeking the prosperity of the gods." He wanted knowledge of the weapons because he wished to avenge his foes (Vana Parva: 38).

What is remarkable in this passage is the recognition, already in that distant period in history, of the need to be physically well-armed in the context of enemies, actual or potential. That need is more urgent than spiritual peace and dreams of heaven: a sad truth in the real world which Hindus have recognized from time to time. But sadly, they have not always been able to actualize it, and with terrible consequences.

Later, Arjuna went in further pursuit of a great weapon in the Himalayas. Here Shiva appeared, disguised as a common hunter who claimed a beast that Arjuna had shot with his arrow. Arjuna engaged the hunter in a fierce fight, impressing Shiva greatly. As soon as he discovered who the hunter really was, Arjuna prostrated to him. In appreciation of his skill in archery, Shiva presented him with a celebrated weapon called *pasupata* (Vana Parva: 40).

Arjuna attended the great *svayamvara* contest for princess Draupadi. An entire subsection of the first book of the Mahabharata is devoted to this (Svayamvara Parva). In a svayamvara, a princess chose her spouse from among competent suitors competing in a contest. King Drupada wanted Arjuna to win his daughter's hand. So he had made the competition especially hard for anyone else. Arjuna excelled everybody with his extraordinary skill with bow and arrow, and won the hand and heart of the princess. Many kings attended the event.

The description of the scene is fascinating in the epic: It is said that thousands of spectators were seated on platforms in the amphitheater which was decked with colorful drapes and garlands of flowers. It was like a festive sports stadium. King Drupada, father of the bride walked in majestically from the north-eastern gate.

Thousands of trumpets resounded, the air was fragrant with black aloes and sandal-paste. The whole place was surrounded by tall white buildings. It looked as if they were reaching the cloud-kissing peaks of Kailasha. The windows of the homes were adorned with networks of gold, the walls set with diamonds and rich carpets and costly cloths. The buildings had wreaths and garlands of flowers all white and spotless, very like the necks of swans. Their fragrance could be felt at eight miles away. Those seven-storied houses with a hundred doors and luxurious beds were reserved for the royal guests who had come to compete. On and on the description goes.

The competitions lasted for several days, reaching a climax on the sixteenth. On that day entered Draupadi, the princess, richly attired and adorned with gorgeous ornaments, and bearing in her hand a dish of gold and a garland of flowers. The officiating priest ignited the sacrificial fire and with due rites poured libations of clarified butter on it. Gratifying Agni by these libations and making the Brahmanas utter the auspicious formulas of benediction, he stopped the musical instruments that were playing all around.

The vast amphitheatre became perfectly still. Dhrishtadyumna, Draupadi's brother, took hold of his sister's arm and placed himself in the midst of that concourse. And he said in a sonorous voice, "Hear ye assembled kings, this is the bow, that is the mark, and these are the arrows. Shoot the mark through the orifice of the machine with these five sharpened arrows. Truly do I say that, possessed of lineage, beauty of persons, and strength whoever achieveth this great feat shall obtain today this my sister, for his wife."

After these words, Drupada's son addressed his sister, and recited to her the names and lineages and achievements of those assembled lords. (Adapted from Adi Parva: 187). Arjuna, of course, won the contest

At one time, when he was taking a dip in the sacred waters of the Ganga, Arjuna was dragged to the bottom of the river by Ulupi, the princess of the Serpent Realm (Nagas). She had been aroused by the God of Desire. Arjuna was now in a beautiful mansion of the King of the Nagas. The Naga princess Ulupi said to Arjuna: "Beholding thee descend into the stream to perform thy ablutions, I was deprived of reason by the god of desire. O sinless one, I am still unmarried. Afflicted as I am by the god of desire on account of thee, O thou of Kuru's race, gratify me today by giving thyself up to me.' Arjuna replied, 'Commanded by king Yudhishthira, O amiable one, I am undergoing the vow of *brahmacharin* (celibacy) for twelve years. I am not free to act in any way I like. But, O ranger of the waters, I am still willing to do thy pleasure (if I can). I have never spoken an untruth in my life. Tell me, therefore, O Naga maid, how I may act so that, while doing thy pleasure, I may not be guilty of any untruth or breach of duty.'

Ulupi answered, "...Thy virtue cannot sustain any diminution (by acceding to my solicitation). Then again, O thou of large eyes, it is a duty to relieve the distressed. Thy virtue suffereth no diminution by relieving me. Oh, if (by this act), O Arjuna, thy virtue doth suffer a small diminution, thou wilt acquire great merit by saving my life. Know me for thy worshipper, O Partha! Therefore, yield thyself up to me! Even this, O lord, is the opinion of the wise (viz., that one should accept a woman that wooeth). If thou do not act in this way, know that I will destroy myself. O thou of mighty arms, earn great merit by saving my life. I seek thy shelter, O best of men! Thou protectest always, O son of Kunti, the afflicted and the masterless. I seek thy protection, weeping in sorrow. I woo thee, being filled with desire. Therefore, do what is agreeable to me. It behooveth thee to gratify my wish by yielding thy self up to me" (Adi Parva: 116).

Arjuna stayed overnight in the sub-riverine palace, and received the boon of invincibility in water for the favor.

On another occasion Arjuna happened to go to a place called Hiranyavindu. He explored the regions with its sacred waters. He came upon the river Utpalini in the Naimisha forest, as also the rivers Gaya and Ganga. He went into the kingdoms of Vanga and Kalinga. Then he slowly reached Manipura whose king was

Chitravahana. There in that king's palace when Arjuna's eyes fell upon the beautiful princess Chitrangada, he experienced an urge to have her. He went to the king and asked for his daughter. Chitravahana explained to him about a boon by which everyone in his lineage would have but one progeny, and he himself only one daughter. So he would readily grant her to Arjuna provided that his son through her would be king of the realm. Arjuna consented to this and married this princess of Manipura. He stayed there for three years during which time a son was born to them. His name was Babruvahana. Then, one day, Arjuna was off again on his exploits (Adi Parva, 217).

I recall seeing a dance drama by Rabindranath Tagore on Chitrangada where the creative poet gave another version of the story line. In the Tagore story Chitrangada puts on the costume of a man to appear to be the ruler of the kingdom. She is an extraordinary warrior who protects her kingdom very ably. Arjuna was very impressed with her abilities. Eventually the two fall in love and wed.

Once Arjuna rode to Dwaraka in his golden chariot. The people of that city crowded by the thousands to get a glimpse of the hero. He was received with great respect and affection, and he went to Krishna's mansion there, which was richly adorned with precious stones and works of beauty. He stayed there with Krishna for many days.

During this stay the two friends went to enjoy a festival. There Arjuna saw Bhadra, the sister of Krishna, beautifully bedecked in sparkling ornaments. Arjuna was smitten again with the desire to have her. He asked Krishna who that lovely woman was, and Krishna told him it was his sister. Arjuna wanted to marry her, and asked Krishna how he could have her. Krishna replied that the svayamvara was not always dependable, for who can predict whom the woman would choose? So he said, "In the case of brave Kshatriyas, a forcible abduction for purposes of marriage is applauded, as the learned have said. Therefore, Oh Arjuna, carry away this my beautiful sister by force, for who knows what she may do at a self-choice." Then Krishna and Arjuna, having settled as to what should be done, sent some speedy messengers to Yudhishthira at Indraprastha, informing him of everything. The strong-armed Yudhishthira, as soon as he heard it, gave his assent to it.

And so Arjuna carried away Subhadra in his golden chariot. There were protests and noises, but Krishna came to Arjuna's defense, though not every modern reader may find his arguments convincing. For he argued: "This Pandava looks upon the system as untrustworthy in its results. Also, who would approve of accepting a bride in gift as if she were an animal? What man again is there on earth that would sell his offspring? I think Arjuna, seeing these faults in all the other methods, took the maiden away by force, according to the ordinance. This alliance is very proper. Subhadra is a renowned girl. Partha too possesseth renown. Perhaps, thinking of all this, Arjuna hath taken her away by force..... I do not see, in all the worlds with Indra and the Rudras, the person that can by force vanquish Partha in battle, except the three-eyed god Mahadeva. His car is well-known. Yoked thereunto are those steeds of mine. Partha as a warrior is well-known; and his lightness of hand is well-known. Who shall be equal to him? Even this is my opinion: go ye cheerfully after Dhananjaya and by conciliation stop him and bring him back...." So they went and brought back the couple who were then formally married (Adi Parva: 221-223).

These feminine conquests of Arjuna may remind one of the character created by Tirso de Molina (*El burlador de Sevilla y convidado de piedra*), who has come to be known as Don Juan in the Western tradition: a veritable playboy whose only accomplishments were, as per a famous Mozart aria (in *Il dissoluto punito, ossia il Don Giovanni*) the seduction of countless women in different countries: Spain, Italy, Germany, and Turkey. But the comparison is only superficial. Don Juan was without character, and he had nothing noble or outstanding about him. He lived in an age in which monogamy was the normal ethical behavior. He was simply carnal, a helpless addict to sensuality. But Arjuna's polygamy was not all that uncommon in the age in which he is said to have lived. He was a man of character and high principles. When a celestial nymph was sent to seduce him, he resisted, reminding her that she was like a mother to the Pandavas who had all heavenly beings as fathers.

Arjuna mastered music from the Gandharva Chitrasena. When the apsaras Urvashi in heaven was charmed by him and came to enjoy him, he respectfully declined, recalling that if he had gazed at her it was because she was a parent of his dynasty. But Urvashi's desire could not be quenched, and she explained that apsaras were free to sport with whomsoever they chose. Others of his ancestors had come there and sported with them, and that was not counted as sin. "Relent, therefore, Oh hero," she exclaimed, "it behoveth thee not to send me away. I am burning with desire. I am devoted to thee. Accept me, Oh thou giver of proper respect."

To this Arjuna simply said, "Oh beautiful lady of features perfectly faultless, listen! I truly tell thee. Let the four directions and the transverse directions, let also the gods listen. Oh sinless one, as Kunti, or Madri, or Sachi, is to me, so art thou, the parent of my race, an object of reverence to me. Return, Oh thou of the fairest complexion: I bend my head unto thee, and prostrate myself at thy feet. Thou deservest my worship as my own mother; and it behoveth thee to protect me as a son." Here we see Arjuna's character. For this he was cursed by the apsaras to the effect that he would have to pass his time among females unregarded, he was to become destitute of manhood and scorned as a eunuch (Vana Parva: 46).

During the battle in Kurukshetra, Lord Krishna served as Arjuna's charioteer. Arjuna's hesitation at the commencement of war is a memorable scene in literary history. There, on the ominous eve, the hero of all heroes, strong and mighty, sharp in mind with dharma on his side to boot, lays down his arms and wonders aloud if the recovery of his immorally seized kingdom was worth all the blood that would soon be spilled. He suddenly turns pacifist, and wants to call it quits. He reveals by his questioning that far greater than military might and conquest is compassion. He is confused about the ethics of war, and beseeches Krishna to counsel him. And what a counseling it was! Never in all of history has there been such an exchange between Man and God.

Here are Arjuna's famous words: "Beholding these kinsmen, assembled and eager for the fight, my limbs are becoming languid, and my mouth is drying up. My body is trembling, and my hair is standing on end. *Gandiva* is slipping from my hand, and my skin is burning. I am unable to stand up; my mind seems to be wandering. I behold adverse omens too. I do not desire victory, Oh Krishna, nor sovereignty or pleasures. Of what use would sovereignty be to us, or enjoyments, or even life, since the preceptors, sires, sons and grandsires, maternal uncles, fathers-in-law, grandsons, brothers-in-law, and kinsmen, for whose sake sovereignty, enjoyments, and pleasures are desired by us, are here arrayed for battle ready to give up life and wealth. I don't wish to slay these though they slay me, even for the sake of the sovereignty of the three worlds, what then for the sake of the earth? What gratification can be ours, Oh Janardana, by slaying the Dhritarashtras? Even if they be regarded as foes, sin will overtake us if we slay them. Therefore, it behooveth us not to slay the sons of Dhritarashtra who are our own kinsmen."

"How can we be happy by killing our own kinsmen? Even if these, with judgments perverted by avarice, do not see the evil that arises from the extermination of a race, and the sin of internecine quarrels, why should not we who see the evils of the extermination of a race, learn to abstain from that sin?" (Bhíshma Parva: 25).

Thus emerged the Bhagavad Gita, a most precious document in Indic heritage, replete with wisdom and philosophy, ethics and metaphysics: A work that in its musical chant has become sacred in the Hindu world. Krishna, we recall, dispels Arjuna's hesitation, and urges him to battle. Irrespective of the veracity or the historicity of this momentous encounter in India's sacred history, what we learn from this scene is that civilization cannot survive without the rule of moral law. And the rule of that law demands that in the pursuit of righteousness and justice, compassion has only second place. Compassion towards those who consistently break the law of righteousness may be commendable on an individual basis and in the plane of moral discourse, but it would be disastrous at the civilizational level. Give in to ruthless usurpers, rapacious intruders, and religious bigots, and you will be doomed. Tolerate evil-doers, hate-mongers, and mindless fanatics who are itching and eager to destroy your culture and heritage: that would pave the way for evil to rule the world. This predicament has been replicated time and time again all through humanity's history.

Gandhára and Gándhárí

On board the ship *Asia* in 1955 which I took on my first voyage to Europe, I happened to meet Daniel Schlumberger, an archeologist who was on his way back to his native France after doing some field work in Afghanistan. He had been working for a decade in Kabul as director of the *Délégation Archéologique Française*. There he discovered a Greek city of the time of Alexander the Great at Ay Khanum on the River Oxus. Schlumberger told me about the discovery of a palace of Mahmud Ghazni, the ruthless plunderer who, in the eleventh century made annual assaults on the rich Gangetic plains, slaughtered thousands, demolished temples, and returned home with obscene amounts of booty which included men and women as slaves.

I was reminded of these conversations when, some years later I read the Váyu Purana where it was said that the subcontinent of India was divided into nine principal regions, one of which was Gandhara (current Afghanistan). Gandhara was once part of the India of the Mahabharata (Ashvamedha Parva: 84). We read in the epic that King Suvala reigned there at one time, that his son was Shakuni and his daughter was called Gandhari: i.e. the woman from Gandhara. When she was betrothed to the blind King Dhitaráshtra of Hastinápura, she blindfolded herself for the rest of her life. She conceived, but the infant was not born for two full years.

When Gandhari heard that Pandu's wife Kunti had become a mother, she struck her womb with vehemence: a hard ball of flesh was ejected. The sage Vyasa, hearing this, came and instructed, "Let a hundred pots filled with clarified butter be brought here right away and be concealed. Let cool water be sprinkled on the ball of flesh…" Then the ball of flesh was broken into a hundred bits and put in the pots. It was from these and from a part that was left that the hundred sons (Kauravas) and a daughter (Dushala) of Gandhari emerged (Adi Parva: 110-115). This was not in vitro fertilization, but in vitro embryonic development.

Gandhari is said to have been a beautiful woman, with character and integrity. Sadly, her sons turned out to be villains. She urged her husband to be more firm with them, and she herself tried to mend their ways, but to little avail. She said of her oldest son Duryodana: "One who is of uncultivated heart and sacrifices both virtue and profit, does not deserve to rule a kingdom." In a sad scene just before the commencement of the great war Duryodana asks for his mother's blessings for victory, but she refuses, because she could not wish for the unrighteous to win. This is nobility of the highest order. Arjuna would rather that the unrighteous win than that he kill his kith and kin in the war. Gandhari would rather that her own sons die than that the unrighteous win. Such exemplary values set the ethical ideals of the Hindu world.

When the war was over and Gandhari saw the Kauravas on the ground as inert corpses, she was stricken with intense grief by the horrific sight that spelled the extermination of the Kuru clan. She tearfully eulogized them (in nine chapters of the epic), recalling the glory days when her son ruled the kingdom. She was pained to see her sons killed and her daughter widowed. "That daughter of mine of tender years is now wailing in grief...." She addressed Krishna, "What can be a greater grief to me than that my daughter of tender years should be a widow and all my daughters-in-law should be without their spouses? Alas, behold my daughter Dushala, having cast off her grief and fears, is running hither and thither in search of the head of her husband!" Then Gandhari's anguish turns to anger at Krishna. "You had the power to prevent the slaughter," she said and cursed, "But you were deliberately indifferent to the carnage. You should reap the fruit of your action.... On the thirty-sixth year from this, after causing the slaughter of your kinsmen and friends and sons, you will perish in a disgusting way in the wilderness" (Stri Parva: 25).

It is interesting to read that even Krishna was not free from the karmic law.

This is one of the most poignant utterances in the epic. It echoes the wrath that so often arises in the hearts of humans towards an omnipotent Divine that allows pain and suffering in the world. Why does not almighty God prevent the disasters that occur each and every day? Could it be, as the scene in the Mahabharata suggests, that all this results from moral misbehavior on the part of thinking humans which, therefore, even the gods cannot arrest? This is surely among the mysteries that no one has yet resolved.

Gandhari is one of the great heroines of Hindu sacred history who seldom get the recognition they deserve. She sacrificed her own sight as a mark of respect for her husband's blindness. She was the victim of an unfortunate turn of events that made her hundred sons evil from the very start. The Kauravas could well have turned to evil ways upon seeing both their parents without sight, who knows! Gandhari did whatever she could to mold the character of her sons for the better, but to little avail. In the end, after experiencing the terrible pain of losing all her sons on the same day in a dreadful battle, she retired to the forest with the mother of the Pandavas and her own husband, and spent her last years in peace and harmony with them. Such was the heroine who came from the land whose Purushapura has become Peshawar today, where Buddhism reigned for centuries, where the renowned university of Takshashila once flourished. That land has seen untold bloodshed and oppression since its occupation by invaders in the seventh century, and it continues to suffer, now under threat from groups that belong to the Dark Ages, but have managed to acquire enough fire power to keep the helpless people of the land under their ruthless control.

Duryodhana

Duryodhana is one of a handful of villains who are held in very low esteem in Hindu lore. First of the hundred sons of the good king Dhritarashtra and his noble queen Gandhari, his name starts with a prefix (*dur-*) meaning bad (like the Greek prefix dys-). *Yodhana* means a fight. Duryodhana could mean a bad fighter or a tough fighter. Sometimes he was also called Suyodhana: Good Fighter.

It is said that when Krishna, Buddha, and Christ were born, the heavens rejoiced. When Duryodhana was born, he brayed like a donkey, whereupon asses, vultures, jackals and crows made loud noises also. The king's counselors, upon hearing these bad omens, advised Dhritarashtra to abandon the infant, declaring that "an individual should be cast off for the sake of the family; a family should be cast off for the sake of the village; a village may be abandoned for the sake of the country; the earth itself may be abandoned for the sake of the soul" (Adiparva: 115). But paternal love was strong, and the baby was not left to die. Thanks to which, the Mahabharata story evolved, and Krishna preached the Gita. Villains in epics are indispensable for the good to shine.

During the time the Kauravas (Duryodhana and his brothers) were fellow students of the Pandavas under illustrious teachers, it was clear that the former were no match for the latter. Moreover, the Pandava Bhima used to taunt the Kauravas. Bhima was mighty strong. With just a gentle kick, he would shake the tree on which Kauravas climbed to pluck fruits, and the whole gang would fall down with some fruits. Duryodhana developed intense dislike for the Pandavas whom he harassed in many ways. "Seeing these wonderful exhibitions of the might of Bhima, the powerful Duryodhana, the eldest son of Dhritarashtra, began to conceive hostility towards him. And the wicked and unrighteous

Duryodhana, through ignorance and ambition, prepared himself for an act of sin. He thought, 'There is no other individual who can compare with Bhima, the second son of Pandu, in point of prowess. I shall have to destroy him by artifice. Singly, Bhima dares a hundred of us to the combat. Therefore, when he shall sleep in the garden, I shall throw him into the current of the Ganga. Afterwards, confining his eldest brother Yudhishthira and his younger brother Arjuna, I shall reign sole king without molestation'" (Adi Parva: 128).

We may take note of two things here. First, that Duryodana's evil nature was not unprovoked. It is a matter of recent finding that many adults who are destructive-minded were bullied when they were young. Early experiences of helplessness in the face of a more puissant competitor can lead to frustrations that may find horrific expressions in later life. It is interesting that this aspect of human psychology was well understood by the author of the Mahabharata. On the other hand, in the ancient categorization of everything into black and white, of bad guys and good guys, the narrative shows little sympathy for Duryodhana even though he had been a victim of the teasing and taunting of the more gifted Pandava brothers.

Once Duryodhana invited the Pandavas to a lodge for water sports which he had built on the banks of the Ganga. There all were treated to fine foods. Duryodhana stealthily mixed poison in Bhima's meal. When the latter, half dazed, lay down by the river, Duryodhana shoved him into the waters. Bhima drowned, but encountered the serpent people down under, who received him, treated him to nectar, and took care of him for a whole week.

Duryodhana could not stand the sight of his cousins prospering in every way. He confessed to Shakuni, his mother's brother, that he was filled with jealousy, and burning day and night, and dried up like a shallow tank in summer. He wanted to fling himself into a flaming fire or swallow poison or drown - so unbearable life had become for the poor fellow.

He tried to kill the Pandavas by arranging to set fire to their palace, but failed. He schemed with his uncle to entice the Pandavas to a gambling game of dice, and won the game. With their defeat he took over their kingdom and forced them into exile. But his hatred of them did not lessen in any way, though he had been crowned king of Hastinapura.

At another time Duryodhana was captured in a forest by a Gandharva clan led by one Chitrasena, and taken prisoner. Yudhishthira, the chief of the Pandavas, rescued him from that bondage. This humiliation only aggravated Duryodhana's fury. On another occasion he lost a combat with Arjuna (Vana Parva: 244). This made him contemplate suicide.

For a brief moment he even became righteous. He went to his brother Dussasana and spoke to him thus: "Alas, led by folly I have done a highly improper and wicked act, for which, fool that I am, I have fallen into such distress. Therefore, I will perish by starving, life having become insupportable to me. Relieved from distress by the foe, what man of spirit is there who can drag on his existence? Proud as I am, shorn of manliness, the foe hath laughed at me, for the Pandavas possessed of prowess have looked at me plunged in misery! Oh Dussasana, accepting this installation that I offer you, be king in my place. Rule the wide earth protected by Karna and Suvala's sons. Cherish your brothers in such a way that they may all confide in you. Let the friends and relatives depend on you like the gods depending on him of a hundred sacrifices. Always you should bestow pensions on Brahmanas, without idleness, and be ever the refuge of your friends and relatives. You should always look after all consanguineous relatives. You should also always cherish your superiors. Go, rule the earth gladdening your friends and reproving your foes."

But Dussasana would have nothing of it. His voice choked in tears, he said with joined hands and bending his head unto his eldest brother, "Relent!" Saying that, he fell down on the ground with heavy heart. "This will never be!," he said, "The earth may split, the vault of heaven may break in pieces, the sun may cast off his splendor, the moon may abandon his coolness, the wind may forsake its speed, the Himavat may be moved from its site, the waters of the ocean may dry up, and fire may abandon its heat, yet I, O king, may never rule the earth without thee" (Vana Parva: 247). The rhetoric here reminds us of Hamlet's epistolary declamation to Ophelia,

> Doubt thou the stars are fire;
> Doubt that the sun doth move;
> Doubt truth to be a liar;
> But never doubt I love.

In every contest and competition with the Pandavas, in every game of skill and intelligence, in every attempt to swindle or kill his cousins, Duryodhana was a miserable failure, except in the game of dice where the Pandavas lost. He never got a praise or a prize, but on many occasions he was humiliated. He inherited a kingdom, but was unfit to rule it. Rather than learn from his blessed cousins, he despised and alienated them. Duryodhana was, one would say, a born loser.

Nowhere else in literature or in life has there been so pathetic an individual. Yet, Duryodhana came from a good family, had loving parents and wise advisors, and could have acquired fame and name. He was mean and greedy, petty and envious, his spirit was eaten away by many base qualities. Krishna said, referring to him, "He, who, following the impulses of lust and wrath, and from darkness of soul, hates and seeks to injure one who is possessed of every good quality, is regarded as the vilest of men." There have always been such people in the world. The epic shows that such a person will ultimately succumb to the wrath of dharma and the rule of karma.

On the last day of the Mahabharata War, Duryodhana hid himself near a lake, but the Pandavas spotted him, and challenged him to battle with Bhima. The fight lasted for a while, but eventually when his thigh was struck ferociously by Bhima's mace, Duryodhana fell down and died.

Sad is Duryodhana's story, but his life was not in vain. In however low an esteem we may hold him for his various vices, we must feel sorry for so unfortunate a character. Moreover, it was his intransigence and hate that provoked the Kurukshetra war. It was in that context that Krishna spoke out the Bhagavad Gita which has lit the Hindu world like a powerful lamp for millennia. Here is the irony: Would the Gita have come to words if Duryodhana had seen right from wrong, been decent and giving, repented and returned the kingdom to the Pandavas? Of all the countless people in the grand epic, we have to be grateful to Duryodhana for having been unwittingly the cause of the Gita.

Draupadi

Every culture has its great women: historical, mythological, religious, and fictional. With its rich history and lore, Indic culture has many such. Draupadi is one of the more illustrious of them. She had a miraculous origin, along with her brother Dhrishtadyumna: both emerging in a supernatural way from the fire altar of a sacrifice performed by King Drupada of the kingdom of Panchala (Páñcála). Also known as Pañcali, Draupadi is described as very lovely with large black eyes like the petals of the lotus flower. Her complexion was dark. The locks on her hair were blue and curly. She looked like a celestial being, like the daughter of a celestial. She had the fragrance of blue lotus. Because of her dark complexion she was also called Krishna. As daughter of king Drupada, she was known as Draupadi. (Adi Parva: 170).

When king Drupada offered Draupadi in marriage to Arjuna, the oldest Pandava Yudhishthira said to the king that he too would like to marry his daughter. The king said, "So be it, then! Or you may offer her to any of your brothers." Yudhishthira said he wanted Draupadi to become the common wife of all the brothers, for their mother had ordered that any jewel that any brother won should be shared by all the brothers. So it was that Draupadi became polyandrous (Adi Parva, 198).

When I first read this story, like most people of our times I too was shocked. Then I was told that this was not unusual in ancient India. I have no idea of how correct this is, because when Yudhishthira made that proposal, there was an immediate negative reaction to it. In fact, king Drupada said: "The practice is sinful in my opinion, being opposed to both usage and the Vedas. ... Nowhere have I seen many men having one wife. The illustrious ones also of former ages never had such a usage amongst them. The wise should never commit a sin. I, therefore, can never make up my mind to act in this way. This practice always appears to me to be of doubtful morality."

But again, Drupada was not entirely right either, because Yudhishthira, after asserting that he could not digress from their mother's order, went on to say: "I have heard in the Purana that a lady by the name of Jatila, the foremost of all virtuous women belonging to the race of Gotama had married seven Rishis. So also an ascetic's daughter born of a tree had in former times united herself in marriage with ten brothers all bearing the same name of Prachetas and who were all of souls exalted by asceticism" (Adi Parva: 198).

More than anything, these exchanges show the complexity of Indian lore, practices, and perspectives.

Another key episode in the story is when Yudhishthira was tempted into a gambling game with the Kauravas. There he lost his kingdom, brothers, and himself. He even staked Draupadi, and lost her too. Now began one of the most dramatic scenes of the epic: Draupadi is ordered by Duryodhana to come to the assembly, and she refuses, asking what right Yudhishthira had to hold her as a wager when he had lost his own freedom. The matter was debated by the men assembled. Now Duryodhana's brother Dussasana, following orders, dragged Draupadi by the hair. She protested and declared that she was having her period. Nevertheless, she was forced into the presence of so many men, and ridiculed. Draupadi exclaimed: "The king (Yudhishthira) was summoned here, and though he was not skilled at dice, was made to play it with skillful, wicked, deceitful gamblers. He was deprived of his senses by wretches with unholy instincts… He could not understand their tricks… Let all of you reflect upon my words, and decide on the basis of what I have said." Bhima was furious at Draupadi's plight, and he spoke angrily against Yudhishthira, for which he was reprimanded by Arjuna.

Then followed the infamous order to disrobe the Pandavas and to peel off Draupadi's garment in public. When Dussasana began that shameful act, Draupadi began to pray to Krishna for help. By Krishna's magic the long cloth that formed Draupadi's robe kept growing in length even as it was being pulled off and peeled away. After one long strip was removed, another of the same kind appeared, covering her. This continued on and on until Dussasana, totally exhausted, gave up. Everyone in the hall, seeing that extraordinary sight, applauded.

I see this scene as a metaphor for Man's treatment of Woman over the ages. Woman has been regarded as property, as object of ridicule and for lust, as deserving of no say on what happens to her life, as unworthy of being heard, as not eligible for justice. All those wise men were sitting mute, adhering to rules like: "If you lose a game where you have staked something, you have to give it up." They represent the silent upholders of injustice towards women on the basis of what the shástras say: No equality, no voting rights, no admission to higher education, etc. because those were the laws for thousands of years of tradition. Dussasana's persistent effort to disrobe her is symbolic of the centuries of oppression that women have suffered, and the never ending robe reflects woman's inner strength which has kept her from succumbing to this. That an author stated it all in one moving and dramatic scene so many centuries ago is indeed a wonder.

Yudhishthira had said that Draupadi "is neither short nor tall, neither spare nor corpulent. She has blue curly locks…. her eyes are like the leaves of autumn lotuses, and fragrant likewise. She is equal in beauty to the goddess (Lakshmi) who delights in autumnal lotuses…She is compassionate and sweet-speeched." He says all this to his opponents in the game of dice for impressing upon them what a great stake he was offering. (Sabha Parva: 65 et seq.).

We may recall in this context the poem *Panchali Sabadham* by the great Tamil poet Subramania Bharati. The epic poem had been composed in 1912, as symbolic of the rape of India by the British and the vow of Indians to avenge the insult. The following lines from that poem (translated by C. Rajagolapachariar) is as relevant today as when they were composed a century ago:

"... What is mere falsehood? A mere petty custom, and a habit of ignorance, this worth on has accepted for Dharma. Alas! Throughout the ages, thus has many a one among us found misery. Fools! Does falsehood become Truth by mere age! You appeal to the past, O-Fools! But how long back do you go for your past? The past is three thousand years ago, and three score years before as well Do you think the countless multitude that crowded like flies on this Earth in the dead past were all sages? Do you think that before you were born there were no fools on this Earth? No, from the beginning of Time, among the myriad lives that appeared here, unnumbered like the raindrops in the clouds, ignorance and Evil always existed. Alas, in this land of Bharata, unmeasured has been the evil wrought by ignorance that mistook false custom for Dharma and the farces of liars for scripture.

Recently, a new English translation of the work has been published. (Rajagopalan, 2013).

Draupadi was a brave and bold woman. When the Pandavas were hesitating to launch a war with the Kauravas, Draupadi firmly told that if they wanted peace with the enemy, they should call to mind her tresses which were seized by Dussasana's rude hands. She added, if Arjuna and Bhima "were so low as to long for peace," her old father would avenge her. And she exclaimed in rightful wrath: "Fie to Partha's bowmanship, oh, fie to Bhimasena's might as long as Duryodhana lives for even a moment....If I deserve any favor at your hands, if you have any compassion for me, let your wrath, O Krishna, be directed towards the sons of Dhritarashtra" (Udyoga Parva: 82). This was before Krishna's preaching to Arjuna, and it could well have been that when Krishna instigated Arjuna to take up arms against a sea of Kauravas, Draupadi's plea was ringing in his ears.

Draupadi was a heroine of extraordinary strength and determination, of patience in the face of hardship, capable of anger when provoked, and unforgiving when deliberate wrong was perpetrated; loyal to the ones she wed, but uncompromising in matters of principle. *Ecce homo*! (Behold the man!) it was said of Christ and of Julius Caesar in sheer admiration. *Ecce femina*! (Behold the woman!), one might exclaim about Draupadi.

V

Song Divine: The Bhagavad Gita

(The Bhagavad Gita) represents not any sect of Hinduism but Hinduism as a whole, not merely Hinduism but religion as such, in its universality without any limit of time or space, embracing within its synthesis the whole gamut of the human spirit, from the crude fetishism of the savage to the creative affirmations of the saint.

- S. Radhakrishnan

    Blessèd wisdom in Sanskrit verse
    Heavenly song in meters terse:
    Arjun receives Krishna's light,
    Gita's mystic message is shining bright.
    As Krishna talks on *dharma*'s role,
    Values, conflicts, body, soul
    Action selfless, contemplation,
    Devotion, death and transmigration,
    God's awareness, matter, mind:
    Insights fed to humankind.
    Through sacred *slokas* are revealed
    Aspects of life on battle-field.

My introduction to the Gita

Vasantha G was the sister of a friend during my college days. She was studying philosophy at Ashutosh College in Calcutta. One of the books she had to read was S. Radhakrishnan's *The Bhagavad Gita*. One day she asked me who Tess was: the one mentioned in a footnote to verse VI.14. Radhakrishnan states that Thomas Hardy described Tess as a pure woman, reminding us that Ahalya, Sita, and Draupadi are all regarded as chaste women in the Hindu tradition, even though attempts had been made to violate them.

This is how I was drawn to Thomas Hardy and to the *Bhagavad Gita*. I found Radhakrishnan's introductory essay to be erudite, and also a pleasure to read. I decided to read thirty pages of the book each day, jotting down some comments as I went along.

Like many Hindus, I have read and heard the Gita countless times. I have also read parts of it in half a dozen translations. In the Mahabharata, several sections (Bhíshma Parva: 25 et seq.) are devoted to it. But over the years, I became more and more persuaded that the Gita is the work of a profound thinker, erudite scholar, and person of wisdom rather than the words of Divinity incarnate, as traditionalists believe. At any rate, I find the work to be far more fulfilling and meaningful from my perspective. It is in many ways a spiritual document in the Vaishnava tradition, and yet in many other ways it transcends sect and denomination, culture and religion.

The Gita is a dialogue between Krishna and Arjuna on the eve of the battle between Kauravas and Pandavas. The confrontation became inevitable since Duryodhana was intransigent, in spite of pleas from Krishna and others. In a remarkably dramatic, not to say science-fictional way, we read that the scene that was transpiring on the battlefield was being seen live by Sañjaya, King Dhritarashtra's trusted counselor while both were in the palace, quite a distance away from where the action was taking place. What this means is that Sañjaya was endowed with the capacity to hear and see what was happening miles away. It is a sad contrast: On the one hand there is Dhritarashtra who cannot see at all; on the other hand, there is Sañjaya who can see distant events miraculously.

This is the first recorded instance in all of literature of what is essentially a tele-visual power possessed by a human. It was not unlike what we can do these days: Watch from our living room what is going on at a place thousands of miles way. Whether such a possibility actually existed in the remote past is not as important as the fact that some thinkers could envisage its possibility millennia ago. Some may look upon this as a powerful example of early science fiction.

That the Gita occurs smack in the middle of the Mahabharata suggests that the book is an integral part of Hindu culture. That is to say, its full import cannot be understood - or only superficially—by those who are unfamiliar with the Hindu cultural and sacred historical framework. Not only is the language Sanskrit, the sacred idiom of Hinduism, but the terms and metaphysics are very much part of the Hindu world. There are references in the Gita to varnáshrama, Vedas, aum, Brighu; Vayu, Yama, Agni, Prajapati, and Brahma; to mantra, Kamadhuk, Janaka, and more. It is fair to say that the non-literate Hindu or alien who extols the Gita after reading it once or twice may be only repeating what he/she has read elsewhere. Thus the epic context and the literal textual verses are quintessentially Hindu. To absorb and appreciate these to the full, familiarity with the Hindu world view is a *sine qua non*. I have often wondered if some of the eighteenth and nineteenth century European admirers of Gita who have written in eloquent praise of the work, and even some modern Hindus who have gone through English translation of the shlokas and rave about it were/are really knowledgeable about the countless allusions in the work.

Be that as it may, the Gita expounds also higher truths, metaphysical and moral, which are universal. What can be more universal in the human experience than war and conflict, confusion and compassion? Interspersed in all the abstract philosophy permeating the work are insights that are meaningful and relevant to one and all, and for all times. In its distilled form the message of the Gita can be understood by non-Hindus as well, its wisdom could interest people of other faiths and cultures also. The Gita is more universal than Hinduism or India, for it mirrors the human predicament at all times. That is why people as diverse as Al Beruni, Warren Hastings, Thoreau, and Annie Besant, and countless more at all times and from different places have acknowledged the enrichment they have derived from reading the Gita.

That the Gita is presented on the battlefield suggests that deep philosophical questions are not just matters for arm chair speculation. Questions about the nature of the self and the goal of human activity are more than matters for classroom discussions. Fundamental problems pertaining to existence and death are not mere intellectual inquiries, of interest only to those sheltered in the ivory tower of academia. Rather, they are human questions, relating to the human condition. Their significance must be related to the harsh problems of life and death. They must be perennially borne in mind through all of life's ups and downs, they must enlighten us in our decisions at every heartbeat of existence, in the rough and tumble of life as in the quiet of the countryside.

The discharge of one's duty becomes difficult when there is conflict between duty and personal desires and interests. Yet, if such a situation arises, the Gita insists, we need to sacrifice our own needs and urges, and do what is incumbent upon us. In the context of civilized society the law of the land should take precedence over political convenience. In the case of individuals, the moral law should take precedence over self-centered inclinations. This is a perennial theme which finds expression in various forms in all cultures. Thus, a character in a play by Pierre Corneille (*Le vieil Horace*, Act II, Scene v) says: *Faites votre devoir, et laissez faire aux dieux:* Do your duty, and leave the rest to heaven. Or again, in the Rossini opera Tancredi, a father (Argirio) has to send his daughter (Amenaïde) to the gallows because she is suspected of treason. But his love for her is also strong, and he is torn between duty and emotion.

The Bhagavad Gita is glorious music. When we hear it chanted in its traditional rhythm and we immerse ourselves in its serene melody, we experience an inner peace such as only the loftiest expressions of the human spirit can afford. When one is listening to Mozart's *Exsultate, Jubilate*, who is thinking of the meaning? The piously simple and the profoundly sensitive are moved by it.

The Gita combines poetry and philosophy, music and religious solace. It kindles subtle thoughts; it also calls for decisive actions. It consoles the bereaved and uplifts the dejected. It thrills the soul and illumines the mind. It presents a vision of the human condition that is lofty and universal. No other work in India's rich literary heritage has accomplished so much for a millennium and more. That is why throughout India's long history, many thinkers, great and modest, lay and religious, have been touched by this work; and thinkers outside of the Hindu tradition have also found meaning and message in the Gita.

Some lessons from the Gita

Arjuna is a robust man with keen intellect. Yet, he is baffled by the confusions of right and wrong, of war and peace. This is to remind us that no matter how intelligent and smart we are, no matter how much knowledge we possess and how many books we have read, ultimate questions as to righteous and unrighteous actions do not have easy answers. Moral problems are not as easily solved as problems in arithmetic and algebra. Questions relating to war and peace are complex, as also the conflicts of everyday life. Who can assert categorically what is right and what is wrong, what is punishment and what is forgiving? Events in the world where we play a major or a minor part may have deeper significance than what we are able to picture, their grander purpose in the scheme of things may not always be clear to our imperfect understandings.

When a young and unknown Mohandas Karamchand Gandhi was asked to get out of a first class compartment of the train at Pietermarizburg in South Africa, he challenged their right to do so, beginning the civil rights movement in that country.

On December 1, 1955, a simple African American woman named Rosa Parks in Montgomery, Alabama, defied a driver's order to vacate her seat in the bus so a white man could sit there, this sparked the Civil Rights movement in the United States, leading ultimately to the election of a black president to occupy the White House.

On December 17, 2010 a Tunisian fruit vendor, harassed repeatedly by the police whom he had to bribe regularly, set fire to himself in utter frustration. This sparked a popular uprising which became the Tunisian Revolution The people rose up "to topple a 23-year dictatorship and march on, demanding radical change in their government" (*New York Times*, January 21, 2011).

The mind can grasp and order things, and it can explain what causes what. But logic alone cannot say what is ultimately good and what is bad. Mathematical decision theory can reveal what will be the outcome of particular courses of actions and with what probability, but it can never tell us what the morally right action is.

The Gita instructs us that in everything we do, we must remember the link between the individual and the universal. There is more to being human than engaging oneself only in self-centered actions which have little relevance in the cosmic scheme of things. If anything, they blur our vision of the grander goals of life and civilization.

The notion that we do this and we do that, as if we are in full control of the world, is a paltry view of what life is all about. It arises from ingrained ignorance, even as the geocentric picture, however convincing to the superficial observer of the skies, is a grossly mistaken appraisal of how the universe actually is. When we begin to recognize that there is something loftier to life than the satisfaction of the senses, our actions begin to take on greater meaning and relevance.

This recognition comes from an understanding of the ultimate nature of the self which is the intangible center of our innermost experience. The self in the embodied state goes through the cycle of terrestrial life many times over before merging with the Absolute. And even when the body ages, grows decrepit, and dies, the self continues to exist for ever, for it is unaffected by the constituents of the physical world.

Having realized this fundamental truth, we must work in the framework of our inborn talents (*svadharma*) and abilities. Only in such a self-discovery will one find true fulfillment, not in actions motivated by imitation or envy. This is how I interpret the injunction not to follow *paradharma*. We all have our respective roles to play in society, our different duties to perform. The spiritual mode is to discharge these duties with a sense of commitment and to dedicate our actions to a higher Spirit that undergirds the world.

But the performance of one's duty alone will not suffice unless it is done with the proper attitude. Our actions must be in the spirit of consecrating them to the world at large, rather than for purely selfish purposes. It is in a spirit of sacrifice that we must play our part in life. This is best accomplished if one develops an abiding love of God. In other words, the deeply felt *bhakti* mode is most conducive to spiritual life. What this means is that for spiritual progress one needs to adopt a frame of mind that does not crave for physical gratification.

The Gita does not propound any one philosophical system as the correct one. It presents a variety of paths and views, some of them seemingly incompatible. At one point Arjuna pleads with Krishna to show him just one way by which he may attain the highest good. Krishna expounds many spiritual modes: ritualism and meditation are extolled, action and detachment are both recommended, pursuit of knowledge and pious devotion are equally praised. If anything, the Gita reveals that there are many ways to find inner peace and fulfillment in life, for no one path is appropriate for one and all, any more than that shoes of a single size will fit all feet. In this most of all the Gita may be regarded as the quintessence of Hindu spirituality whose underlying affirmation is that there are multiple paths to spiritual fulfillment, which is a radically different view from many other religions.

Perspectives on the Gita

The Bhagavad Gita has been approached from a variety of perspectives. Volumes have been written by scholars on interpretations of the Gita. To many traditional Hindus, it is the voice of God, revelations of ultimate divine knowledge to mortals *via* Arjuna. The verses of the Gita are regarded as capsules of esoteric wisdom, the spoken syllables of the Lord in human aspect. Tilak (2002) entitled his book as *The Secrets of the Gita*. Krishna himself asserts this in his dialogue with Arjuna:

> Thus, knowledge more secret than all secrets
> Has been imparted to you by Me. (XVIII.63)

Some have heard the voice of Krishna directly. Sri Aurobindo once had a mystical experience which he described thus: "It seemed to me that He spoke to me again and said, 'The bonds you had not the strength to break, I have broken for you, because it is not my will nor was it ever my intention that that should continue. I have had another thing for you to do and it is for that I have brought you here, to teach you what you could not learn for yourself and to train you for my work.' Then He placed the Gita in my hands. His strength entered into me and I was able to do the sadhana of the Gita. I was not only to understand intellectually but to realize what Sri Krishna demanded of Arjuna and what He demands of those who aspire to do His work, to be free from repulsion and desire, to do work for Him without the demand for fruit, to renounce self-will and become a passive and faithful instrument in His hands, to have an equal heart for high and low, friend and opponent, success and failure, yet not to do His work negligently. I realized what the Hindu religion meant" (Sri Aurobindo's Uttarpara Speech, 30 May 1909).

Bhaktivedanta Swami Prabhupada considered the Gita to be the words of God which ought to be accepted literally, and without questioning. He felt that the Gita contains all that is worthy of knowing. Had not Krishna Himself declared this?

> I will declare to you in full, this wisdom together with knowledge
> By which there shall remain nothing more to be known. (VII-2)

This revered Swamiji who has done more for the propagation of the message of the Gita in the Western world than anyone in history, went further and declared that scholarly dissection and intellectual analysis of the Gita are uncalled for, and also impertinent, not to say blasphemous. More exactly, those who do not belong to the Krishna consciousness tradition, he went on to declare, have no right to interpret the Gita. Their "unauthorized interpretations.... are so many stumbling blocks in the path of spiritual understanding." The reason for his position is that "the deluded interpreters do not surrender unto the lotus feet of Srí Krishna, nor do they teach others to follow this principle" (Prabhupada, 1975, 385). This statement may be warranted on the Vaishnava spiritual plane. It also echoes similar assertions by devout Muslims regarding the Holy Qur'an.

But there are other levels and perspectives from which the masterworks of spiritual traditions can be and have been approached. The *bhakti* mode is no doubt the most powerful and popular in all traditions. It deserves all our respect. Though it does not appeal to all, it's great strength and appeal lies in that it can and does afford inner peace and fulfillment to many spiritual aspirants. This is a valid time-honored mode with parallels in all religious traditions. From this perspective, inconsistencies or contradictions within the Gita, if and when such are perceived, arise from one's inability to understand the deeper esoteric meanings; which, in turn, is due to one's low level of spiritual evolution.

Even if the religious fundamentalists are absolutely right in their assessment, and understandable in their condemnation of outsiders who dare to comment on their scripture, not everyone buys it, as the expression goes. More seriously, if such a view is enforced by religious authorities, there can be more persecution and pain than knowledge and liberation in any culture. This should be evident to anyone who has studied the history of religions and considers what is going on in some societies today.

Indeed, if Western governments had adopted a similar perspective on the Bible and disallowed other religious modes, the eminent propagator of the Gita would have been politely asked to leave the country where he did much of his evangelical work.

Those who are so committed to their scriptures as to deny others the right to think for themselves or call for the silencing of diverging views are doing more disservice and harm to the tradition than they realize. Being anchored to a tradition is different from being fettered by it.

Associated with, but not identical to, this approach is the view of the book as scripture. One author has described the Gita as a scripture for all humankind (Tapasyananda, 2005). Christians feel the same way about the Bible and Muslims about the Qur'an. But, in this context, it is good to recall what Sri Aurobindo, enlightened mystic that he was, said with great insight: "… the letter of the Scripture binds and confuses us, as the apostle of Christianity warned his disciples when he said that the letter killeth and it is the spirit that saves; and there is a point beyond which the utility of the Scripture itself ceases. The real source of the knowledge is the Lord in the heart" (Aurobindo, 1950, 84).

For ages, the Gita has been regarded as one of the three pillars of Hindu canonical works, the Brahmasutras and the Upanishads being the other two. The philosopher T. M. P. Mahadevan put it this way: "The Upanishads, the Bhagavad-gita, and the Brahama-sutra (are) together referred to as the prasthána-traya, the triple canon of Vedanta. Since the Upanishads are the summits of the Veda (shruti-shiras) and therefore are parts of it, they are described as shruti-prasthána (*prasthána* means foundation). The Bhagavad-Gita comes next only to the Upanishads.... As this text forms part of the Mahabharata which is a smriti (remembered, i.e. secondary text based on the Veda) it is called smriti-prasthána. The third of the canonical texts is the Brahma-sutra which is regarded as the nyaya-prasthána, because it sets forth the teachings of Vedanta in a logical order."

Because it is regarded as scripture, in the Hindu world it replaces the Bible as a book on which one takes oath. Recently, the first Hindu congresswoman in the United States swore allegiance on the Bhagavad Gita, just as a few years ago a Muslim congressman did his oath on the Qur'an.

Pious reading of the Gita is a religious exercise that is said to be conducive to one's spiritual evolution. Lord Krishna states this explicitly:

> He who hears this (the Gita) with faith, who does not just argue, he too,
> Liberated, shall attain the higher region attained through meritorious deeds. (XVIII-71)

Like the Bible, the Gita can serve as a guide in moments of difficulty. Mahatma Gandhi was one of many who vouched for this: "When disappointment stares me in the face and all alone I see not one ray of light," he wrote, "I go back to the Bhagavad-Gita. I find a verse here and a verse there, and I immediately begin to smile in the midst of overwhelming tragedies -- and my life has been full of external tragedies -- and if they have left no visible or indelible scar on me, I owe it all to the teaching of Bhagavad-Gita" (Gandhi, 1925, 1979).

The Gita enunciates many basic Hindu doctrines, such as the nature of the soul and reincarnation. It also lists the virtues and vices of human beings, righteous and unrighteous conduct. It is a guiding light in a variety of contexts, a source of insight into the nature of life and death, and of human action and experience. It speaks about human qualities and responsibilities, and prescribes steps by which one would ultimately achieve liberation. For many Hindus in today's world the Gita symbolizes the essence of Hindu spirituality.

Then again, the Gita may also be looked upon as a popular work on certain classical Indian philosophical systems, presented in the form of a dialogue so as to make the exposition more interesting and understandable. From the point of view of the history of ideas, the Gita contains theories about the nature of body and soul, about food and the phenomenal world as they were in that age. The discussions are all cast in the framework of a spiritual worldview of matter and spirit, of life and death. There are references to the five elements in the Gita, to the concepts of mind and matter, and to the world beyond. The verses tell us of how Indian thinkers of past centuries thought and discoursed upon matters of perennial significance. In other words, the Gita is not only propounding a perennial philosophy, but it also serves as an invaluable source book for the thought currents and the sciences of past generations.

The Gita has also been looked upon as an allegorical poem on the predicaments governing life. This view has been expressed by many thinkers and saints, of whom Sri Aurobindo is a prime example. In Swami Yogananda's analysis we find one of the most lucid and penetrating insights in this regard. He clarified the idea that the Bhagavad Gita is "an allegory of the inner conflict between man's base materialistic instincts and his innate yearning to attain the blissful spiritual consciousness of the oneness with the Divine" (Yogananda, 2007).

In life's journey, there are conflicts between good and evil. The Kauravas represent human attachment to material things and to human weaknesses which outnumber the higher qualities represented by the Pandavas. Though temporarily subdued, the good qualities will ultimately triumph. Krishna is the enlightened Mind that wields the reins of the horses which are straying along directions in which the mind wanders. Kurukshetra is the human heart and mind where the battle rages day in and day out. The Gita tells us how to attain tranquility amidst all the stress and turmoil of mundane existence.

Commentaries and Translations

The Bhagavad Gita has provoked more scholarly commentaries and analyses, more discussions on its contents and significance than probably any other Hindu work. In the classical world, eminent thinkers and saints like Adi Sankararacarya, Ramanujacarya, Madhavacarya, Vallabhacarya and Nimbarkacarya wrote commentaries on the work. Since the nineteenth century, B. G. Tilak, Sri Aurobindo, Mahatma Gandhi, Vinobha Bhave, Swami Sivananda and scores of others have commented, and continue to comment, on the Gita in English, Hindi, Tamil, and other languages.

Lay, scholarly, and saintly people have interpreted the masterpiece from their different visions, sometimes drawing practical lessons to guide their own lives. Swami Chidbhavananda gave an excellent simile. He compared the Gita to a mirror, each person seeing in it a little bit of his/her own reflection (1992 ed.).

In the exposition of the great Shankaracharya, the karma that Krishna speaks of refers to Vedic rituals, activities one ought to engage in with meticulous attention in order to achieve spiritual progress. Centuries later, karma came to be interpreted differently. Tilak saw in the Gita the philosophy of the nineteenth century scientific notion of energism, as popularized by W. Ostwald and others in the world of physics. For Tilak, karma was action rooted in knowledge and leading to liberation; selfless action, no doubt, yet day to day action for a noble purpose, not routine rituals. The Yoga of the Gita is an exercise, Tilak suggested, a modus operandi for the effective performance of action. Jñana and bhakti are there, but it is action in the real world that is most important. Tilak did not look upon renunciation favorably (Tilak, 2002). A recent study explores the interpretations of the Gita by three major thinkers of the tradition, Tilak, Gandhi, and Radhakrishnan (Pani et al., 2009).

For Gandhi, Kurukshetra is supreme symbolism, poetic imagery and not a call for killing. It is a sublime metaphor for the eternal conflict between good and evil. Gandhi felt that each person could see his own meanings in the Gita, irrespective of what literal translations might suggest. He justified his non-violence in terms of the Gita, for in his view the war that Krishna was urging Arjuna to wage was not a physical war with weapons and bloodshed, but an ethical and spiritual struggle. The Gita was a personal experience for Gandhi, inspiring him to a commitment for right action (Gandhi, 1998).

On the other hand, political revolutionaries during the British Raj, such as Veer Savarkar, sought inspiration from the Gita to take up violent arms against alien rule. Damodar Chapekar had a copy of the Gita with him when he assassinated a British official in the 1890s.

Vinobha Bhave's interpretations are linguistic. From the meanings of the words in the text, he constructed meanings for whole passages. He analyzed the syntax and word combinations of the verses to draw his own interpretations. He was convinced that there are subtle meanings in the Gita verses that are not evident to the superficial reader (Bhave, 1964).

The value of the Gita lies in its many insights, even if some are mutually irreconcilable. Its messages may be adapted from age to age, and from context to context. Like a great work of art, it is satisfying to people in different ways from different perspectives. Each serious student can find appropriate quotes from the work, and interpret them suitably, to justify or vindicate his or her own position (Agarwal, 1998). This is the genius of any great work.

No one knows where the original manuscripts of the Mahabharata and of the Gita are, or what happened to them. But at least 125 manuscripts of the *Bhishma-parvan*—Book V of the Mahabharata which contains the Gita—are known to scholars. The earliest published version of the Gita in Devanagari script goes back only to the seventeenth century.

Today we have translations of the Bhagavad Gita in many different languages of the world, several times into some, and in various versions. Thus there are at least 70 Tamil, 150 Telugu, 132 Marathi, 384 Bengali and 300 Hindi versions of the work. There are some 25 French, 28 German, and more than 270 English translations of the Gita. Aside from the major languages of the world, the Gita has also been rendered into such not so widely known languages as Santali, Serbo-croatian, Finnish, Ho-Mundari, and even in Esperanto. It was reported in 1983 that there were in all some 1891 translations of the Gita in 75 different languages. It is of interest to note that Old Javanese and Arabic were the first languages into which the Gita was translated, and this was in the eleventh century, even before the first Indian languages. Marathi adopted it in the close of the thirteenth century and Braj Bhasha in early fourteenth century.

Every reader may have his or her own favorite verse or verses from the Gita. Perhaps the most frequently quoted verse is the one which expresses historical optimism. It says in effect that as and when injustice and inequities come to dominate, a selfless leader will emerge to harness the positive potential of the people and subdue and eliminate the harmful elements:

> *yadá yadá hi dharmasya glánir bhavati bhárata:*
> *abhyutthánam adharmasya tadá átmánam srjám aham:*
> Whenever indeed dharma becomes decayed, oh Bharata,
> And on the rise is adharma, then do I come forth.
> (XVIII-71)

Basic messages

Though there are many meanings and messages, essentially the Gita says the following:

(a) Do your duty.
(b) Act selflessly.
(c) Resist all desires
(d) Sever attachments to worldly things.
(e) The soul is immortal.
(f) Be devoted to (a bhakta of) Lord Krishna.
(g) The true bhakta will attain liberation.

These ideas are expounded in great detail in seven hundred shlokas. This is done in a dialogical mode, often as answers to legitimate questions.

When one reads the verses carefully, noting their meanings, one finds that these basic ideas are repeated several times throughout the work. One almost gets the impression that the author of the Gita is trying to teach some fundamental truths, and in the process, like all teachers, he keeps repeating these fundamentals that need to be learnt.

VI

Thoughts Sublime: The Upanishads

All this is verily Brahman. This self is Brahman.

- Mundaka Upanishad

Introduction

Like many Hindus I cannot recall when I first heard about the Upanishads. I seem to have known all through my adult life that they are part of the sacred writings of the Hindu world. What this means is that they should be approached with respect and reverence. I realized only later in life that some of the ideas in the *shlokas* (sacred verses) I had learned as a youngster are in fact from the Upanishads.

Scholars say that many of the Upanishadic writings were composed during the period between 800 BCE and 200 CE, and that there are over 150 pieces of writing that were once referred to as the Upanishads (Olivelle, 1996).

In the eighth century CE Adi Shankaracharya listed 108 of them: the authentic Upanishads. He also wrote learned commentaries of twelve of these which have come to be known as the *Principal Upanishads*. These twelve are read and discussed more often than the others. They bear the following names: *Aitareya, Brihadaranyaka, Chandogya, Isha, Kaivalya, Katha, Kena, Mandukya, Mundaka, Prasna, Svetasvatara, Taittiriya*.

Hindus are generally anchored to the Vedas as the fount of their religion. Actually, the quintessence of Hindu beliefs and doctrines are found in the Upanishads even more so than in the Vedas. The law of karma, transmigration of the soul, the esoteric significance of *aum*, the notion that we are all sparks of the undergirding cosmic principle: all these find full expression and explanation in the Upanishads, rather than in the Vedas.

The formats of the Upanishads range from simple prose to didactic dialogues and subtle poetry, and cover a broad spectrum of topics. The texts embody lofty thoughts and profound reflections pertaining to human existence, its origins, and its relation to cosmic mystery. They speak of God and spirit, of world and Being, not in poetic and pictorial ways, nor as problems or puzzles, but as revelations of the Infinite.

The Upanishads tell us that we are more than the gross matter (atoms and molecules) that constitutes our physical body, and the energy that sustains it. Though we are subject to the limitations of space and time, and restricted by the constraints of causality, yet, say the Upanishadic seers, there is something in us that transcends all of this. They remind us in no uncertain terms of our links to the eternal. To ignore our cosmic connection would be as pathetic as the plight of the homeless vagabond who roams the roads in poverty when, in fact, he is heir to a billionaire.

Perhaps the most potent of all the terse aphorisms is which says, *tat tvam asi*: that thou art, in the Chándogya (VI.8.7) meaning that each one of us is none other than a part of the grand cosmic consciousness. This is perhaps the most lofty appraisal of the human condition in the history of thought. It recognizes our finitude, but paints our fleeting existence on a cosmic canvas. This is not picturesque mythology, nor a promise of heaven or threat of hell. Rather, it is a magnificent vision that raises human consciousness to a sublime level.

When this great saying (*mahávákya*) is fully assimilated, every human being will be recognized as a spark from the same Divine. As one scholar put it, the Upanishadic seers "first realized the profound truth (of the identity of the infinite, but material Brahman and the finite, but spiritual Átman) through their own—direct, existential, and hence authentic—non-dual mystical experience, transcending the senses and the intellect" (Puligandla, 2002, 16-17).

Many people know how to say or quote this great truth. But most of us have difficulty internalizing it, if only because that is not easy to do. To repeat a great saying, however often and however fervently, is not the same as living up to it. When we truly regard fellow members of the human race in this light, we are transported to a higher level of perception. From there, how can we classify people on the basis of caste and creed, as *dvijas* and dalits, as Christians, Jews, Hindus, Muslims, and Buddhists?

In the nineteenth century, Arthur Schopenhauer who understood the philosophical depth of Upanishadic thinkers intellectually, if not experientially, wrote famously about the Oupnekhat (Upanishads) in the preface to one of his major works: "From every sentence deep, original, and sublime thoughts arise, and the whole is pervaded by a high and holy and earnest spirit. Indian air surrounds us, and original thoughts of kindred spirits. And oh, how thoroughly is the mind here washed clean of all early engrafted Jewish superstitions, and of all philosophy that cringes before those superstitions! In the whole world there is no study, except that of the originals, so beneficial and so elevating as that of the Oupnekhat. It has been the solace of my life, it will be the solace of my death!" (Schopenhauer, 1968, lxii).

But it is also a fact that this great admirer of Upanishadic wisdom "habitually dined well at a restaurant; he had many trivial love-affairs, which were sensual but not passionate; he was exceedingly quarrelsome and unusually avaricious" (Russell, 1945, 758). In a peculiar way, Schopenhauer symbolized what so many of us do. We are profuse in singing the glories of our heritage, in paying homage to our sage-poets, and announcing to the world what great wisdom lies in the philosophy and spirituality of our culture. But when it comes to practice, we go about our chores and challenges with a business-as-usual mind-set, small and self-centered in our different ways, deeply prejudiced at the core, and susceptible all too often to the anger and pettiness that humans are prone to. Reading grand ideas and listening to eloquent sermonizers can sometimes numb us into the conviction that we ourselves are as evolved as the thoughts we entertain in our minds. I have never been able to reconcile the divide between what I have observed in the practices of some Hindus and what I hear in the moral high ground of their proud pronouncements. It is poor consolation that this dichotomy is not peculiar to Hindus, for Christians and Jews, Buddhists and Muslims are no less immune to this. Wherever high religious ideals are articulated with pride and passion, there it is more likely to this awkward dissonance.

Prayer for light and nature of perfection

People who grow up in the Hindu tradition hear many sacred stanzas: the *shlokas* and *mantras* of the tradition. Once these were uttered only by the initiated at appropriate times and occasions. Today, though there are still controversies about privileges as regards the sacred thread, practically any Hindu may learn and recite any of the canonical prayers. This has happened because of two factors: First, we have overcome the prejudices of keeping sacred stanzas within hearing reach of only a privileged class of mostly upper-caste men. The second factor is largely due to modern science and technology which have come up with many voice recordings and sound-reproducing devices.

Not everyone may be familiar with the sources of the prayers which have acquired considerable sanctity and frequent repetition over the centuries.

Consider, for example, the following:

> *asatomá sad gamaya;*
> *tamasomá jyotir gamaya;*
> *mrityormá amritam gamaya.*
> From the unreal, lead me to the real;
> from darkness, lead me to light;
> from death lead me to non-death.

This is a magnificent expression of the human spirit, recognizing its state of ignorance and finitude, and its longing for knowledge and ultimacy. Few Hindus who have grown up in the tradition have not heard this inspiring invocation.. This prayer is from Yajus verses in the *Brihadáranyaka Upanishad* which is regarded as the oldest of all extant Upanishads. The lines are in fact from the last part of the *Satapatha Bráhmana*. It is prescribed that while the priest is reciting mantras during a sacrifice, one who is performing the sacrifice should be chanting this. In our own times this has become one of the most widely chanted *shlokas* in the Hindu world, recited by one and all in temples, sometimes prior to dinner in homes.

In the Upanishad it is explained that unreal and darkness mean death; real and light mean immortality. The prayer is to seek release from death and to attain immortality.

I prefer to interpret *asad* or the unreal as an illusory understanding of the true nature of reality, as happens when the ephemeral is taken for the eternal and the perishable for the never-decaying. The prayer is to enable us to understand the deeper aspects of this passing world of experience, for in that recognition we become wiser and more balanced in our perspectives.

I am reminded of a Tennyson line here: "The prayer was 'Light—more Light—while Time shall last;'" and also the line in Luke (i.79) which says: "To give light to them that sit in darkness."

I take *tamas* or darkness to mean ignorance, not just of spiritual truths but of the nature of physical reality as well. In modern terms, this is a prayer for a clearer and scientific understanding of the physical world, rather than the superficial and often mistaken views we have, whether of the rainbow or of an eclipse. We can only obtain correct knowledge of the phenomenal world when we move away from the darker superstitions of a bygone age into the lighted regions of science. The *jyoti* or light that one seeks is not just the physical light that helps us to see things and the knowledge-light revealed by science, but also the moral light and enlightenment: a vision of life and society that respects others, is caring and compassionate, is guided by reason and understanding, and not misled by unthinking adherence of outworn worldview and practices.

Finally, the plea to be taken from death to immortality is asking to be released from the cycle of birth and death so that one may merge with the Cosmic Whole.

The wisdom of sacred texts is not in their literal interpretations, but in the commentaries of revered thinkers, and in the meaningful interpretations that are relevant in new days and ages. Here is where tensions arise between traditional theology and evolving commentaries. In most dynamic cultures, both the forces are always at work.

What is interesting in the Hindu world is that many sacred verses have an intrinsic spiritual appeal which gives fulfillment to the faithful even when one does not fully understand the message they convey.

Another oft-repeated Upanishadic prayer is:

> *púrnam adah púrnam idam, púrnát púrnam udatcyate*
> *púrnasya púrnam ádáya, púrnam eva vashishyate*
> Complete is that; Complete is this.
> Out of the Complete, the Complete emerges.
> From the Complete, (when) the Complete removed,
> The Complete still remains.

These lines are form the opening reflection of *Ísá Upanishad*, also known as *Ísávasya Upanishad*. This prayer also occurs in Brihadáranyaka Upanishad.

Priests recite these lines on auspicious occasions and worshipers recite them collectively after the *árati*. The shloka sounds like the exclamation of one who has had a mystical experience in which one recognized perfection (*púrnam*) all around: here, there, and everywhere. In that experience, the mystic sees the entire cosmos as a manifestation of Fullness, Completeness, Perfection. Though this vast universe has emerged from the boundless Supreme, the latter remains undiminished by it.

If we replace the term complete/full (*púrnam*) by *infinity*, the *shloka* expresses the idea that infinity can emerge from infinity, and that infinity minus infinity is again infinity: an insight with which mathematicians will resonate.

Hindu thinkers envisioned the Divine as that which is without end (*ananta*) and without beginning (*anádi*), like the number system (positive and negative). They also considered various categories of infinity, like nominal infinity (referring to extraordinary greatness), epistemic infinity (referring to boundless knowledge), one dimensional infinity (observation along an uninterrupted line of sight), numeric infinity (fraction with zero in the denominator) and temporal infinity (eternity). These prayers transcend sects and religions: People of all faiths can recite them.

Resolution, invocation, prayer

Most Upanishads are offshoots of Vedic literature, and are linked to the Áranyakas and the Bráhmanas. Thus, for example, the invocatory prayer in the Taittiríya Upanishad. pays homage to the Vedic deities Mitra, Varuna, Áryamán, Indra, Brihaspati, Vishnu, and Brahmá. It declares Váyu (Air) to be the perceptible Brahman, recognizing that air is the most fundamental element for the sustenance of life. The invocation has the format of a determination, a resolution:

> *ritam vadishyámi; satyam vadishyámi;*
> *tan mám avatu; tad vaktáram avatu;*
> *avatu mám, avatu vaktáram...*
> I will speak about what is right; I will speak the truth.
> May that protect me! May that protect the speaker!
> Let that protect me! Let that protect the speaker!...

We note here the insight that ultimately what matters in life are right conduct and truthfulness. Our highest ideals should be adherence to ethical principles and to truth. That would keep us safe and sound in life, no matter what. In history, there are forward and backward steps on two planes: the conduct plane and the knowledge plane. Positive steps along the conduct plane is what non-denominational enlightenment is all about: the kind of actions, whether by individuals or by nations, that are kindled by caring, compassion, respect for others, kindness, and all that is beneficial to others. They transcend religions, doctrines, and scriptures.

Positive steps on the knowledge plane lead us to better understanding of the world. We acquire this knowledge from dispassionate inquiry and through the methodology of science. The pursuit of science can be colored by emotional factors and past misconceptions. When one rids oneself of such constraining factors, the resulting apprehension of truth would be clear and mind-freeing.

Uttering this prayer daily is a mode of reminding ourselves of these values on a regular basis. This can help even those who do not attach importance to routine rituals, to visiting temples, or fasting on appropriate days. We are reminded of something that John Locke wrote in a letter: "To love truth for truth's sake is the principal part of human perfection in this world, and the seed-plot of all other virtues" (Snowden, 1912, 82).

Consider next another shloka which too is a widely used invocation:

> *sa ha náv avatu—saha nau bhunaktu*
> *saha víryam karavávahai*
> *tejasvi nav adhítam astu*
> *má vidvishávahai*

May He protect us! May He be pleased with us!
May we labor together with vigor!
May our studies bring us enlightenment!
May there be no discord among us!

Actually, this is a prayer that a master and pupil are supposed to offer together, so that the *us* stands for both of them. But it is also usually chanted by groups. Taken literally, one would not recite it when one is alone in a worship mode. This invocation starts with the customary appeal for security which is a motivation for most prayers, but it quickly expresses the wish that the Divine be pleased with us. This is a poetic way of saying that we need to act responsibly, righteously, and in non-hurting ways. Ethical principles are to be defined, not by what we think, but by universal standards. This is what is implied by the statement that the Divine must be pleased by our actions. The prayer reminds us of the work we must do. The idea of working together reflects a sense of community, of working for the common good. Furthermore, the prayer distinguishes between the acquisition of knowledge and the wisdom that must accompany it. All the knowledge in the world would be useless if it is not nourished by enlightenment. Finally, the prayer seeks peace and harmony in the world.

During my years of teaching at the university, I used to recall the following lines from the Tatttiríya Upanishad which is a prayer appropriate for a teacher:

> *á máyantu brahmacárinah sváhá,*
> *vi máyantu brahmacárinah sváhá,*
> *pra máyantu brahmacárinah sváhá,*
> *da máyantu brahmacárinah sváhá,*
> *sa máyantu brahmacárinah sváhá.*

I used to have my own rough translation of this, making it relevant to my situation. The word *brahmachárin* traditionally refers to an unmarried male student and seeker of spiritual knowledge. The term *sváhá* is a ritual invocation at the altar of a sacrifice. For my purposes, I rendered these lines as:

> May students come to me from everywhere! Amen.
> May students come to me in different ways! Amen.
> May students come to me well prepared! Amen.
> May students come to me with self-discipline! Amen.
> May students come to me in peace! Amen.

I cannot say that my prayers were always granted, or rather that my wish was always fulfilled. But I felt good when I started the semester with a quote from an Upanishad which, in my translation, seemed contextually meaningful.

Traditionally one utters these prayers in their rhythmic Sanskrit meters in religious contexts in a worshiping mode. This is fine. But when one also reflects on their meanings, they become even more beautiful.

Levels of consciousness and *aum*

All our awareness of the world recedes into temporary oblivion when we fall asleep. What is the nature of the reality that we experience when we are in the sleep state relative to the one that impresses us in our waking state? The question has intrigued keen minds since time immemorial.

Recall the famous story in Chinese philosophy about Chuang Tzu who is said to have dreamt that he was a carefree butterfly hopping happily from flower to flower. When he woke up suddenly and realized his human aspect, he wondered if he was Chuang Tzu who had dreamt he was a butterfly or a butterfly which was dreaming it was Chuang Tzu.

The Upanishadic seers had a different view on the matter. The Mándúkya Upanishad (3-7) offers a theory of the modes of human awareness. Human beings, it says, can be in one of three possible states: the waking state, the dreaming state, and the profound dreamless sleep state. It names these as *vaishvánara*, *taijasa* and *prájña* respectively.

While awake, we interact with the external world through our sensory organs, feeling pleasure and pain. What we experience in our dreams are not material things. They are subtle, creating the impression of being real. Here, we still have the deep desires in which we are often enmeshed. We are still touched by pseudo-enjoyments and unpleasant experiences. At the level of very deep sleep, all distinctions between experiencer and the experienced are dissolved. There is merger of the separated consciousness with Totality. Though this is bliss, one is not aware that one is a part of the Whole: a case of bliss in ignorance, rather than the usual ignorance in bliss.

The Mándúkya Upanishad goes on to say that there is a fourth stage. It is known as *turíya*, and it is the purest state of awareness. This is the real legitimate state of the self. In this state, consciousness transcends all categories, and becomes cosmic consciousness, and it defies verbal descriptions. It is the pinnacle of spiritual enlightenment. This does not happen with all brains, but only with some. *Turíya-yoga*, which the Siddhas are said to have practiced, promises such experiences. I must confess that I write about this stage as other writers and preachers have done, on the basis of what I have read and heard, and surely not from direct experience.

All these states belong to the continual changes to which all finite and perishable things are subject. Modern science has revealed two stages in sleep: One with the rapid eye movement (REM) which occurs several times when we dream. The other is the non-rapid eye movement (NREM) stage with which sleep starts. During these phases, different types of brain activities are known to occur. It is interesting that Indic thinkers of ancient times recognized different phases of sleep, and interpreted them as stages of awareness. This translates in current paradigm into different types of brain activity. The insight of Hindu thinkers was in considering sleep state as another mode of awareness, suggesting that awareness is a function of the type of processes occurring in the brain.

The Mándúkya Upanishad also relates *aum* with the states of consciousness. Phonetically the sound *aum* may be analyzed into three constituent sounds: A-U-M. It says that Vaishvánara or the waking state corresponds to the A sound; *taijasa* or the dream state to the U sound, and *prájña* or deep sleep to the M sound. And the sacred syllable, taken as a whole, represents the fourth state of *turíya*. It stands for ultimate realization, for supreme spiritual knowledge, for the transcendental experience of cosmic consciousness (I.9-12). This is why *aum* is invoked on all spiritually significant occasions.

The most universally recognized sound associated with Indic traditions is *aum*: a prolonged sonorous invocation which is as much Buddhist as Hindu. Its representation as a written symbol resembling the number three with a curly appendage with a crescent with a dot is as much a signature of Hinduism as the star of David and the Cross are in other traditions. No one knows the origin of this ancient sacred Vedic sound which has been reverberating in the Hindu world for ages.

Other Upanishads also speak about *aum*. The Taittiríya Upanishad says that *aum* is Brahman (I.8.1). The Shetáshvatara Upanishad says that using the body to chant *aum* is like using a stick to rub against a surface to generate fire: In this case, the fire of the Divine (I.14). The Chándogya Upanishad begins by saying that we should meditate on *aum* (I.1-10). It also says that this is a syllable of assent, of agreement. In the same Upanishad we read that this sound emerged from Prajapati (Lord of the People), the progenitor of humankind. "As the leaves are all held together by the stalk;" it says, "in the same way all spoken words are held together by *aum*."

Finally, the Mándúkya Upanishad also says that all the past, the present, and the future are enshrined in *aum* (I.1). In other words, *aum* is a capsule-sound of what was, is, and will be; a transformation, as it were, of temporal eternity into an audible vibration. As much as for their spiritual loftiness, it is in such poetic, profound, and provocative conceptual sweeps that Upanishadic insights become most interesting.

It may be noted that in ancient Tamil, one used to agree to things by repeating *aum* twice: *aum-aum*, which later become *ámám* (word for *yes* in current Tamil).

Dialogue on a grand mystery

As we live through life we learn many things, and our knowledge is steadily increasing. But there are matters about which we know next to nothing. There are questions which stand out impressively as questions, but they have no definite answers though many are given in various religious traditions. One such question pertains to death: What happens to the individual consciousness after the body dies? It is a grand mystery hanging as a backdrop in life.

There is a famous passage in the Kathopanishad (I.1) where this mystery is presented as a story. Vajashrava performs a sacrifice, offering all his possessions to the gods. His son Nachiketas asks the father, "To whom will you offer me?" Vajashrava is upset by the question, and he says he would offer the son to the Yamá, God of Death. Nachiketas goes to Yamá's abode where he waits for three days, and confronts the Death-God. Upon his return, Yamá, realizing that the young brahmin had been waiting, promises him three boons to compensate.

Nachiketas wants his father not to be ill-disposed towards him, and he wishes to return home. This is granted. Then he seeks the secret of the altar of a particular fire-sacrifice that leads men directly to heaven. This too is revealed to him. Finally, for his third boon, Nachiketas asks: "According to some, a person continues to exist after death, but others do not believe this. I wish to know what happens to a person when he dies." To this, Yamá says: "Ask for cattle and horses, for elephants and gold. Ask for progeny that will live a hundred years. Ask for lands and possessions, kingdoms and power, beautiful damsels and perennial pleasures, but don't ask for the secret of Death."

This insightful passage declares in simple and rhetorical terms that while there are no limits to human knowledge and achievements, we can never know what will happen to the individual experience after the last breath is heaved.

But the human spirit is not satisfied when boundaries are drawn on its quest. So Nachiketas does not accept Yamá's answer and he persists. He refuses to take any other boon. The implication is that ultimate knowledge about the hereafter is of such significance that it is preferable to every conceivable possession or experience. And the human spirit will never stop probing.

Finally Yamá, instead of answering the question directly, explains to Nachiketas that our actions could be for achieving one of two things: fleeting satisfactions, or what is intrinsically and everlastingly good. Work for attaining passing pleasures, and you will get nowhere. Work toward the greater good, and you are on the right track to immortality. Yamá goes on to say that the foolish and the short-sighted imagine this world to be the only and total reality. They think that the world will dissolve from their field of experience when they die. This is because they do not understand the true nature of the átman. For this, one must have a master who has himself realized the Truth, for higher spiritual knowledge cannot be attained by mere reading and reasoning.

This is a crucial idea in the tradition. In order to fully grasp the significance of the truths implicit in the sacred texts, one needs a guru. It is through a guru that occult meanings become clear to the seeker. Those who read and study on their own can learn much in many fields, but not in the spiritual. Here, intellectual knowledge is inadequate, and may even be unsatisfying.

I can vouch for the truth of half of this. I have acquired some knowledge through readings and reflections. I have never had a traditional guru. As a result I have no spiritual knowledge. As to whether I could have attained it with a guru or not, I don't know for sure: I have met people who have had the benefit of gurus, but do not seem to have acquired spiritual knowledge or wisdom.

In any case, the non-spiritual reader may find this story in the Upanishad to be interesting, but not quite revelatory about the mystery of death itself. However, a guru might explain that the episode does give an answer to the question: Nachiketas' return to his father symbolically refers to reincarnation, for re-birth is essentially a return to where we came from before reaching the realm of the dead. The reference to the sacrificial fire which enables one to go to heaven means that by leading a proper life, one obtains liberation. In other words, both re-birth and *moksha* are possible for one who dies.

Yamá also explains to Nachiketas the importance of the mystical mantra *aum* whose apprehension reveals the nature of Brahman. He states that the átman is smaller than the smallest imaginable unit, and grander than all of physical space. Yamá compares the physical body to a chariot, our reasoning to the charioteer, and the mind to the reins. The senses are the horses that take the charioteer here and there. As the good charioteer controls the horses with the reins, and does not let them drag him where they will, our reasoning mind should control our senses and not let us go astray. This simile is used in many traditional literatures in the Hindu world. Nachiketas learns other spiritual truths from Yamá and becomes immortal, it is said, having attained the knowledge of Brahman.

Though Nachiketas is a student in this exchange, in the Upanishadic tradition he is regarded as a teacher of esoteric wisdom. Shankaracharya called him an acharya of brahmavidya, comparing him to a bridge that helps us cross the waters of samsára: another oft-repeated image. This is because he has determination, earnestness, sincerity, in the quest for higher truths. One normally considers these as characteristics of a student. Actually, they should be of a teacher no less.

Empiricism in the Upanishads

The route to ideas, knowledge, and convictions about the world is through three paths: revelation, reflection, and observation. Traditional religious scriptures offer us revealed knowledge. Thus, the truths proclaimed in the Vedas, the Bible, and the Qur'an are taken as truths by the adherents of the respective religions. Faith is fundamental in the acceptance of revealed knowledge. Philosophers engage in insightful reflections which are discussed and debated by other analytical thinkers. Such are the views of Plato and Kant, Shankara and Ramanuja, for example; although some would claim that unlike Plato and Kant and other Non-Hindu thinkers, the likes of Shankara and Ramanuja had spiritual revelations. More exactly, intuition plays a role in the elaboration of speculative knowledge. Finally, we have modern scientific methodology where empiricism is fundamental. Here nothing is accepted as valid unless it is supported by extensive observation, experimentation, and verification. This is the hallmark of modern science.

In the Western tradition, Aristotle was one of the earliest to insist that everything we know about the world comes from what we observe. But it was not until many centuries later—from the seventeenth century—that this came to be adopted in a systematic way as a criterion in the acquisition of knowledge about the world. Thus, in modern science empiricism (observational, and verification routes to knowledge) is crucial, though it is not the only mode of grasping knowledge. Intuition and insight also play important roles here.

It was long believed that Indian thinkers, like their counterparts elsewhere, relied primarily on revelation and reflection in constructing their worldviews. To a large extent, at least this is the impression one gets from many ancient Hindu writings, and their interpretations by most scholars. However, there is a passage in the Chándogya Upanishad (VI.7), dating back to the sixth century BCE or earlier—which talks about a sage who understood very well the significance of empirical knowledge.

This Upanishad speaks about ritual chants and the primordial significance of the sun, of breath and food, of the genesis of Vedic hymns and much more. In the midst of all this, we encounter a personage by the name of Uddálaka Áruni. His son Shvetaketu returns home after twelve years of intense study under a guru. The youth now displays the conceit of a fresh graduate who thinks he has learned everything. The father detects this, and tells him that with all his guru-given knowledge, Shvetaketu had not learned about the essence of reality.

The point here is that the traditional wisdom one gets from gurus which one repeats parrot-like is often only superficial knowledge. It does not reflect any depth of understanding. There is too much of this in all religious contexts. Now Uddálaka teaches his son about the ultimate. He explains that beyond the pot which has form and name is the clay which is its essence. Beyond the golden articles, there is gold which is the essence. Beyond rain and grain there is water, which is the essence. From the minutest of seed arises the mammoth tree. Recognizing the hidden truth behind appearances is true enlightenment.

Next Uddálaka asks his son to sprinkle salt in some water. The next day the son returns, and he can see no salt in the water, but he is able to taste it. We cannot see or touch the salt in the water, but we can experience it. So it is with Brahman, explains the father.

Then Uddálaka tells Shvetaketu that a person is made up of sixteen entities. He asks him not to eat solid food for fifteen days. His breath, which consists of water, will not be affected, he says. The son does just that and returns, only to discover that he cannot recall any of the Vedic chants he had learnt. Then the sage asks the young man to eat for fifteen days and return. The son obeys, and now he is able to recall the chants. The father explains: "Just as, in a huge lighted fire, if a single ember small as a firefly is left, and it can be made to blaze by enclosing it in a heap of straw, the little fire that was left in you, when covered with food, blazed again.

So you remember the Vedas now. The mind consists of food, the breath consists of water, and speech of heat."

Thus Uddálaka Áruni experimentally proved to his son what he had stated. This interesting episode is extremely important in the history of science in its unusual empirical methodology. In no contemporary writing elsewhere does one find such a dramatic illustration of the observational verification of a theory. Because this is buried in a mountain of metaphysical musings in a work that is regarded as of primarily spiritual significance, its scientific relevance had escaped detection until a few decades ago.

Interestingly, it was European scholars like J. D. Bernal, Herman Jacobi and Walter Ruben who were among the first to uncover the materialistic, naturalistic, scientific spirit that is hidden in the heaps of spiritualism that has dominated the writings of Indic thinkers for ages. More importantly, this analysis by Bernal *et al.* gives an entire new twist to the history of science. It had generally been accepted in the nineteenth and twentieth centuries that Thales of Miletus was the first to think of naturalistic explanations. Debiprasad Chattopadhyaya, a scholar and historian of Indic science, drew attention to the scientific import of passages from the Upanishads which had been taken for too long to be no more than articulations of the mystic quest.

Chattopadhyaya has argued that the exchange between father and son in the Chandogya Upanishad entitles Uddálaka, rather than Thales of Miletus, to be reckoned as the first scientific thinker in history. Uddálaka Áruni, he wrote, "did in fact boldly knock at the gates of natural science to be opened," for which effort he deserves to be called "the first rational natural scientist in the history of the Indian subcontinent, if not in global history" (Chattopadhyaya, 1991, Ch. VII).

The question why in spite of such keen and inquiring minds positive sciences did not emerge with great force in the Indian subcontinent has been raised and pondered by some scholars.

How Many Gods?

Once I was in a friend's home for dinner. The guests included some Americans. One of them asked during a conversation if it was true that Hindus believed there are millions of gods. The host gave a polite smile which implied how naïve the questioner was, but another lady guest (Hindu), who was a physician, lashed out, saying that most ignorant Westerners think Hindus are all fools. The gentleman apologized profusely for his question, saying he had read it somewhere that Hindus do worship many gods, and was ready to grant that it was a mischievous distortion. He apologized for this question and said he just wanted to know what Hindus thought of this.

I asked the lady who had taken offense at the question why, in her opinion, people get such impressions about Hinduism. I heard the usual answer: This was due to British and Christian anti-Hindu propaganda. Then I asked if anywhere in Hindu sacred works it was mentioned that there are thousands of deities. No one present seemed to know that the origin of that perception or misperception may be found in statements from within the Puranic framework, and when one visits a Hindu temple (Patel, 2006).

We read in the Puranas and in the Mahabharata that there are eight Vasus (Dwellings), namely: Prithví (Earth), Agni (Fire), antariksha (Intermediary Space), Váyu (Air, Life Breath), Dyaus (Sky), Súrya (Sun), Nakshatra (Stars), Soma (Moon); eleven Rudras (Lords of annihilation; twelve Ádityas (Lords of Phenomena), Indra (Thunderbolt), and Prajápati (Lord of

Progeny). They add up to 33. Each of these is regarded as a manifestation of the Divine. But ultimately, they are all manifestations of the same single Divine principle. This view is elaborated in the Brihadáranyaka Upanishad (III.9.1-26) in the following conversation between the sage Viddagdha Shakalya (VS) and Yájñavalkya (Y).

> VS: *kati deváh*, Yájñavalkya? (How many gods are there, Y?)
> Y: As many as are mentioned in the invocatory hymns of the scriptures, which is three hundred and three, and three thousand and three. (*trayas ca trí ca shatá, trayas ca trí ca sahasreti*).
> VS: Yes, but how many Gods are really there, Y?
> Y: Thirty-three
> VS: Yes, but how many Gods are really there, Y?
> Y: Six.
> VS: Yes, but how many Gods are really there, Y?
> Y: Three.
> VS: Yes, but how many Gods are really there, Y?
> Y: Two.
> VS: Yes, but how many Gods are really there, Y?
> Y: One and a half.
> VS: Yes, but how many Gods are really there, Y?
> Y: One. (*eka iti*.)
> VS: Yes, but which are those three hundred and three and three thousand and three (which you mentioned earlier)?

At this point Yájñavalkya goes on to say that those are all manifestations of the thirty-three primary gods of the Vedic framework., and then he explains who the Rudras, the Ádityas, etc. are.

What is interesting in here is that when Yájñavalkya comes up with these large numbers, though the answer is based on Vedic statements, the latter doesn't take him seriously. This suggests that it is not always wise to take what we read in the scriptures literally. The persistent questioning by Shakalya means that one needs to probe more and more to fully understand what the core meaning of it all is.

The final answer to the effect that there is but one God is as true as the initial one that there are more than three thousand gods, because the one God is manifest in countless different forms in air and water, on earth and sky, in the sun and moon and stars, with countless different names. This is another way of saying that God is omnipresent: The Divine is implicit in every aspect of the perceived universe. This vision of a unity behind the multiplicity is at the core of the Hindu vision of the Divine.

God, in the Hindu framework, is too grand and magnificent to be declared as One, and just left at that. To say that the Divine has only one Prophet is even more restrictive of the capacity of the Divine for self-expression or communication. If anything, manifestations of God, whether as minute atoms or as mammoth stars, as mindless animals or as thinking humans, as poets or prophets, have to be vast in numbers.

Thus, it is quite true to say that in the Hindu framework there are millions of gods. It is equally true to say that there is only one God. The Divine is like music. There is but one Music, but it finds countless expressions. It is through a particular song or sonata that we experience music. So it is that we get a glimpse of God through every form or name.

Some Greek Parallels

Worldviews from places far apart have often overlapped. There are similarities between Norse and Roman gods, between Babylonian religion and the Judaic tradition, between Hindu deities and the Greek pantheon. It is known that there have been mutual interactions and influences among ancient peoples, but questions as to who influenced whom, and where an idea first arose are still matters of controversy, often colored by nationalistic sensitivity and cultural hegemony. I have seldom been interested in such matters because, on final analysis, we all belong to *Homo sapiens*, trying to figure out what it is all about, and interesting ideas have arisen in brains all over the world.

Wisdom is not the monopoly of any one people, any more than that intelligence is the characteristic of any one race or caste. So, just as we have our *rishis* and *kavis*, the Greeks had *hoi sophoi* (the wise ones) and *hoi poietai* (the poets). Thales of Miletus was the foremost of the Seven Wise Men (*sapta rishi*) of Greece. According to Diogenes Laertius, Thales believed that "Water constituted the principle of all things" (Laertius, 2006). This reminds us of the idea expressed in the Upanishads that water is Brahman. This is one example of the parallels between some Upanishadic visions and those of some ancient Greek thinkers.

Anaximander, a fellow Miletian, spoke of an immaterial *apeiron* as the *arche* (beginning) of everything. His book *On the nature of things* begins with the statement: "That from which all things are born is also the cause of their coming to an end" (Kahn, 1960). He imagined that in the beginning a seed of hot and cold was separated from the boundless *apeiron*, whence emerged a huge sphere of flame around the air, like the bark of a tree. There are similar cosmologies of *agni* in the Upanishads also.

Anaximenes talked of *pneuma*: air as the ultimate substance. *Pneuma* refers to something more than physical air. It is the life-principle, and corresponds to the *qi* (*chih*) of the Chinese and the *prána* of the Upanishads. It says in the Kaushítaki-Bráhmana Upanishad (II.2), *práno brahmeti*: The breath (breathing spirit) is the Creator.

Heraclitus of Ephesos declared that fire is at the root of all changes (Robinson, 1987). This reminds us of the passage in the Brihdáranyaka Upanishad where it says that Agni is in the sun, in the rain-bearing cloud, on earth, indeed that men and women are also fire. Heraclitus also spoke of opposite tensions by which everything was characterized by the coexistence of opposite tensions which were normally in a state of balance. The balance is upset when one of the forces gets the upper hand. The break in the equilibrium causes change. This is like the three-guna theory in Hindu thought.

Parmenides was the greatest of the Eleatic philosophers. His famous line is *hen ta panta:* all things are one (Scott, 1986). This very simply sums up the *advaitic* worldview. But then we do observe changes. Parmenides explains this by saying that these observed changes are not real. They appear to be so because of our inability to recognize the unchanging principle beneath it all. For him, the universe was a large, unchanging, unmoving body which remains the same forever and forever. This was Ultimate Reality, which again is not unlike the Upanishadic *Brahman*. The universe with all its changes is an illusion in the minds of those who have not realized that Ultimate Reality, Parmenides added. The Shvetáshvatara Upanishad also reminds us that the phenomenal world (*prakriti*) is an illusion (*máyá*) (IV.10). Parmenides also argued, like some Hindu thinkers, that instead of trying to explain lightning and the rainbow, we must strive to uncover the true nature of reality.

Empedocles of Acragas was a physician, philosopher, poet, and physical theorist (Wright, 1995). He believed that he had been a bird and a fish, even a shrub, in previous incarnations, reminding us of the Shaiva mystic Manikkavasagar (Raman, 2011). He was not the only Greek thinker to subscribe to reincarnation. According to one interpretation of his writings, he propounded the notion that the world passes through four successive stages which repeat themselves. In the first stage, Love reigns supreme. All the elements were fused together. In the second stage, Strife gradually enters the scene, and begins its disruption. In the third stage, Strife takes over completely, and the elements are separated out. In the fourth and final stage, Love re-enters: little by little, the elements come back together. This was his idea of the *cosmic cycle*. Parallels with the Hindu concept of the *yugas* are inescapable. One can go on and on.

Clearly, the visions of the Upanishadic seers were not unique to them. Other thinkers in other regions and climes had similar inklings as to the ultimate. The urge to see unity behind multiplicity, commonality beneath diversity is an ancient urge that inspires the human spirit in its quest for meaning in existence and purpose to life. The sages and seers of the ancient world, like scientists in our own times, knew no boundaries of nation or religion. They expressed in the language of their times the deepest insights they came upon whether through reflection, intuition, or meditation. Ideas must certainly have seeped from region to region, culture to culture, and undergone local variations. It is therefore not surprising at all that we find parallels between Upanishadic visions and the writings of Greek philosophers.

VII

The Puranas (Puránas): Lore and legends nourishing the Culture

Purá api navam Puranam: Though
ancient, still new is Puranam.

-Sanskrit saying

Introduction

The word *purana* refers to something old or ancient. Thus *puranagíta* means a song sung by the ancients, *puranaprokta* would be something declared by ancient wisdom, and *puranadvitíya* means a former wife.

There is an important body of classical Sanskrit literature which are known as *puranas*. [The term used in Tamil is *puranam*. But the word has a slightly different connotation there.] The goal of the puranas is said to be to elaborate upon and corroborate Vedic truths. That they are very old is obvious from their name. Centuries of scholarly probes haven't been able to date their history, let alone origin. Some of the extant Puranas clearly belong to the Common Era. But all the major puranas mentioned in the Mahabharata were certainly composed BCE. The epics are also sometimes regarded as *puranas*: *itihasa puranas*. The author of the first *purana* (whoever it was) could not have called it a *purana*: How could it have been called old if it had just been created? This suggests that the *puranas* are compositions based on very ancient oral traditions that must have existed in the subcontinent for ages.

Indeed, in the sense of something too ancient to reckon, Hinduism itself is a living *purana*, for in cultural antiquity it surpasses practically any known religion. Tradition attributes all the *puranas*, as also the epics and the classification of the Vedas, to the great and venerable Vyasa, but this may well be a way of saying that all these are edited works.

Purana as a genre of sacred literature is supposed to have five characteristics: *pañchalakshna*. The five topics they are meant to treat are cosmogony (*sarga*) or how the universe came to be; re-creation (*pratisarga*) or how it periodically dissolves and re-emerges; royal and divine dynasties (*vamsha*) or genealogies of kings and gods of yore; eons and epochs (*manvantarani*) or stretches of time corresponding to various Manus or Mind-born sons of Brahma; and the stories of the dynasties (*vamsanicaritra*) or narratives of kings and gods. But as often happens, there are wide divergences between theory and practice. Not all Puranas deal with all these five themes, and some deal with lots more unrelated topics. What is true is that most of the *Puranas* are legends pertaining to the principal divinities associated with the *trimúrti*, and all are regarded as being part of sacred history.

Canonical classification puts eighteen principal (*mahá*) *puranas* into three separate boxes which are affiliated to the three principal members of the Hindu pantheon: namely, Brahma,

Vishnu, and Shiva. Rather than simply extol the divinities in the abstract, they are given form and qualities, which makes it all very interesting. However, these works were composed by adherents to one sect or another. Hence, while glorifying one divinity here and another there, we also find unfriendly innuendos about one another. This diminishes their spiritual content, but they also reveal that sectarian rivalries existed in the classical Hindu world between Shaivas, Vaishnavas and those who considered Brahma as primary (Mani, 1975).

Sectarian glorification of the gods, especially of Vishnu, is strong in many puranas. In one system, gunas (intrinsic natures) are attributed to the various puranas in a hierarchical mode: Thus, puranas associated with the name of Brahma are said to be rajasic (energetic and dynamic); those with the name of Vishnu are sattvic (enlightened and peaceful); and those named after Shiva are regarded as tamasic (dark and lethargic).

In addition to the eighteen *mahapuranas*, there are also eighteen *upapuranas* or secondary ones. All this shows that there were countless creative writers in classical India whose energies were directed to traditional gods and spiritual worldviews, often with sectarian zeal. Taken as compositions of a distant age they are fascinating, but regarded as divine history, they may not strike all modern readers as spiritually uplifting. Nevertheless, some of the puranas continue to have impacts on the religious worldview of many. A number of beliefs and rituals in our own times are derived from the puranas (Shastri, 1995).

Agni Purana

As per sacred history, *Agni Purana* was revealed to sage Vasishtha by the Vedic God Agni (Chaturvedi, 2004). In it may be found one list of the ten avataras of Vishnu, and details on each. In the Matsya avatara, for example, Vishnu appears to Manu as a fish that gradually grows in size, and He says, "I must punish those that are evil and protect those that are good." He then informs Manu that there would be the grand deluge a week later, and says a boat will come to save Manu. He instructs Manu to take the saptarshis (seven sages) on the boat as also seeds for grains. This reminds one of the story of Noah's Ark in the Old Testament. Either such stories spread from culture to culture, or there was indeed a global flooding at one time, like the global warming that is threatening humanity now.

There is a retelling of the Ramayana and the Mahabharata in this Purana. Incidentally, other puranas do this also, often with minor variations. The Agni Purana says something about the Buddha: that it was *Mahamoha* (the Great Deluder) that incarnated as the son of Suddhodana. He created such illusions that the *asuras* who till then had followed the Vedic path, now abandoned it and became Buddhists. It refers to Buddhist ceremonies as a pathway to *naraka* (the nether world). This is an obvious reference to the spread of Buddhism within India, and it shows how this was looked upon by Hindu thinkers.

The Agni Purana describes Kali Yuga as one in which people become immoral, cowardly, and materialistic. Unbelievers rule the world, it says, and they would also become cannibals. Then, at last, Kalki would be born to Vishnuyasha, and he would decimate all the infidels. After this, the era of righteousness (*satya yuga*) will be established again. It is important to remember that puranas are essentially narrations of received lore. This promised advent of Kali is somewhat like the Book of Revelation in the Bible.

The Agni Purana says that Vishnu must be depicted as riding eight-armed Garuda and He too must have eight arms, holding sword, mace, shield, discus, and conch shell. The eighth hand is for granting a boon. To his right are Lakshmi and Sarasvati. Those who have seen Ravi Varma's painting of Vishnu may recognize the Agni Purana inspiration in it.

The creation story in this work is very similar to what one finds in other puranas: Brahma and the Cosmic Egg. It is said that the texts of the Vedas emerged from Brahma's body. Though Vishnu is described as the Lord of creation, preservation, and destruction, this is still a Purana of the Shaiva category. There are references to the lingam which is to be made of the earth, iron, jewels, gold, silver, bronze, or mercury. This reveals the knowledge of metallurgical craftsmanship of the age.

The purana mentions sacred rivers like Narmada and Ganga, as also places of pilgrimage like Pushkara where Brahma is said to reside, Kurukshetra where Vishnu comes periodically, and Prayaga where the gods are always present. Then again, Shiva once told Parvati that he never leaves Varanasi. The Agni Purana says that this sacred city got its name because it is at the conjunction of two holy rivers: Varana and Asi.

As per its sacred geography, there are seven *dvípas* (island regions) in the world: *Jambu, Plaksha, Shalmali, Kusha, Krouncha, Shaka* and *Pushkara.*, and they are surrounded by seven seas: *Lavana, Ikshu, Sura, Sarpih, Dadhi, Dugdha* and *Jala*.

The Agni Purana is impressively encyclopedic in the sweep of the topics it covers. These topics range from poetry and grammar to architecture, arts of war, astrology, and more. Like all puranas, in this day and age it is far more interesting and worth reading as an ancient literary work, than as scripture, though many people continue to do just that. The following is among the many invocations to Agni we find in the Agni Purana:

> Great Agni, though thine essence be but one:
> Thy forms are three, as fire thou blazest here,

As lightning flashest in the atmosphere,
In heaven thou flamest as the golden sun.
By art of sages skilled in sacred lore
Thou wast drawn down to human hearths of yore
And thou abidest a denizen of earth.

Bhagavata Purana (Bhágavata Purana)

If there is one Purana that stands above all others in the prestige it enjoys and the impact it has had, it is *Bhagavata Purana*, also known as *Shrímad Bhagavatam*. It is more cogent in its content than most other puranas, although, in the view of some scholars, it does not quite fit in the category of puranas. Many parts of it were clearly inspired by the contents of *Vishnu Purana*. This purana exudes love for the Divine in the incarnation of Lord Krishna: bhakti in the purest mode. Besides being a composition of great spiritual significance, it is also a work of extraordinary beauty from a literary point of view.

The Bhagavata Purana says that Vishnu had twenty-four incarnations, the first was as a Brahmin; next was *as varaha* (boar) to save us from *naraka*. Then Nárada came and preached the worship of Vishnu. Next, there was the dual aspect: *Nara* and *Narayana*. The incarnation of Kapila came next, and he was followed by Dattatreya. After this came Svayambhuva Manu and Rishabha. Then, in answer to a prayer (*prarthana*), the Divine appeared as Prithu. After this, earth came to be known as *Prithví*.

The purana narrates the deeds of Krishna: the fondness of Nanda's son Krishna (*Nanda-kumara*) for butter which he sometimes stole (*Navaníta-chora*), his captivating the hearts of gopis (*Gopi-manohara*) in Vrindavan (*vrindávana sañcari*) on the banks of the Yamuna, his lifting Mount Govardhana (*Govardana-giri-dhári*): all these have inspired devotional songs.

The purana is in the format of a dialogue between Shukadeva Rishi and King Parikshit who had insulted a holy man. The latter's son cursed the king to die from a snake-bite within a week. To atone for the sin the king listens to the Bhagavata Purana

The concept of dharma is complex and varied in the Hindu tradition. Its range of meanings includes duty, righteous conduct, and religion. The Bhagavata Purana says that dharma is desireless worship of God—*nishkama bhakti*, one might say—reminding us of Krishna's *nishkama karma*. Historians of Hindu culture have pointed out that this vision of dharma, enunciated in this Purana, was a milestone in Hindu spiritual life.

The purana lists deities, prescribing who is to be worshiped for which purpose: *Prajápati* for children, *Aditi* for food, *Ashvins* for longevity, *Uma* for conjugal bliss, etc. In the metaphysics of this purana, the Divine is pure consciousness, but it created the physical universe through *máyá*. Maya is a positive power for Vaishnavas. For Advaitins it is deluding: the world is unreal and illusory, like the feats of a magician.

The Bhagavatam refers to Tamil Srivaishnava mystic saints (now called *ázhvars*), which has led some scholars to suspect that it was probably authored by a South Indian mystic. Also, from the fact that the great Ramanuja (twelfth century) makes no reference to this quintessentially Vaishnava work, and from the fact that Madhva (thirteenth) century does refer to it, one is led to conclude that the work was composed in the intervening period. One devout commentator declares that *Shrímad Bhagavatam* mentions Sri Chaitanya Mahaprabhu as the avatara of Vishnu in the Kali Yuga; but I have not been able to find any reference to this saintly soul in the Bhagavata Purana. In fact, he was born a few centuries later.

No matter who wrote it or when, the Bhagavata Purana's impact has been as great on Hindu spiritual life as the *Ramacharitmanas* of Tulsidas, especially in Northern India, and among many South Indian Vaishnavas. To this day, this inspiring work is recited by countless Vaishnavas and presented by rhapsodists to audiences all over the world. Unlike other puranas which glorify Vishnu, the central thrust of the Bhagavata Purana is that Krishna is the one who appears in incarnations (*Krishnastu Bhagavan Svayam*).

Many works have been written on this purana. If one wishes to learn about the full spiritual perspective on this purana one should go through the multi-volume work on it by Bhakti Vedanta Prapbhupada (Prabhupada, 1999). In this series, Book Seven of the work is entitled *The Science of God*. Clearly, the word science means something quite different here from what it usually connotes.

Bhavishya Purana

The word *bhavishya* refers to that which is about to happen. [It is derived from the verb *bhú to be*.] *Bhavishya-kála* means future tense. Therefore, the title of *Bhavishya Purana* means *Purana about the Future* (Bhavishya Purana, 1959). One is thus inclined to think that this is a Hindu Book of Revelation, telling us about things to come. However, when one looks into the contents of the extant versions of this Purana one discovers that it is more about rites and rituals, about the duties of various castes, about festivals, etc., with very little of any prophesy.

This is the only purana that refers to Zoroastrianism. Buddha and Buddhism are mentioned in a few other puranas. This one says that the Magas have their ancestry in a person called *Jarasasta*: Zoroaster or Zarathushtra; It describes those people as wearing girdles around their waists. The Magas were sun-worshipers. They are referred to as the Magi in the Bible, and their names have left a stamp in the English word *magic*.

The *Bhavishya Purana* also talks about the magnificence of the Sun. Recognizing the sun as divine, it says that the sun is a visible divinity. Because we see things with the aid of sunlight, the sun is also described as the eye of the world. Because the day is born with sunrise, the sun is called the maker of the day. Because it seems to have been and will be forever, the *Bhavishya Purana* describes the sun as eternal. For these reasons, it is said that no other deity can be compared to the sun. Moreover, since we reckon time by the rising of the sun and the seasonal changes caused by it, the sun is called the source of time. The centrality of the sun in the universe is recognized in this purana when it says that planets, stars, Vasus, Rudras, Váyu, and Agni, and all other Gods are parts of him.

The Creation myth in this Purana is very like the one in *Manudharma Shástra* where it is stated that the universe existed as primeval darkness, unperceived, destitute of distinctive marks, unattainable by reasoning, unknowable, wholly immersed, as it were, in deep sleep. Then the divine Self-existent appeared with irresistible (creative) power, dispelling the darkness, and making (all) this, the great elements and the rest, discernible.

In 1897 there appeared a spurious version of the *Bhavishya Purana* which incorporated totally new materials, clearly with the intention of creating the impression that the author of that purana was a seer who saw well into the future. Whereas the quatrains of Nostradamus were merely vague, and could be interpreted in many soothing ways, in this nineteenth century fake of the Bhavishya Purana, specific names are given. We read about "Adam and Eve, Noah's Ark, the fall of Sanskrit and coming of other languages, the coming of Buddha, Madhavacharya,

Chandragupta, Ashoka, Jayadeva, Krishna Chaitanya and Kutubuddin and the Shahs ruling Delhi."

Obviously penned by a man familiar with the Bible, Islam, and Indian history, this book talks about Medina which is described as a place of pilgrimage and about Mahamada (Mohammad). It says that the followers of this mleccha-dharma will practice circumcision, and will not have any tufts of hair, and will be known as Mussalmans.

Many people, simple-minded and some professed scholars, have been fooled by this fraudulent version (Knapp, 1998). One author, who is too shy to reveal his name, has added new names to the alleged predictions in a website where he goes so far as to claim that the *Bhavishya Purana* "speaks accurately of the British controlling India, Hitler fighting the world, and Max Mueller misrepresenting the Vedic teachings." Western scholars are not the only ones who distort and mangle Hindu sacred texts.

When one talks about puranas one rarely mentions *Bhavishya Purana*. Not only do we know very little of interest or relevance about Brahma, Vishnu and Shiva from this work, but some passages in the new version are also embarrassingly false and overtly racist.

The Brahma Purana

Also known as *Ādi Purana*, *Brahma Purana* is regarded as the first of all Puranas. It is said to have been revealed by a certain Lomaharshana to an assembly of rishis in the Naimisha Forest. But the version that we now have is probably of much later vintage. Other puranas are said to have been revealed in the same way. Today, all Puranas are revealed via the internet.

The Rig Veda, in its *Hymn of Creation* (X.129), contains one of the earliest visions of cosmogony in the Hindu world.

Not unlike Thales of Miletus, the Brahma Purana also says that water pervaded the primordial universe. It proposes the Cosmic Egg/Womb hypothesis by which the Golden Embryo (*Hiranyagarbha*) emerged in the primeval waters, from which Brahma was self-born (*svayam-bhú*). From that egg arose *svarga* (Heaven) and *prithivi* (the Earth). On earth arose time, language, the senses and much more.

Though categorized as a Brahma Purana, this purana also speaks of Vishnu and Shiva. We read that Vishnu was resting on the primordial waters in a cosmic bed, that *nara* means water and *ayana* means bed, whence Vishnu came to be invoked as *Náráyana*. The birth of Umá, the deeds of Krishna, as well as other interesting stories are found in this Purana.

The Brahma Purana lists the *saptarshi* who emerged from Brahma's mind. It mentions a man called Svayambhuva Manu, and a woman called Shatarúpa: One with a hundred forms, who emerged from Brahma. Their three sons were Vira, Priyavarata, and Uttamapada. All human beings have their origins in Manu, not unlike Adam in the Judeo-Christian tradition. Since all came from Manu, human beings are known as *mánava* (derived from Manu). These puranic views on cosmogenesis and anthropogenesis are barely known to the masses, even scholars seldom refer to them.

This purana also speaks about seven continents and seven seas, exactly as some others do. Of these, India is *Jambudvípa*. Eight huge mountains were created here by Brahma: *Sumeru, Kailash, Malaya, Himalaya, Udayachala, Astachala, Suvela* and *Gandhmadana*. He also created rivers and lakes.

It is sometimes claimed that the caste system was introduced by the British in India. It may be noted in this context that the Brahma Purana explicitly mentions the varna classification of society. It says: "Their names are brahmana, kshatriya, vaishya and shudra. The duties of a brahmana are to donate alms, perform tapasya, worship the gods, perform yajñas and study the Vedas. To earn a living, brahmanas are authorized to teach and act as priests at sacrifices. The duties of a kshatriya are to bear arms and protect the earth, donate alms and perform sacrifices. A kshatriya is also permitted to study the shástras. The duties of a vaishya are agriculture, animal husbandry and trade. That apart, vaishyas should donate alms, perform sacrifices and study the shástras. The duties of a shudra are to serve brahmanas. Shudras can also be shopkeepers and artisans.

In times of emergency, a brahmana is allowed to adopt the livelihoods of kshatriyas or vaishyas to earn a living. In similar fashion, a kshatriya is permitted to adopt the livelihoods of vaishyas or shudras and a vaishya is permitted to adopt the livelihoods of shudras."

This purana mentions the four stages of life (*catur-áshrama-dharma*): The first of these is *brahmacharya*. During this period, the student spends his days with his guru and studies the Vedas. He has to serve his guru appropriately and live on alms. The next ashrama is that of *grihasthya*: the householder's phase. One is married and has children. During this stage the person serves the deities, sages, ancestors and guests. Householders provide alms for sages and hermits. The third ashrama is known as *vanaprastha* (forest-dwelling). One retires to the forest and withdraws one's mind from worldly matters. A man may leave his wife in the care of his sons or take her with him. He is expected to live on roots, fruits and leaves and make a bed for himself under the trees. He is not allowed to shave or cut his hair. His clothes are of bark or skins. The fourth ashrama is *sannyasa*. Now he severs all associations with the world and he lives in solitude. He feeds himself by begging. He is not allowed to spend more than one night in a village. It would appear that the last two phases are more ideal than practical. We do not have these as records of the society when the majority of the people followed these to the letter.

There is mention of a certain Brahmin named Somasharma who once conducted the ceremony of the sacred thread before he himself had become a dvija. This grievous sin resulted in a penalty for him: upon his death he became an asura. In this purana there are also discussions on the theory and practice of yoga. Here may be found the definition of yoga as a meditative mode by which the individual soul unites with the supreme one, thus enabling one to recognize unity behind the diversity.

According to the geography given here, at one time Bharatavarsha referred mainly to northern India (Ch. 18-20). The purana talks about Ondra (the current Orissa), and refers to its population as religious (Ch. 28). It gives a description of the famed Konarak Temple around which were numerous trees, though there was much sand all around. The mention of this temple, which is known to have been built in the twelfth century, dates the extant version of the Brahma Purana as not earlier than that century.

The icon of Surya in the temple is called *Konaditya*. The twelve names of *Aditya* (the Sun) are listed in this purana as *Indra, Dhata, Parjanya, Tvashta, Pusha, Aryama, Bhaga, Vivasvana, Vishnu, Amashumana, Varuna* and *Mitra* (Ch. 30). Rules for worshiping the Sun icon are prescribed with the assurance that this would be a sure way of erasing all the sins of the past seven births. Early morning worship is recommended.

Brahmanda (Brahmánda) Purana

The word *andam* literally means an egg. *Brahmanda* means the immense egg (egg of Brahma) which is a metaphorical way of describing the principle of cosmic creation. Thus the *Brahmanda Purana* is said to narrate, in principle, how the universe came to be. In other words, we may expect it to be a treatise on cosmology. However, the work has a great many other stories, some more and some less interesting than the others. The notion of *brahmanda* is an important conceptual element in Hindu thought, representing the macrocosm of which each of us is in some ways a micro-reflection.

In the Brahmanda Purana we read about the *saptaloka* or seven spheres: the earth, the sun, the moon, the stars, the planets, Ursa major, and the Pole Star. Here we also read the story of Parashurama getting into a fight with Lord Ganesha during which his axe was broken; in revenge, he broke one of Ganesha's tusks, making the God *ekadanta* (single-tusked). In this purana, there is also the story of Sage Agastya who is said to have brought the Vindhya Mountains to size since they were growing tall and proud. This rishi of modest dimensions traveled all the way to the Tamil country. He performed penance in Kancheevaram, and Lord Vishnu appeared before him as *Hayagríva* who revealed to him that the way to attain moksha (salvation) is either by complete renunciation of everything, or by constant worship of Vishnu in the form of the Mother Goddess.

Then there is the story of how at one time Indra became so powerful that even Shiva lost his primacy. So Shiva instructed Rishi Durvasa (Durvása) to meet Indra in heaven. On the way Durvasa, in the attire of a mendicant, happened to encounter a celestial nymph who, upon seeing him, paid her respects to him and gave him the garland she had acquired at the temple. When Durvasa saw Indra riding on his magical elephant Iravata, the rishi offered the garland to Indra who contemptuously threw it on his elephant. The elephant threw it to the ground and stepped over it. The enraged Durvasa cursed Indra whereby his power and grandeur diminished considerably (II.2.25 et seq.).

The Brahmanda Purana is famous for its *Adhyátma Ramáyana* which begins with a prayer to Rama who is described as the light of consciousness, immaculate, adored by the gods, and so on. The narrative is as in Valmiki. But here Rama is Divinity more than a hero. The work evokes the bhakti sentiment more than literary appreciation. Its advaitic leanings have led some scholars to suspect this part to be a post-Shankara interpolation.

There are magnificent descriptions of the palaces where the Mother Goddess resides. Called Srípuras, they are separated by seven walls of incredibly long circumference. The mere mention of the materials of which the walls are made reveals a knowledge of many metals: *alasya* (iron), *tamra* (copper), *sísa* (lead), *arakuta* (bronze), *pancaloha* (alloy with five metals), *raupya* (silver), and *hema* (gold).

Then there were square compounds serving different functions which are embellished by *pushyaraga* (topaz), *padmaraga* (ruby), *gomedhika* (agate), *vajra* (diamonds), *vaidurya* (cat's eye), *indraníla* (sapphire), *mukta* (pearl), *marakata* (emerald), *vidruma* (coral), *manikya* (gem), and *navaratna* (nine precious stones). There were also other compounds, named as of the mind (*manomaya*), of the intellect (*buddhi*), of the ego (*ahamkára*), of the Sun (*súryabimba*), of the moon (*candrabimba*), of eroticism (*sringara*), and desire-yielding gems (*cinntamani*). These show the sheer splendor with precious stones and the imagination the authors of the puranas had. In such conceptual grandeur of poets one can legitimately experience the richness, color, and magnificence of Indic lore.

Brahmavaivarta Purana

This is another of the Mahapuranas that takes the worship of Lord Krishna to the highest levels. The length of this purana is of the order of 18,000 verses (Sen, 1974). It has some interesting legends too, such as the story of Balarama and of how the sage Narada was cursed by Brahma to lead a life of sensuality. In this latter context, there is the view that Krishna instructed Prakriti to be transformed into Durga, Lakshmi, Sarasvati, Savitri, and Radha.

The purana has four sections. Perhaps the most fascinating one of these relates to cosmology. The universe (*prapañcha*) is seen as a transformation of Brahman, whence the name of the purana. The term *vaivarta* is derived from the root word *vivarta* which refers to something that is revolving or changing. Conceptually we may interpret this to mean that the universe is the unfolding of its innate essence, like the unrolling of a curled up sheet of map.

The Purana tells us about the various spheres (*lokas*) which include *Vaikuntaloka*, *Shivaloka*, and *Brahmaloka* where Vishnu, Shiva, and Brahma reside. But the triune principles are no longer there during the periodic dissolution of the prapañcha when all the lokas except these cease to exist.

The Brahmavaivarta Purana speaks of a still higher imperishable realm. It is the dwelling place of Brahman in the aspect of Krishna. Called *Go-loka*, it is not affected by the periodic eon-dissolution. In that realm is a secluded place called *Rasamandala*. Here, from Krishna's left, emerged the eternal Radha, and from her body came innumerable gopis, while from the body of Krishna arose as many men, and they are all in perennial ecstasy. In another chapter Radha is adored by Ganesha, Brahma, Shiva, and Ananta.

As per another imagery painted in this Purana, Vishnu came from Krishna's right side and Shiva from his left side, while Brahma came forth from Krishna's navel. Again it was Krishna who brought forth the consorts for the Trimurti: Sarasvati for Brahma, Lakshmi for Vishnu, and Durga for Shiva.

Next, from Vishnu's ears, out of the wax it contained, shot forth two horrendous demons, Madhu and Kaithba. The demons started on a rampage to attack Brahma, but Vishnu promptly destroyed them. He gave their corpses to Brahma who used them in his creation of the planet earth. Such is the narrative of cosmogenesis and geogenesis, according to this purana. If this is not poetic fantasy, there may not be another one.

According to this purana again, Vishnu did come down as Rama, and Lakshmi as Sita. During the Krishna avatara, there were two phases. In the first phase Radha was Krishna's consort. However, as a result of a curse, the two were separated for a whole century during which Krishna was king of Dwaraka, and had Rukmani (or Rukmini) as his queen. She too was an incarnation of Lakshmi.

The Brahmavaivartara Purana deals with a hundred other topics, ranging from dietary rules for brahmins and a day in the life of a shudra child to Brahma's injunctions as to a Brahmin's duties and the story of Savitri. In the body of this purana we also find discussions on medicines, as well as theories of matter. The purana tells us about how the *tulasi* plant and the *salagrama* stone acquired their sanctity.

Garuda Purana

The *Garuda Purana* was narrated by the mythical bird Garuda to Rishi Kashyapa who passed it on to Vyasa. The purana talks about the avataras of Vishnu, and says that the first incarnation was as the eternal youth: *Sanat Kumar*. Next Vishnu appeared as *Varah* (the boar) to salvage the world from the miscreant *Hiranyaksha*. We learn from this purana further that Vishnu also incarnated as Narada, and it was then that the doctrine of *nishkama karma* (desireless action) was expounded.

Usually this is regarded as Lord Krishna's advice in the Bhagavad Gita. The sixth incarnation was as *Kapila,* and its goal was to protect the *Sankhya* school of philosophy. [In the *shad-darshana* system, Sankhya philosophy is attributed to the sage Kapila.] Then we read about other incarnations: *Yajña Deva, Rishabha Deva, Prithu,* and *Matsya* (fish), *Kurma* (tortoise), and so on. In this reckoning, the sage Vyasa too was an incarnation of Vishnu, while Rama was the eighteenth and Krishna the nineteenth avataras.

This purana mentions five divinities, instructing how they are to be worshiped. The five are Vishnu, Shiva, Durga, Surya, and Ganesha. It is interesting to see how, over the centuries, worship modes and divinities have been changing in the Hindu world.

The Garuda Purana is also known for its detailed exposition of the post-mortem phase. It speaks at length about where the soul goes, and its descriptions of hell. The litany of all the horrible torments we read here are not much different from the Christian or the Islamic centers of torture. The purana tells us about omens that portend death, and also prescribes rules for the treatment of the corpse prior to cremation: some of which are followed to this day. For this reason, in some parts of India, passages from this purana are recited when there is death in the family. This purana mentions sati explicitly, showing that the concept, if not the practice, had been there in the Hindu framework for a very long time.

There is a passage in this purana that describes the different colors of whatever goes with Vishnu: Garuda is white like a lotus; Vishnu's mace is dark. The earth goddess has the color of the acacia flower. Lakshmi is golden. The conch has the color of the full moon. Vishnu's jewel has the color of dawn, whereas his discuss is like the sun. The lock of hair on his head is dark like *atasee* flower. His garland has five colors. His serpent is white, his arrows are like lightning.

There is a passage in which Vishnu asserts his omnipotence to Shiva: "O Rudra! I am the Master of all the devas. I am the one who controls everything that occurs in the Universe. I am the one whom all mortals worship to obtain liberation. But for me the universe will not exist. I am the creator, the sustainer and the supreme destroyer also. I am there in sacred mantras and in their meanings. People meditate on me. The material world is no more than a manifestation of me."

After the physical universe was created the five elements came to be, of which sound (*shabda*) was one. Then came the sense organs as well as instruments of action. Then followed immovable entities like mountains and trees. After this came animals and birds. Then followed various deities and celestial beings. After this came human beings. What is to be noted here is the insight of a gradual (temporal-evolutionary) process in the world.

The legend of Daksha is related in the Garuda Purana. We read that he arose from Brahma's right thumb whereas his consort Prasuti came from Brahma's left thumb. They were the first to begin populating the world by sexual union.

We note that each Purana gives its own slightly different theory of origins. Clearly many thinkers in India were reflecting on these questions over the ages, and giving their own interpretations. Their creativity in speculating on these fundamental questions commands our admiration. One reason why modern science did not emerge from all this was that the ideas were invariably tied to religion, and were not subjected to public debates, discussions, and critiques.

Kurma (Kúrma) Purana

Of the principal avataras of Vishnu on earth, the Kurma (tortoise) avatara was one. The Kurma Purana derives its name from the sacred historical fact that it was narrated to Narada by Vishnu himself when he had taken on this aspect. What is chronologically inconsistent is that other (yet to occur) avataras, including that of Rama, the greatness of Varanasi, Prayag, and holy rivers, are narrated here. This purana recounts the famous episode of the churning of the ocean (*samudra mathana*), talks about king Indradyumna who was re-born as a Brahmin to whom the Goddess Lakshmi once appeared. Indradyumna wanted to know who she was, and Lakshmi told him that she was none other than Vishnu, and that she was Vishnu's power of maya through which the physical universe is generated.

The purana talks about castes and their origins. It prescribes the duties of each. It talks about the four *ashramas* or stages in life, and the corresponding responsibilities: *brahmacharya* (celibate student stage) for the study of scriptures and service of the guru; *garhasthya* or *grahasthya* (house-holder stage) when one is to continue studying, serve guests, give alms, keep the yajña-fire burning at home, raising a family, etc. Next comes *vanaprastha* (forest-dwelling stage) during which one studies the scriptures, meditates, and lives on fruits and roots. In the final *sannyasa* (renunciant stage) one curbs all desires and meditates on the Divine. In this stage one lives on the charity of householders: this was the ancient equivalent of the Social Security Service system in the United States where householders (working people) contribute moneys which are used to maintain retired people. This ideal *chaturáshrama* described here was, like many other privileges and recommendations, only for dvijas, as the three upper castes are called.

The purana says there are anti-Vedic religious texts in the world. Those who adopt them are bound to go to naraka.

We also have here a version of the classic Daksha episode. Recall that Daksha was Brahma's son. One of his daughters was Sati, and she was married to Shiva. Once, during a visit to Shiva, Daksha felt slighted, and for this he chastised his daughter severely, saying that she had a terrible husband. Hearing this, Sati immolated herself. This gave her name to the practice of widow self-immolation. Shiva in turn cursed Daksha to be re-born as the son of the Kshatriya Prachetas. Sati was re-born as the daughter of Himavana: Parvati. The Kurma Purana contains a thousand names for Parvati. The list includes Paramashakti, Avyaya, Vidyá, Satyá, Amritabha, Shánti, Chinmayi, Támasi, Vishála, Mahágarbha, Soumya, Jaganmáta, and more. Some of these have been adopted as Hindu names for girls.

This Purana also gives a whole section on time-classification from *nimisha, kashtha* and *kála* to *áyana, yuga*, and *kalpa*.

There are stories in this purana which reflect poorly on some rishis, and even on the gods. The story of Gotama is one such. This man had been generous to many rishis, but was made to suffer by the ungrateful rishis out of sheer jealousy. Other stories recounted here are those of Hiranyakashipu, his four sons Prahlada, Anuhrada, Samhrada and Hrada, and of the Narasimha avatara.

Then there is the story of Andhaka, who, while Shiva was away, tried to abduct Parvati. But she was protected by the Nandi-bull. Nandi used his trident to keep Andhaka away. But this demon generated a thousand more like himself, and they went on a rampage. Finally they were all killed by Shiva and Vishnu.

The Purana gives the etymology of Rudra as from the root *rud*, to weep: He is Rudra because he causes people to cry.

Linga Purana

The Linga Purana is dedicated to Shiva. It too talks about cosmogenesis. It includes the narratives of the Varaha and the Narasimha avataras also. It formulates the principle that all procreation involves the union of an experiencer and an experienced, and it is by understanding the intricacies of this mystery that one can grasp the nature of reality.

This purana contains some omen-mongering assertions: If one can't spot the Pole Star one will die in a year (one might wonder about people living in the southern hemisphere); a dream in which gold is vomited means ten more months to live; if there is a sudden loss or gain in weight, there are but eight months to live, etc.

Among the cities the purana lists as sacred the first is Varanasi, for it was there that Shiva himself lives with Parvati and Ganesha. There are five other such sacred spots: Kurukshetra, Shriparvata, Mahalaya, Tungeshvara, and Kedara.

In this purana we find a thousand names for Shiva, such as: Bháva, Ishána, Ganeshvara, Vishvamúrtí, Suresha, Pashupati, Bhútavahana, Nílagríva, and Achintya, suggesting that (by now) Shiva is essentially a Sanskritic deity.

The Linga Purana talks about the yuga system of reckoning eons, and says that during Kali Yuga Shiva appears as an avatara. It is said that there have been twenty-eight Kali Yugas during the present kalpa. The twenty-eight avataras of Shiva, called Yogeshvaras, are listed. They bear such names as Shveta, Madana, Kanchana, Dadhiváhana, Gautama, and Sahisnu. This purana also gives the names of the rulers of the solar and lunar dynasties (Súryavamsa and Chandravamsa).

In one episode, when Brahma and Vishnu were engaged in combat, there arose a bright linga. It seemed to be rising indefinitely upward, as well as downward. Intrigued by this, Brahma took on the aspect of a swan and flew up. Vishnu took on the form of a boar (varáha) and dug downward. But neither of them could find an end-point for the linga in either direction. What is interesting here is the concept of linear infinity (one-dimensional unbounded Euclidean space): a straight line that extends indefinitely in either direction which is a geometrically sophisticated idea. Brahma and Vishnu realized this was an extraordinary power, and they prayed to the linga with a resounding aum. At this point Shiva emerged from the linga as the sage Vedanáma who explained that the linga was the source of cosmogenesis, for it was from there that the *brahmanda* (primordial egg) came. Shiva initiated Brahma and Vishnu to the gayatri mantra, explained that Brahma, Vishnu, and Shiva were all one and the same, just three manifestations of the same Brahman.

Shiva's consort is to Shiva what word (instrument) is to meaning (substance). The former can exist without the latter: there can be a word without meaning; but the latter cannot exist without the former: there cannot be meaning without a word. On the other hand, the former, without the latter would be irrelevant, if not useless: a word without meaning has no relevance to us. This is a profound reflection on word and meaning. Then again, Shiva is described as the Lord of Creatures (*Pashupati*). The twenty-four *tattvas* (life-principles) are the *páshas* (reins).

Elsewhere, Vishnu claims to be the lord of everything, for which he is reprimanded by a certain Virabhadra who declares Shiva to be the most supreme. Then there was Tárakásura who was going on a rampage, waging war on Vishnu for twenty thousand years. It was to get rid of this asura that Karttikeya was born to Shiva and Parvati.

In another story, pleased with the munis of Devedáru forest, Shiva visited the place, in the guise of a naked ugly ascetic. The wives of the hermits were drawn to him. The angry hermits spoke to Shiva in harsh terms. When they told Brahma about this, the latter rebuked them, and said Shiva had gone to test them. They had forgotten the sacred rule that no guest is to be treated with dishonor.

Markandeya Purana (Márkandeya Purána)

The Markandeya Purana is reckoned as one of the most important, if not the most ancient of all the puranas: important because it narrates stories from the tradition without being sectarian, and ancient because it speaks about Agni and Surya rather than Shiva and Vishnu. In a homage to the Sun, the Markandeya Purana says: "I pay obeisance to the embodiment of the universe, the light on which the practitioners of yoga meditate."

It describes the sun as the matter of which the gods are the soul. It says that the river Yamuna is a manifestation on earth of Yamí, the sister of Yama. In its vision, India is said to be resting on the back of a huge tortoise (kúrma). This may be likened to the modern view of tectonic plates. In recounting the story of Dattatreya, the purana describes how the gods described that sage: "No blemish can stain the heart which has been awakened by true learning and wherein the light of knowledge has penetrated." How applicable this is to many enlightened souls!

This is the only purana that is named after a person: Markandeya, an eminent rishi who is mentioned in the Mahabharata. The context of the Purana is as follows. The sage Jaimini once went to Markandeya with four questions relating to the Mahabharata. The first was: why was it that Divinity, the ultimate source of the whole universe, came down as an avatara here below. The second related to Draupadi's polyandry. The third question had to do with Balarama's brahminicide, and how this was expiated. Finally there was the question about the premature death of Draupadi's sons.

Sage Markandeya replied that he was too busy at the time to answer the questions, and directed Jaimini to certain magical birds, which could recite the entire epic, for they would be able to answer them. He went on to explain how those birds (actually incarnations of heavenly beings) happened to possess such knowledge. Birds have a special significance in Hindu mythic visions.

The interesting story of Vipaschit occurs in this Purana. Vipashchit was an honorable king who, nevertheless, was dispatched to the nether world. The reason for this harsh punishment was that he had not been with his wife at a time when she could have conceived. In this context Yama (the God of justice) explains the consequences of one's karma. After a brief period in naraka, Vipashchit was going to be taken away from there to svarga (heaven). But the dwellers in hell pleaded with him not to go because his breath somehow assuaged the torture they were undergoing. So Vipashchit refused to leave. But the Lord of Dharma insisted he should go to heaven for that is what his karma had earned him, as the denizens of hell were reaping their karma. The number of good deeds he had done was like the number of drops of water in the ocean and stars in the skies and sand grains in the Ganga. The similes for uncountably large numbers are interesting.

Vipashchit said that those poor souls were not sinners but sufferers, and insisted on staying with them. Finally Yama agreed to allow them all to enter heaven with him. This is a beautiful story showing the nobility of compassion and self-sacrifice. Legends like this reveal the lofty ethical heights which some ancient Hindu thinkers reached. Some of the morals in puranic legends are more sublime than the legends themselves.

In this purana we read a gruesome description of the black goddess Chámunda who is said to have sprung from the forehead of Durga. She wore a garland of corpses, and her garb was an elephant-hide. Her tongue hung out of her open mouth, and her eyes were blood-shot. She is said to have annihilated two terrible demons by the names of Chamda and Munda, whence her name. The interpolated version of Markandeya Purana contains the famous *Devimahatmya* which is one of the classic hymns devoted to the goddess Durga. It is recited to this day during the festival of Durga, especially in Bengal. We may note in passing that though Buddha himself is said to have ignored the question of the existence of God, Chámunda is reckoned as a goddess by some Buddhists.

Mastya Purana (Mátsya Purána)

In the canonical listing of the avataras of Vishnu, Matsya or the Fish avatara is reckoned as the first one. In the Matsya Purana, we read that list as *Matsya, Kurma, Varaha, Nara-simha, Vamana, Parashurama, Rama, Krishna, Buddha,* and *Kalki.*

Vishnu incarnated in pisciform after the mahapralaya (the Great Deluge). Manu was the only one who was saved in the global flood. Manu in a boat and Vishnu as Matsya in the waters sailed along. Tradition has it that this purana was narrated by Vishnu Himself during the flood. The purana says that Vaivasvata Manu, son of Vivasvan, the Sun-god, was the seventh Manu of the era. His son was Ikshváku. The Purana also gives other genealogies, some of which have clearly historical roots.

This purana also has many legends, such as the story of Shukrachárya and Savitri, and it also sacred cities such as Prayaga and Varanasi, as well as the names by which Shakti is known in these 108 places. To give but a few examples, the Goddess is worshiped as Vishalakshi at Varanasi, Lalitadevi at Prayaga, Jayanti at Hastinapura, Radha at Vrindavana, Devaki at Mathura, Sita at Chitrakuta, Parvati at Shivasannidhana, Indrani at Devaloka, Sarasvati at Brahmamukha, Prabha at Suryabimba, and so on. It also mentions Sati's self-immolation after reciting these names.

While narrating the story of Pururavas and Úrvashi, the Matsya Purana refers to the traditional triple goals of life: upholding the values of civil society (*dharma*), pursuing activities for acquiring economic well-being (*artha*), and seeking enjoyment in life (*kama*). In this Purana we read that Pururavas was cursed by the gods of Artha and Kama because he was more devoted to dharma than to them. Later, Pururavas rescued Urvashi—the celestial nymph affiliated to Indra—from the demon Keshi.

We are also told here that Bharata gave the blessings of music and dancing to humankind, and assigned Menaka, Urvashi, and Rambha to exemplify these. While they were doing this, Urvashi was charmed by Pururavas and missed a dancing step. For this she was cursed to spend fifty-five years on earth. During this time she married Pururavas and bore him eight sons. The Urvashi-Puruvaras amour is mentioned in the Rig Veda (X:95), and is also the theme in a play by Kalidasa.

The yuga division of cosmic time is given here, as also the features of each yuga. Thus, the varnashrama and the four-stages-of-life system were already there in the treta yuga. In this yuga there was no disease, and no one was poor. People lived happily wherever they wanted. It was only in the next dvapara yuga that hatred and jealousy began to seep in, and people began to violate the strictures of the varnashrama dharma, especially endogamy. It was to counteract such corrupting influences that the Vedas were introduced. Astronomy and medicine came into human societies during this yuga.

The present Kali yuga is, of course, the worst of all. Because of evil such as selfishness, cheating, inter-caste mixing, shudras reading the Vedas, and the like, natural calamities like diseases, draught and famine began to occur.

Architectural principles are enunciated in this purana for homes, palaces, and temples, with technical terms for various types of houses, with reference to their window locations. According to the Matsya Purana, it was Brahma who authored the first treatise on architecture. The purana spells out prohibitions on the type and placement of trees near a house, and prescribes woods that must be used for construction. For instance, trees should never be planted in front of a house. The wood from neem and mango tree should never be used for house construction, etc. Some of these guidelines are followed to this day.

The Matsya Purana is reckoned among the very old Puranas. It is estimated that it dates back to between 250 and 500 BCE. Again and again we are impressed and surprised by the richness of the mythic visions of ancient Indians.

Narada Purana (Nárada or Náradíya Purana)

This is another of two Puranas named after a sage. Narada was the universal traveler who went, not just from place to place here on earth, but from sphere to celestial sphere. The notion of a jet-setter in cosmic terms is implicit in this major personage in Hindu lore. This sage is also known affectionately as a trouble maker. There is a story in the Bhagavata Purana to the effect that Narada once instigated Vayu (the Wind-God) to chop off the top of Mount Meru. Vishnu's vahana Garuda spread his wings and protected the mountain. But, at a time when Garuda was absent,

Vayu succeeded in his mission: a slice of Mount Meru flew off and fell in the ocean in the distant south of the subcontinent, giving rise to the island of Sri Lanka. The idea that an island in the sea is the top of a mountain beneath is implicit here.

According to the Brahma Vaivaitara Purana, Narada was condemned by Brahma to a solitary life of sensuality, but the Mahabharata (Book X: *Shanti Parva*, xxx) says that he married Sukumari, the daughter of Sriñjaya. Puranic references to mythic personages are not always mutually compatible.

The *Narada Purana*, generally regarded as the extension of a more ancient and highly sectarian work called *Vrihannáradíya Purana*, is more interesting than the one which is regarded as its source. The latter is unabashedly sectarian.

The traditional assignment of roles to the trimurti in Hindu cosmology is spelled out in the Narada Purana, along with the manifestations of Shakti. Thus Brahma and Sarasvati are responsible for *srishti* (creation), Vishnu and Lakshmi for *sthiti* (sustenance), and Shiva and Parvati for *laya* (dissolution)

The Narada Purana gives us a version of ancient Hindu cosmography and geography. According to it, there are fourteen realms in the universe, seven higher and seven lower. The higher realms are known as *bhúloka, bhuvarloka, svarloka, maharloka, janoloka, tapoloka,* and *satyaloka*; while the lower realms are called *atala, vitala, sutala, talatala, mahatala, rasatala* and *patala*. All these worlds are inhabited by different beings. Our earth (*bhuloka*) has seven land masses and seven oceans. The land masses are called *Jambudvípa, Plakshadvípa, Shalmaladvípa, Kushadvípa, Krounchadvípa, Shakadvípa* and *Pushkaradvípa*. The seven seas have the names *Lávana, Ikshu, Súra, Sarpih, Dádhi, Dughdha* and *Jala*.

There is also some astrology in this purana. Here we read, for example: "Orb of the Sun appearing like a pot will cause famine (in the country); if it is like an arch, it will cause the destruction of the capital; and, if it is like an umbrella, it will cause the destruction of the country. A spilt Sun will cause the death of the monarch. If at sunrise or sunset, there occur (against the sun's disc) lightning, meteor and thunder, then one can foretell the death of the king or fight between kings."

Many Indian rivers, such as *Godavari, Sarasvati, Kaveri* and *Shatadru* are listed here as sacred. But Ganga is the most sacred of them all. We read that one who anoints himself with the clay from the bank of Ganga becomes like Shiva, one reason why some ardent Shiva devotees cover their bodies or at least their foreheads with ash.

It states in this Purana that those who are born in *Bháratavarsha*, which is described as *karmabhúmi*, work without thinking of the fruits of their actions (*nishkama karma*). Lands where only enjoyment is in the minds of people are called *bhogabhúmi*. Those born in *Bháratavasrha* are very fortunate, the purana says. Chauvinism and nationalism are not new in cultural history, nor unique to any people.

Narada Purana prescribes punishments for various sins, but these depend on the caste of the perpetrator. The worst sin is the killing of a brahmin by a shudra; the corresponding penalty is also terrible. It also says: "in times of danger or calamity, it is permitted that a brahmana take up the occupation of a kshatriya or a vaishya. Similarly, it is permitted that a kshatriya take up the occupation of a vaishya. (As seen earlier, this thought is expressed in other puranas too.) But under no circumstances should an individual belonging to one of the first three classes take up the occupation of a shudra. A person who does this is to be regarded as a chandála.

The Narada Purana says that Shakti divided herself into *Vidyá* (knowledge of the identity between Brahman and the

Cosmos) and *Avidyá* (ignorance of this). In her different aspects Shakti is known as Sarasvati, Lakshmi, and Umá.

The names of the *panchabhúta*s (*elements* in ancient science) are given in this Purana as *kshiti* (earth), *apa* (water), *teja* (energy), *marut* (wind) and *vyoma* (sky).

We read in the Narada Purana that Markandeya—son of Mrikundu—was the only one who survived the flood, and that he floated on the waters "like a dried up leaf" for a thousand *mahayugas*. In this context the purana gives its yuga measurement of time.

Like the other puranas this one also sheds considerable light on the social norms, worldviews, and values of the people of India more than 1500 years ago.

Padma Purana

The Padma Purana, bearing the lotus (*padma*) appellation, is one of the Brahma Puranas. We recall that Brahma Himself is known as *Padmayoni*: Lotus born, and is envisioned as seated on the lotus flower.

The Bengal recension is the main source of information on this work. It consists of five principal parts which deal with *Srishti* (creation), *Bhúmi* (the earth), *Svarga* (heaven), *Pátala* (nether world), and *Uttará*: a last part, which deals, among other things, with the descent of the sacred Ganga.

The purana is in the form of a revelation from Pulastya to a certain Bhíshma Sutji. It tells us at first that three kinds of egos were created from the *mahat tattva*, and it was from these that the sensory organs as also the organs of action, and the five elements were created. From these arose the material world (*prakriti*). It is said that it is Vishnu in the aspect of Brahma who effects all Creation.

The *yuga* division of time, which is unique to Hindu chronology, is mentioned here too, with its millions and billions of years, as in other puranas.

This purana also mentions the origins of chaturvarna (four castes) much like what one reads in the Purusha Sukta: Brahmanas and Kshatriyas from the Cosmic Purusha's mouth and chest, Vaishyas and Shudras from his thigh and feet. Then came the *mánasaputras* (mind-born sons) *Bhrigu, Pulah, Kratu, Angira, Marichi, Daksha, Atri* and *Vasishtha* the purpose of whose creation was to propagate the human species.

At first there were no females, and the *manasaputras* were without any desire. This angered Brahmá, whereupon Rudra appeared from his forehead, and from Rudra emanated both males and females. There are in the same purana other stories about how scores of daughters were born who became mothers, and how gradually the population of the world increased. We read that the demon *Hiranyáksha* had four sons each of whom had 270 million sons and grandsons.

In another passage we are told that Bhrigu's wife Khyati had a daughter, and this was Lakshmi, the consort of Vishnu. Elsewhere, the legend of the churning of the ocean is narrated in this purana, wherein the other (traditional) genesis of Lakshmi is explained, very much as in the Mahabharata.

In its section on Naraka, we read about the serpent world and Ravana. Here Rama's life is retold, inspired by Kalidasa's Raghuvamsha. We also read episodes from Krishna's life. We find here the *Vishnu Sahasranama* of the Mahabharata, as also a thousand names of Rama. There are sections on the geography of India, both actual and mythical. The purana talks about Lake Pushkara and mentions the Durga festival of those days.

There is a story here in which a wife shows extraordinary chastity and loyalty to her husband during his absence on a pilgrimage, in spite of many provocations. For her virtue, her husband receives a boon from the gods. When a woman like Ahalya does something wrong, she is severely punished, but when she does something right, her husband is richly rewarded. This may seem to be a somewhat mixed up value system from current frameworks.

We see in the enunciation of the Padma Purana that all the other puranas were also mentioned, suggesting that this recension must have been of a much later period, after the appearance of all the other puranas.

Among other matters we see in the Padma Purana a mythic explanation for the lunar phases. Describing how Yama appears to the virtuous, it says that he is riding on Garuda. The story of how Chitragupta, the divine ledger-keeper, sprang from Brahma, is told here. The etymology of Rudra from *rud*: to weep, occurs here too. It says that Vác (goddess of speech) was Daksha's daughter. The dwarf-nature of Agastya is also mentioned here.

Skanda Purana

Skanda is the son of Shiva. He has other names, like *Guha, Kumara, Karttikeya, Mahásena, Gangaputra, Shanmukha, Subrahmanya,* and *Murugan* (in the Tamil world). The Skanda Purana narrates the genesis and deeds of Skanda. It is the only Purana that is not dedicated explicitly to the veneration of Brahma, Vishnu, or Shiva. With 81,000 verses, it is reckoned as the longest Purana. The extant edition is believed to have grown over the centuries (Tagare, 1996).

Skanda was born to rid the world of the demon Tarakásura. The genesis of Skanda, as we read here, is similar to the one in Kalidasa's Kumarasambhava. When Shiva was with Parvati, his sperm fell in fire. The fire took it to Ganga which flowed into a forest of reeds (Sara-vana). The embryo that emerged got split into six parts. These were nurtured by six Krittikas (presiding female deities of Krittika—the Pleiades). Hence Skanda has several names—*Agniputra* (son of Fire), *Gangaputreya* or *Gangeya* (son of Ganga), *Kárttikeya* (son of the six Krittikas), *Shanmatura* (one with six mothers) and *Saravana-bhava* (one who was born in a forest of reeds). Today there is a Tamil restaurant nearing this last name of Skanda with branches in many cities and countries.

Scholars and mystics have seen esoteric meanings behind the legend of Skanda's genesis, such as that the sparks from Shiva represent the six chakras and that Uma's embrace signifies their integration into a single personality. Every myth has a deeper meaning, often seen or brought out by scholars.

As in some other puranas, here too there is geography and references to holy places. In the *Káshí Kánda* of this Purana, some fifteen thousand stanzas are devoted to the holy city of Varanasi. Here we read that there are thirty-five million apsarases. Vishnu's thousand names are popular. Shiva's thousand names are also known. But in the Skanda Purana, there is a hymn for the sacred Ganga with a thousand names for the river (*Gangásahasranamam*).

One book of this purana describes the sacredness of the region we call Odisha with a reference to the Lingaraja Shiva temple at Bhuvaneshvar.

As per the Skanda Purana, the linga represents *akasha*, and *prithivi* is the altar. All the gods reside therein. As in other puranas one finds here the genealogies of some gods: Thus Soma (the Moon) was born to Atri and Anasúya; numerous episodes from the lore are presented here. We read about Indra's seduction of Rishi Utathya's wife, and the price Indra had to pay for this. Here we also read that Shiva put a curse to the effect that Brahma would never be worshiped in temples because Brahma had lied that he had reached the pinnacle of the Linga. There is also the story of Abhinandana who neglected to invite Indra to a great sacrifice, for which he was eventually punished. It was in this context, as per this purana, that Ganesha came to be prayed at the beginning of all undertakings (*punyaha-vacana*). We read here too that Brihaspati prayed to Shiva for a thousand years, for which he was made into the planet Jupiter.

Interestingly, in one of books of this purana we read about Krishna's rasa-dance with the gopikas. Eminent Vaishnava scholars like Vallabhacharya and Baladeva wrote commentaries on this.

The *Skanda Purana* has an elaborate Tamil equivalent. This important work in the Tamil Shaiva tradition is known as *Kanda Puranam*. Here Kandan (Skanda) marries Valli and Deivayani. His mission was to rid the world of the asura named Surapadman (of Sri Lanka). Kandan was the equivalent of an avatara in the Shaiva tradition.

Vamana (Vámana) Purana

The Vamana Purana derives its name from the Vamana (dwarf) avatara of Vishnu. There is the long story of Vamana's arrival in Kurukshetra where Bali was performing a sacrifice. When asked why he had come there, Vamana said he wished to make a sacrifice for which he needed a small piece of land in the measure of only three steps that he would take. Bali's counselor Shukracharya advised him against making any hasty promise to Vamana. Nevertheless, Bali agreed to give Vamana three steps of land. No sooner did he make this promise than Vamana grew to his cosmic expanse. In one step he covered the entire earth. The second step swept the higher realms. There was no place for the third step. Bali offered his own head for that. When Vishnu put his foot on Bali's head, the latter was pushed into patala, suggesting that Vishnu covered the nether world too. The story beautifully illustrates the all-pervading grandeur of the Divine, and the limited intelligence of humans.

This powerful myth is retold in various ways in the Bhagavata Purana, the Matsya Purana, the Agni Purana, the Padma Purana and the Brahma Purana.

In the Vamana Purana we read about the fabulous city of immeasurable wealth and abundance in the nether world that was built by Vishvakarma for the demon Bali. While the hedonists there were in the height of sensual pleasures, Vishnu's *sudarshana chakra* entered Bali's palace and, after dimming all their radiance, it returned to its source. Then, in accordance with the advice of his grandfather Prahlada, Bali arranged to build a magnificent temple for Vishnu and Lakshmi. Here he prayed regularly.

Another story we read in this purana says that Vishnu discovered Shiva with three eyes, wearing a *rudraksha* and holding a *trishúla* (trident). In a confrontation between Shiva and Brahma, each one was insulted by the query of the other as to their respective identity and origin. In this context, Shiva severed one of Brahma's five heads. Shiva regretted this act and went to Vishnu for redress. Vishnu asked Shiva to hit Vishnu's left arm with his trident. When this was done three mighty rivers resulted. The first was *Ákashganga* (the Milky Way) in the heavens; the second was the river *Mandakini*. The third one fell on Shiva's head, which eventually became *Ganga*.

As per this purana, the Maruts were the sons of Kashyapa and Aditi. The puranic etymology of Maruts is found here too. They are said to have been weeping, when they were told, "*Ma rud!* (Do not cry!) oh powerful ones! You will be called Maruts."

It is said that a certain Sukeshi, who had received blessings of invincibility from Shiva, once asked some sages for the secret of respectability and contentment. The answer was that one had to follow dharma. But what is dharma? The answer was that dharma included performing rituals, studying various things, especially the Vedas, and devotion to both Vishnu and Shiva. The demons had qualities like jealousy and envy, but they were also devoted to Shiva, the sages added.

Then he wanted to know about naraka (hell). He was told there are 21 hells, and these were listed as Raurav, Maharaurav, Tamistra, Andhatamistra, Kalchakra, Aprathisth, Ghatiyantra, Asipatravan, Taptakumbh, Kootshalmali, Karpatra, Swabhojan, Sandansh, Lohapind, Kalmasikta, Kshaarnadi, Krimibhojan, Vaitarninadi, Shonitpayabhojan, Kshuraagradhaar, Nishitachakra and Sanshoshan. No other mythology has a richer elaboration of hell.

Five special names for Vishnu are given in the Vamana Purana: *Karanavámana, Naráyana, Amitvrikrama, Shargangadhkra,* and *Charkrin.*

Varaha (Varáha) Purana

The Varaha Purana's title refers to the third avatara of Vishnu. It is said that at one time the demonic Hiranyáksha carried away Prithivi to a different realm. Vishnu, descending in the boar form (Varaha avatara), rescued her from there. The astounded Prithivi posed many questions to Vishnu about cosmogenesis and the ultimate fate of the universe. Vishnu opened wide his mouth and there Prithivi could see all the splendor of the cosmos, as astronomers do when they peer into a powerful telescope.

The avataras of Matsya, Balarama, and Kalki are also recalled here. As we have been seeing, many legends overlap in puranic literature.

In its creation story we read that at first there was total darkness. Then arose five types of ignorance: *tamasa* (inertia), *moha* (confusion), *mahamoha* (great confusion), *tamisra* (darkness), *andhatamisra* (pitch-darkness). Then were created immovable things like mountains and trees. These are called *mukhya sarga* (principal creations). Then followed *tiryaksrota* (quadrupeds), after which came the sattvik ones: deities. Humans came after these as *arvaksrota* (embodiment of Dawn). According to the Vishnu Purana arvaksrotas were primordial beings which had crooked alimentary canals. They were ignorant of their own nature. It is interesting that the idea of evolving human beings is implicit here.

Only then were the *anuraghs* (sages and seers) created. After this emerged the kumáras (adolescent beings). Finally, ten mind-born sons of Brahma arose: Marichi, Angira, Atri, Pulah, Kratu, Pulasya, Pracheta, Bhrigu, Narada and Vasishtha. Initially, Brahma had created *Ardhanarishvar* (half male and half female). It was Rudra who split himself into a male and a female.

As in other Puranas there are a great many legends here too. The story of Nachiketas (which we read in Kathopinshad) is presented here. In this context there is a listing of some of the sins that will take one straight to hell. These range from lying, greed and jealousy to criticizing one's teacher or the Vedas and selling alcoholic drinks. Here again we read details of heaven and hell. The city of Yama is said to be made of gold. It has two separate entrances: one for the saintly ones and one for sinners. There are rivers there, but also the screams of agony from the sinners who are being tortured. One is reminded of Dante's Inferno. Just as there is the picture of a joyous pleasure-filled heaven, there is also one of an extremely painful and torturous hell as in the other major religions of the world.

A story about Ganesha: Once the deities went to Shiva for redressing some difficulties. They were invariably encountering hurdles in their undertakings. Shiva is said to have laughed when he heard this, and from his mouth a divine and lovely child emerged. Parvati was so charmed by it, she stared at it without closing her eyelids even for a moment. Shiva became jealous and angry and cursed the child to have the face of an elephant and also a pot belly. He also cursed the child to have a snake around his shoulders. It is difficult to know if such tales were spun in amusement or in seriousness.

There are some beautiful hymns in this purana as also a whole Mahatmya on Mathura, the city where Lord Krishna was born.

In this purana we find a recipe for a preparation for offering to Vishnu. Called *madhupark*, it is made up of honey, curd, and ghee. God's name should be chanted while it is being made. One attains salvation by properly offering it to the Divine. Rules are spelled out for worship, for obsequies, and also for the installation of idols. Here it is said that the svastika mark must be etched on the forehead of the icon. The svastika mark is a sign of auspiciousness; so the devotee must keep this in mind while giving shape to the idol.

Vayu (Váyu) Purana

The Vayu Purana is so called because it is said to have been recited by the Wind God Vayu (Bhatt, 2005). In its creation story the cosmic egg contained the earth and the planets, the deities and everything else in the universe, all implicit and unmanifest.

This purana also gives the yuga classification, giving descriptions of each. Thus, for example, in the satya yuga there were no seasons or rains. The people were beautiful and prosperous and cheerful. Everyone was dharmic. The earth produced juices which kept people healthy and youthful. There were no vices, not even anger and jealousy.

In the next (treta) yuga, people's attention changed from dhyana (meditation) to jñana (pursuit of knowledge). Trees (*kalpavrikshas*) grew with fruits on them. Their barks were used for covering the body. But slowly vices began to affect people. People started to fight over ownership of trees. They built houses, leading to measuring systems which ranged from angulis (finger-length) to yojanas which were 8,000 dhanus (bow-lengths). Villages and cities came to be. Herbs and grains grew. It was then that chaturvarna (four-caste system) began. Brahmins who knew the nature of Brahman, Kshatriyas who bore arms and protected the good and punished evil forces, Vaishyas who were dedicated to agriculture and trade, and Shudras who were to serve the others. Note that this is an interesting account of pre-history, albeit speculative and mythological, as well as of cultural regression.

This is one of the puranas where one learns that a kalpa consists of 4.32 billion years. It gives still more inconceivable time periods. Thus, a thousand kalpas constitute a Brahma-year. Eight thousand kalpas make a yuga for Brahma. A thousand yugas make a savana. A trivita is two thousand savanas, and this is a measure of the longevity of Brahma. The purana also lists the names of more than thirty kalpas. These include names like Bháva, Havyaváhana, Oushíka, Vairája, Akuti, and Krishna.

While the four-headed Brahma created mortal beings, Shiva created the immortal Rudras. But Shiva also taught yoga to one and all. Yoga's goal was to unite the jivatman with the paramatman. This purana lists five rather than the customary eight aspects of yoga: pranayama (breath-control), dhyana (concentration of mind), pratyahara (control of senses), dharana (intense focusing of mind), and smarana (remembering the Divine at all times). We are warned that if one does yoga while ignoring the strict prescriptions, without proper guidance and at places at random, consequences would be disastrous: deafness, blindness, insanity, etc.

Aside from legends like that of Daksha and Sati, the Vayu Purana has also its fantasy stories, such as that of King Vrihadashva who had twenty-one thousand sons, and of the demon Dhundhu. When Dhundhu exhaled—which was just once a year—blinding sand storms were generated, as also earthquakes lasting a whole week. Then there is an episode in which Dhanvantari, who emerged during the churning of the ocean and is said to have brought medical science to humanity, asks Vishnu to give him a place amidst the gods. Perhaps this story is to suggest that medicine may be regarded as equal to the nectar of the gods in that it saves human lives and reduces human pains.

The sacred histories of Parashu-Rama as well as of Dattatreya are told in this purana. The number of apsarases is countless, and they form different ganas. In Hindu lore there are supernatural beings of all kinds. One group of ferocious beings are the yatudhanas. The Vayu Purana gives the names of twelve of them. It also gives a list of fourteen ganas. There are some internal inconsistencies in the stories, suggesting that the whole purana was not written by a single author. Perhaps this is true of many other puranas as well.

Shiva Purana is a variation of Vayu Purana. Whereas a Vayu Purana is mentioned in the Mahabharata, the Shiva Purana refers to Gupta kings of the fourth century CE.

Vishnu Purana

The Vishnu Purana is another very old Purana. It is the quintessential source of Vaishnava worldviews and worship. It is also known as Vaishnava Purana. It is mentioned in the writings of the great Vaishnava philosopher-saint Sri Ramanuja. It enjoys the highest esteem among Vaishnavas, and is referred to as *Purana Ratna*: Purana gem.

Here too we read about cosmogenesis, yuga classification, and sacred geography. The golden Mount Meru is the abode of the Gods and Jambudvípa is the Indian subcontinent. Some episodes from Hindu sacred history, such as the churning of the ocean are told. There is a poetic description of Lakshmi. In the Prahlada-story occurs a formulation of the highest ethical principle: One who causes pain to others through thought, word, or deed sows the seeds of a future birth which will be wrought with pain. Another interesting injunction here is that truth should always be spoken except when it has the potential for hurting people, in which case one should not say anything. The Vishnu Purana narrates the story of Dhruva whose intense and unwavering meditation on Vishnu immortalized him as the fixed star Dhruva (Pole Star).

The Purana talks about the four varnas and their respective responsibilities, as also the four ashramas. In this context it prescribes some interesting rules of conduct for the householder. Aside from worshiping gods and cows, one should respect wise and learned people. One shouldn't steal or lie, nor point to the faults of others. We also read here some other interesting injunctions: One shouldn't climb a tree, nor yawn without covering one's mouth, and one should meticulously avoid the shadows of divine icons and flags. It is important to pay obeisance to a divine symbol before stepping out of the house. It is interesting that many of these principles are followed to this day in the Hindu world.

When I first read this passage it occurred to me that it reflected a unique feature of the Hindu world and of the puranas: They contain many nuggets of wisdom and also many ridiculous things. One can appreciate and also be amused by the puranas, but it is difficult for some people not to take them literally or seriously. They are a rich source of ancient worldviews, and deserve to be read at least for this reason.

Many rituals for sacraments, such as wedding and funeral, are spelled out in detail in this purana, and these too are adhered to in our own times.

One surprising item mentioned in the Vishnu Purana about the *shraddha* (funerary) ceremony is this: An odd number of Brahmins must be fed. If the food is simple, the departed souls are satisfied for a whole month. If it has fish, they are satisfied for two months. Rabbit meat will satisfy them for three months, fowl for four months, pork for five months, mutton for six months, venison for seven months, and so on, including lamb and beef. But the meat of the vardhinasa bird will satisfy them forever. Some have suggested that this might be a desha-chara: interpolation to suit local customs.

The Vishnu Purana is quite sectarian, emphasizing the primacy of Lord Vishnu. It regards Brahma and Shiva as aspects of Vishnu. It is explicit in its condemnation of Buddhism and Jainism which are regarded as heretical creeds (from the Hindu perspective). It warns its adherents against interactions with such blasphemous sects with the story of the devout Vaishnava king Shatadhanu who once exchanged a conversation with a heretic, for which offense he was reborn variously as lowly beasts and birds.

The Vishnu Purana says that Kubera was the grandson of Rishi Bharadvaja. It also says that Vishnu's chakra represents the universal mind, his arrows are the senses. Vishnu's garland (*Vaijayantimala*) with five rows of flowers represents the five senses. Earthquakes and tidal waves result when Vishnu's serpent Ananta yawns.

The Vishnu Purana says that the puranas were revealed to a rishi from Patala, who gave them to Pramati who gave them to Jatukarna. Then they spread to others. Finally, it was through Rishi Vasishtha and Parashara that the Vishnu Purana came down to us.

Many modern Anglo-Hindus who argue that the four-varna system was not part of classical/ancient Hindu social history, that castes are based, not on birth but on qualities, that Hindus are all vegetarians, and that Hindus never eat beef, generally have not read the puranas. If the great epics shaped the ideals and values of the Hindu people, the puranas shaped a number of social practices and rituals. Ironically, the details of their contents are known to very few practicing Hindus.

Concluding Thoughts

There was a time when I used to listen to puranic tales with very great interest, and even entertained the idea that they were authentic accounts of what had once happened. Later in life, after looking into the details of some of the stories, it became more and more difficult for me to take them seriously. As relics of the ancient world they are no doubt great. As classical compositions they attest to the creativity and prolific imagination of ancient Hindus. As narratives they do form a corpus of sacred history which countless Hindus still regard with reverence. As stories, some of them are quite interesting, others somewhat naïve, not to say puerile.

No matter how one considers them, puranas are intrinsic parts of Indic lore and culture. Not one in a thousand may read them in their original versions, but a good many Hindus are familiar with the fables that enrich the panorama of Hindu Gods. In no matter which religious tradition, works that reach the pedestal of sacred scriptures cannot be dethroned easily to the level of imaginative poetry or fantastic fiction. So it has been with the puranas.

VIII

Sage-Poets: Rishis of Ancient India

To the rishis, bliss (ánanda) was more than the expansive feeling of ecstasy. It was the basic vibration, or hum, of the universe, the ground state from which all diversity springs...

- Deepak Chopra

Since remote times, sages in India have been speaking on life and existence, on death and after-life, on soul and god. They undertook austerities in their efforts to obtain answers to the mysteries that torment inquiring minds. They acquired insights from years of reflection and meditation. These pioneering spiritual leaders and moral teachers were the *rishis* of India.

Rishis were scholars, philosophers, sages and poets. And they were more. They were practitioners of techniques by which they are believed to have gained glimpses of loftier levels of reality behind the phenomenal world. They spoke with exuberance about the nature of Truth and the Ultimate. The general view is that they broke through the veil of ignorance that keeps ordinary mortals in confusion, delusion, and misunderstanding about the surrounding mystery.

Rishis were extraordinary individuals who explored the human potential for spiritual experience. They were serene personages at peace with themselves and the world. They were inspired seers who uttered wisdom in aphorisms and poetry. They composed hymns to the powers of the universe, framed rules and laws for society, discoursed on philosophy, counseled kings, and initiated the young. Individually and collectively, the ancient rishis laid the foundations for the complex culture, sophisticated civilization, and colorful religious tradition that is known as Hindu today.

Indian sacred history is replete with the names of many rishis whose achievements rendered them superhuman in the estimate of the people. In due course, fantastic stories and incredible time spans came to be associated with the deeds and dates of rishis: One was born of Brahma's thumb, another had a hundred sons, one fathered a bird, another did penance for a thousand years; one pulverized an army by staring at it in anger, another made a mountain prostrate in submission, and such. All this may seem reasonable when one accepts that rishis were a species much superior to the human. However, minds molded, constrained, or awakened by the perspectives of the scientific age may find it difficult to imagine all this to be true. Nevertheless, a good many Hindus, like their counterparts in other religious traditions, do not feel they are in this quandary. They accept the episodes associated with the rishis as to have actually occurred.

Be that as it may, it is difficult to be untouched by the events and episodes we read about rishis. Many of these stories are etched in Hindu collective memory, and have become indelible patches in the quilt of Indic cultural lore. There are similar fantastic anecdotes in the Bible and in the Qur'an. The devout of those traditions take their own puranas to be literally true also. After all, what one usually refers to as mythology is the lore relating to another person's religion.

Truth to say, we know but little of historical validity about the remarkable rishis who once walked on the land and dipped in the sacred waters of India, who first recited magnificent mantras and performed magical sacrifices. But we do know that the Ramayana and the Mahabharata are major literary works authored by eminent rishis. The Vedas, the Brahmanas and the Upanishads: all these and more are attributed to so many rishis. The Narada Purana is named after a rishi, as also the Markandeya Purana. Such works are among the ever-lasting legacies of the great rishis who illumined the Hindu stage.

In ancient India, as also in our own times, rishi was also an honorific: a title for great thinkers and spiritual leaders. The texts mention various kinds of rishis, depending on their qualities or function, as in Brahmarshi and Rajarshi; sometimes, on the spiritual level, as in Devarshi, Maharshi, and Paramarshi; some were called Shrutarshi, meaning that they had heard esoteric wisdom. Brahmarshis are believed to have been created directly by Brahma Himself. They are among the initiators of various *gotras*, and are invoked in the daily prayers of dvijas who belong to their spiritual lineage. They include such names as Kanva, Bharadvaja, and Kashyapa. The names of some rishis are well known, such as Vishvamitra, Vasishtha, and Agastya. Others, like Marichi, Kardama, and Gritsamada, are not as widely recognized. To this day I recall with reverence the name of the saintly Kaundinya Rishi when I recite the gayatri mantra.

Every great religious tradition has at its roots profound thinkers. Sometimes they appeared as prophets carrying a spiritual message: revelations from Beyond. They take their people along new paths. Thales of ancient Greece, Gautama

Buddha, Vartamana Mahavara, Moses, Jesus Christ, Mohammed, and Guru Nanakdev were all such exceptional men, endowed with inscrutable charisma. What is unusual about Hinduism as a religion—perhaps unique in history—is that it emerged in an uncertain age from the utterances of exceptional sage-poets: rishis who came from a variety of social and cultural backgrounds. That is why it may be said that Hinduism has not one, but many founders. Not all rishis always agreed on everything among themselves. This accounts for the ancientness as well as the richness of the tradition. This has also resulted in unsurpassed diversity in the Hindu world. It may also explain the doctrinal tolerance that is, in principle, an intrinsic feature of Hindu religious visions.

Saptarshi

Of the scores of rishis, real and legendary, who have graced the Hindu world, seven are preeminent. They are known as *saptarshayah* or *saptarshi* (seven rishis). They are already mentioned in the Rig Veda (X.130). We recall that the Greeks too had their seven wise men (*hoi hepta sophoi):* Thales, Cleobulos, Bias, Pittacos, Solon, Periandros and Chilon. As in the Greek tradition, not all ancient works list the same names for the Big Seven. Thus, according to the *Satapatha Brahmana*, the saptarshi were: Gotama, Bharadvaja, Vishvámitra, Jamadagni, Vasishtha, Kashyapa, and Atri. These rishis are the ones who are said to have received the Vedas.

According to the Mahabharata, however, the saptarshi were Marichi, Atri, Angiras, Pulastya, Pulaha, Kratu, and Marichi's son Kashyapa. The Vishnu Purana adds Daksha and Bhrigu to the list. These original rishis are considered to be the progenitors of humankind: the prajápatis.

The saptarshi are regarded in many contexts not as ordinary humans, or as gods, but as cosmic principles. It is clear from their names that they are symbols, rather than individuals. The Brhadaranyaka Upanishad (2.2.4) relates the seven rishis to the seven apertures on the human face. At the same time, they also have many personified aspects. We read about these in the epics and in the puranas. The transformation of symbols, concepts, and truths about the human condition into tangible names, forms and persons is part of mythopoesy.

Consider Angiras Rishi. He is said to have arisen from Brahma's mouth. His name appears in the very first hymn of the Rig Veda in which Agni (as the household priest and sacrificial god) is invoked. We read here that whatever blessing Agni bestows upon whosoever worships him materializes through Angiras. The Anukramanika, which is a kind of index for the Vedas, ascribes scores of Vedic hymns to this rishi. It has been said in some Buddhist traditions that Lord Buddha was a descendent of this Rishi (Thomas, 2007), just as Guru Gobind Singh stated in his Vichitra Natak that Gutu Nanak descended from the lineage of none other than Sri Rama himself (Lal, 1992, p. 4559).

Angiras is a personification of Fire (Agni). In Vedic vision, Agni is not simply a raging fire or the slender flame in a lamp. Rather, it stands for force and strength, for energy and passion and life itself: indeed it is the root of all that is dynamic and vivifying in the world. Agni is eternal while the heat and light of even the sun and the stars will fade away some day. It also stands for esoteric knowledge, for the hidden wisdom behind the passing panorama of things. In the Yajur Veda, we encounter again and again the phrase, "I take thee, in the manner of Angiras." Angiras is also regarded as one of the rishis to whom the Atharva Veda was revealed.

The lore ascribes to Angiras two principal wives, and other minor ones. The two principal wives are known as Shraddhá (Devotion) and Smriti (Tradition). Perhaps it is suggested through these names that in the ritual mode, tradition and devotion go hand in hand with the sacrificial fire. Angiras is said to have had four sons and four daughters.

Ursa Major (Great Bear) is perhaps the best known constellation in the (northern hemisphere) sky. Every ancient culture has a mythology about it. In the Hindu vision, the seven stars of Ursa Major are the celestial presence of the saptarshi. That is to say, the seven great rishis were transformed into the stars of that constellation in the heavens. This translation of the saptarshi into the firmament was the basis for a chronological system that prevailed for long in some parts of northern India. It arose from the idea that an important astronomical event occurred in 3076 BCE and that the constellation of Ursa Major moves around each of the 27 nakshatras (lunar asterisms) once every hundred years. This led to a 2700 year cycle which was taken as a theoretical unit of time in the saptarshi chronology.

We may note a peculiar circumstance of sounds and words that may have given rise to the name of *Ursa Major* (Great Bear) in the Western world, or perhaps even to the stellar saptarshi in the Hindu world. A Sanskrit word for star is *riksha* (neuter noun). But *riksha* (masculine noun) also means a bear. It is quite possible that in India the word *sapta riksha* (seven stars) became *saptarshi*. On the other hand, riksha was probably translated as ursa (bear) into the Greco-Latin languages. This is not the only instance of word confusion leading to conceptual changes.

In the jargon of modern astronomy, the association of the seven visible stars of Ursa Major to the saptarshi is as follows: Alpha Ursa Majoris: *Kratu*; Beta Ursa Majoris: *Pulaha*; Gamma Ursa Majoris: *Pulastya*; Delta Ursa Majoris: *Atri*; Epsilon Ursa

Majoris: *Angiras*; Zeta Ursa Majoris: *Vasishtha*; Ita Ursa Majoris: *Márichi*.

The spouses of the rishis have also found places in the sky as stars in constellations. Thus, for example, the star Alcyon in the constellation Pleiades (sometimes, Alcor, the companion star of Zeta Ursa Major or Vasishtha) is identified with Arundhati, Vasishtha's wife. Even today, as part of the marriage ritual, the bridegroom symbolically points this star to his bride to remind her of Arundhati's devotedness to her husband. (Actually neither the groom nor the bride, nor the officiating priest knows where or what is Zeta Ursa Major.) Some say that this is a vestige of the practice in olden times by which the groom would slowly gain intimacy with his bride by showing her a faint star at night, getting gradually closer to her.

Atri Rishi

Rishi Atri is another prajapati. He is said to have emerged from Brahma's eyes. But then, when Brahma's sons were killed by a curse from Shiva, and Brahma performed a sacrifice, Atri came again from the fires of this sacrifice. In this way, he is said to have had two incarnations. In the first of these, he had three sons. One of these was Soma: the Moon. In the second he had a son and a daughter. The son's name was Áryamán. The daughter was called Analá. Such are his puranic biographies.

There are hymns in the Rig Veda (I: 112.7) which describe how Atri was rescued from a fiery pit into which he had been thrown. This probably referred to the treatment that some of the so-called Tribals of India gave to the leaders of Vedic culture. It is difficult to re-construct the history of events that occurred more than 3500 years ago, especially when reports of those events are couched in mytho-symbolism. In another hymn (V: 40) we read that when the sun was attacked, Atri did the rituals for the protection of the gods. This probably refers to early reactions with magical incantations when eclipses came to pass.

In the Mahabharata (Anusasana Parva: 156) this Rig Vedic reference is embellished into a story in which Bhishma tells Arjuna that during one of the periodic conflicts between the gods (devas) and the demons (danavas/asuras) Rahu pierced Surya (the sun) and Soma (the moon) with his powerful arrows, plunging the universe in utter darkness. The gods went to Atri Rishi and appealed to him for help. The rishi asked the gods how he could be of any assistance. The gods suggested that he should become the sun and the moon himself. Atri did just that. This ascetic Brahmin who was clad in deer skin and who subsisted only on fruits, it says, assumed the aspects of the sun and the moon and illumined the entire universe. He also pulverized the evil ones, and restored order in the world. He cast the appropriate spells to root out the demon which was haunting the sun. The echo of this episode still reverberates in India whenever an eclipse comes to pass.

Atri is mentioned in various Puranas. We read about him in the Padma Purana (Sarga Khanda) where it says that the rishi practiced austerities for three thousand years. In the course of this penance, his semen slowly inched upwards, reached his head, was transformed into immortalizing amrita, and then it was ejected from his eyes. This then split into ten portions which illuminated the ten corners of space. So the sun and the moon were born. Not many myths can match this in its sweep of the universe from a supernatural human body.

In the Ramayana, Atri becomes very much a normal rishi. Here we read (Ayodhya Kanda: 117) that Rama, Sita, and Lakshmana, after leaving Chitrakut during their exploration of the forest, went to the hermitage of Atri Rishi. The sage was dwelling peacefully with his wife Anasúya. Her name means: one who is uncomplaining, who bears no spite. Anasuya gives a little talk to Sita on the glory and responsibilities of a chaste wife. In the course of this sermon she says: "For women blessed with noble character, husband is the highest deity, irrespective of whether he misbehaves, is licentious, or is without any riches." This innocuous statement may refer to an episode in Markandeya Purana (XI): A man named Kaushika is said to have expressed a desire to enjoy another woman. Because Kaushika was too weak to walk to his pleasure-lady's house, his faithful wife Shandili carried him on her shoulders to his desired destination. On the way, she accidentally stepped on a holy man named Mandavya. The angry sage cursed the couple to be dead before dawn. Shandili prayed that the sun may never rise again. The godly beings were frightened, and they approached Anasuya for help. Anasuya persuaded Shandili to retract with the promise that Mandavya's curse wouldn't materialize. For this, the gods offered Anasuya three boons. She responded by asking for the moksha of herself and her husband. As a third boon she wanted the Trimurti (Brahmá, Vishnu, Shiva) to become her sons. This was granted in a mystical way: From Atri Rishi's eyes shot a radiant energy which served as the seeds for three incarnations of the Trimurti as Soma, Durvása, and Datta.

Another version of this legend is no less interesting: At one time, the gossip-mongering prankster rishi Narada went to the three great Shaktis: Sarasvati, Lakshmi, and Parvati, and spoke to them very highly about the chastity and loyalty of Anasuya towards her husband Atri. The goddesses grew envious, and dispatched their spouses to tempt Anasuya. Disguised as mendicants, they came to the lady and begged for food, but on one condition: They wanted her to serve them in the nude. Anasuya retreated into the kitchen, prayed to her husband, disrobed herself, and came with some food, clad only in air. The guests had turned into babies. She embraced the infants and fed them milk from her breasts. Rishi Atri returned home and was very pleased for he knew that these babies were Brahma, Vishnu, and Shiva. He took them all in his arms, and they became one. As it was a gift, the child was named Dattáttreaya (Given to Atri).

Pulastya Rishi and his progeny

In the biological world with which we are familiar there are many birds and beasts, insects, mammals, and so on. These are different *species* of life forms. In the Hindu mythic world, there are also special types of creatures. Some of these are anthropomorphic and do not belong to any of the commonly known biological species. How did they come about?

In the puranic framework, they had supernatural origins. Let us consider four such classes of beings: *yakshas*, *rakshasas*, *vanaras*, and *kinnaras*. Like the nymphs of Greek mythology, yakshas are creatures that live in forests. They are fond of trees that are held sacred. Some yakshas are good, and some are bad. They are believed to be real creatures, but invisible to ordinary mortals; therefore, they have to be feared, and they are sometimes worshiped. Some yakshas have attained reputation as important characters in the epics. Perhaps the most famous of them is Kubera, the god of wealth.

Then there are the rakshasas. The term is related to the root, *raksh*: to guard. It is believed that they were created to watch over the elements when they were first formed. In the mythologies, rakshasas are superhuman beings with subhuman qualities. In other words, they have enormous physical and even mental capacities, but generally speaking they are evil in inclinations and prone to destruction. The puranas trace their origins in different ways. One view is that it was Rishi Pulastya who gave rise to them. Elsewhere, Kashyapa Rishi is credited with their genesis. According to another purana, they arose from Brahma's toenail.

Rakshasas appear in all shapes and shades. Some are grotesque and ugly, but some are fair and friendly. Some are huge and monstrous; others are less frightening. Many are cruel and bloodthirsty, but some are also calm and peaceful. Some are fat and some lean, some are dwarfish and others gargantuan. In the Ramayana we read that Hanuman saw all kinds of rakshasas, some with just one eye, some with pendulous breasts, some with huge protruding teeth, some with crooked thighs, etc. Such variety and numbers of Rakshasas in Sri Lanka is no surprise since Ravana, its ruler, was a rakshasa himself.

Then we have the vanaras or forest-denizens, represented with tails and monkey faces. Hanuman is the best known of them. Historically speaking, the term could well have referred to another aboriginal tribe that lived in the southern regions of India. From this perspective, the battle between Ravana and the vanaras in the Ramayana was actually a confrontation between two families of half-brothers (rakshasas and vanaras).

Finally, there are the kinnaras, corresponding to the Greek centaurs. These are beings hippanthropes, with human-like bodies and horse-like heads. Again, it has been suggested that the reference was probably to some aboriginal people who used horse masks in their festivities.

It is said that once Bhishma, the grandsire in the Mahabharata, did many years of austerities. At the end of this period Pulastya appeared before him and promised him any boon of his choice. There is a long chapter in the Mahabharata (Vana Parva: 82) in which Pulastya explains to Bhishma the importance and benefits of making pilgrimages. Specifically, he explains, whereas it requires considerable wealth to perform great sacrifices which, therefore, can be done only by kings and other rich people, even the very poor can go to a *tirtha* (place of pilgrimage with a sacred river or pond) and achieve the same benefits as from a sacrifice.

Pulastya is said to have had three wives and several sons. The oldest of his sons was the great Vishrava. In the Uttara Kanda of the Ramayana (Sarga II), Agastya speaks about the austerities of Pulastya whom he describes as a renowned and mighty Brahmarshi, very much like Brahma himself, of whom he was born (*prajápateh putra*). Pulastya went to the ashrama of Trinabindu which was on Mount Meru, and stayed there, performing many austerities. It was a wonderful place graced by maidens and nymphs who sang and danced joyfully. They distracted the rishi. Pulastya was angry and warned them they would become pregnant if they showed up there again. So they all disappeared, but Trinabindu's daughter strayed into the rishi's presence by mistake, and promptly became with child. Her father married her to Pulastya.

It is thus that Vishrava was born. He married Devavarnini, a daughter of Rishi Bharadvaja, but through a series of circumstances the rishi also begot children through his other wives. Vishrava is remembered in the tradition as the father of many major characters in the Ramayana. These include personages like Ravana, Kumbhakarna, Vibhishana, Kubera, and Shurpanakha: all members of the Sri Lankan royal family.

Kashyapa rishi

In the midst of all the political turmoil tarnishing the beautiful valley of Kashmir, one sometimes forgets that the name of that idyllic spot enshrines one of the prajapatis: Kashyapa. Scholars have reminded us that according to the Nílmat Purana,

King Níla was once a ruler of Kashmir. There was a huge lake (míra) there, whence Kashyapa-míra became Kashmir.

Etymologists have argued about Kashyapa's name. It means, among other things, deer and also tortoise. In the Atharva Veda it refers to beings that regulate the sun's course. In the Shatapata Brahmana it is a rishi's name. According to the Vishnu Purana, Kashyapa was Vishnu in the Kurma Avatara, instigating the of humankind. We read elsewhere that Vishnu incarnated as the son of Kashyapa and his wife Aditi in the Vamana Avatara.

Unlike other prajapatis, Kashyapa was not directly born of Brahma, but was his grandson through Maríchi. In Upanishadic symbolism, Marichi is light, and Kashyapa is Vision: God created light which bestowed vision on human beings.

In the Ramayana (Áranya Kanda: 14) we read about Kashyapa's mythological aspect. He married eight daughters of Daksha. Of these, Adití, Dití, Dánu, and Káláka were closest to him. Through Aditi he gave rise to 12 Adityas, 8 Vasus, 11 Rudras, and 2 Ashvins. Through Diti he was responsible for the Daityas, through Danu came the Dánavas. Other species arose from other wives: including birds like owls, hawks, vultures, and swans; mammals like antelopes, elephants, cattle and horses; and so on. Jatáyu, the leader of the vultures, was the grandson of Kashyapa through his son Aruna whose mother was Vinatá. The Puranas say that Kashyapa married thirteen daughters of Daksha, and that through them he generated every kind of being, from ordinary people to awesome ogres. Nágás, rishis, gándharvas, all had their origin in Kashyapa. One cannot but be amazed by the zoological sweep in such narratives, showing the wealth of knowledge and imagination of the poets who composed them. One might say that in the ancient framework, Kashyapa stands for a primordial biological cell from which all living organisms arose.

In the Mahabharata (Ádi Parva: 14), there is the story of Kashyapa's two wives who were daughters of Brahma. They were called Kadru and Vinata. Kashyapa was so pleased with them that he offered them boons of their choice. Kadru wanted a thousand splendid snakes as her sons, whereas Vinata wished for only two sons who would surpass those of her co-wife in splendor. It was thus that the Nagas were born to Kadru, including Sesha and Vasuki. One of Vinata's sons was Garuda, the lord of the eagles. In the lore, legends abound about Garuda, whose name and images have gone beyond the shores of India: to China, Japan, and Korea. The Indonesian Airlines is named after him.

The blurring of symbolic entities bearing specific names with anthropomorphic beings bearing the same names occurs in puranic and epic works. In the case of Kashyapa we must distinguish between Prajapati and other personages who bear his name. The latter are known as Kashyapa. Thus, in Valmiki's Ramayana (Bala Kanda: 8), Káshyapa is listed as one of the four principal preceptors of King Dasharatha.

Another such rishi is mentioned in the Mahabharata. He had magical powers too. In one story (Ádi Parva: 43), when he was on his way to save Parikshit, he was distracted by the serpent king Takshaka who challenged him to revive a banyan tree which the serpent bit and turned to ashes. Káshyapa, by his prowess, brought the tree back to full life.

In another passage in the epic (Vána Parva: 21) we read about Kashyapa's discourse on forgiveness (*kshama*), reminding us of Portia's words in Shakespeare's *Merchant of Venice* to the effect that mercy "is an attribute to God himself." He says, "Forgiveness is dharma, forgiveness is Vedas, forgiveness is shruti. One who knows this can forgive anything. Forgiveness is Brahma, forgiveness is satya; forgiveness is the punya that comes from tapas. Forgiveness is sannyasa; forgiveness is holiness. The whole universe is held together by forgiveness. It is the might of the mighty, it is yajña and peace of mind. The man of wisdom should always forgive, for then he attains Brahma. The world belongs to those who are forgiving. Forgiveness and gentleness represent eternal virtues." Such passages reveal the ethical ideals in classical Hindu framework. We may recall in this context the Sermon on the Mount in the New Testament (Matthew: V.39) where Jesus says: "… whosoever shall smite thee on thy right cheek, turn to him the other also." We may also recall in the same book (Matthew V:7) the line: "Blessed are the merciful, for they will be shown mercy."

One of the six classical schools of Hindu philosophy is the Vaisheshika system. Scholars date it back to 700—600 BCE. Here we find one of the earliest articulations of Indic atomic theory. Its originator was a certain Kanada: who is also referred to as a Kashyapa. Perhaps this was a different personage. With so many accounts and legends, it is difficult to be sure about when and where Kashyapa and Káshyapa lived. But they have been very influential in Indic culture.

Narada (Nárada)

Narada is a most interesting rishi. The puranas give different accounts of his genesis. According to the *Nárada Pancha Ratra*, the sage was born of Brahma. The Vishnu Purana says that he was one of Kashyapa's progeny. The Bhagavata Purana regards him as Vishnu incarnate. Many fascinating stories are told about this great personage in Hindu lore.

Metaphorically speaking, as I noted earlier, Narada was the first jet-setter in history, for he traveled widely, not just all over this planet of ours, but to heaven and hell as well. For this reason he is known as *triloka sanchári*: traveler of three worlds. But he was no passive tourist. In epic and puranic literature, Narada is often described as a messenger. In this capacity he fed secret information which led to quarrels and misunderstandings among friends. This won him the unfavorable epithets of *Kalikarana:* strife-maker and *kalahapriya*: one who likes misunderstandings. In the Hindu world, a person who gossips with the intention of provoking quarrels is sometimes called *Narad-muni*. But the term is used in an affectionate sort of way.

Brahma once advised Narada to get married and settle down. Narada said Brahma was not a good teacher since devotion to Krishna was the path to felicity. Brahma cursed Narada to get addicted to erotic delights. (Brahma-vaivarta Purana) Narada first wept at this severe malediction; when he gained his composure, he cursed Brahma to become incestuous with his own daughter, adding, "You will not be worshipped for three yugas." Then he tempered by saying, "After that, you will be worshipped for you are worthy of it."

In the Vayu Purana Narada tells the sons of Daksha (who were about to multiply) that they were foolish to undertake this without even knowing how big or small the earth is, for without this knowledge how would they determine if they were overpopulating or underpopulating the world? Daksha cursed Narada for this.

In the Mahabharata, there are many references to Narada. In one episode, he explains the origin of death thus: When Brahma created the universe, he soon recognized that people would be everlasting. This might not be good, he thought, and became very angry. His anger expressed itself as a universal conflagration which destroyed everything. At this Rudra advised him that he should not destroy everything at once. So, Brahma created the personification of Death who would destroy individual lives at various times, rather than all at once. That is why not everybody dies at the same time.

In the Padma Purana Narada talks about eight flowers (*ashta pushpa*) which are ahimsa (non-violence), indriyanigrahana (self—control), sarvabhuta daya (compassion towards all creatures), kshama (forgiving), shanti (peace), tapasya (ascetic focusing) and dhyana (meditation). In another episode in the Mahabharata (Shanti Parva), Narada tells a story whose thrust is to preach ahimsa. In that story Dharma, who had disguised himself as a deer about to be sacrificed by a Brahmin in a yajna, says: "The slaughter of creatures does not conform to the ordinances of yajnas... Injury to animals is no part of yajna." We also read here that a full-fledged religion is one which abstains from doing harm (*himsa*). This is interesting in that the Mahabharata is supposed to have been written before Mahavira of Jainism.

Besides being a scholar, Narada was also a great lover of music. He is said to have invented the veena. He is also remembered as the one who initiated the art of dancing. Being so versatile, he was not always modest. Once he told the Divine principle (*Narayana*): "I always respect my elders; I have never spoken to others about secrets; I have read the Vedas studiously; I have practiced severe austerities; I have never uttered untruth; I have always been virtuous; I have always treated both friends and foes alike; I always adore the Divine." By these, he claimed his right to see the Divine in person.

Valmiki's Balakanda begins with the poet asking Narada: "Is there anyone who merits to be called a perfectly virtuous man? Is there anyone who understands fully the power of ethical comportment? Who is there that fully realizes the value of selfless service, who always speaks the truth, and is also firm in his resolutions?..." Narada answered by saying, "Yes, indeed, I do know of such a hero, one who has all the noble qualities which you have mentioned." He then went on to narrate the saga of the great Rama which Valmiki wrote for us all to read.

This inspired a saintly personage to write: "In Brahmaloka, Ramayana has 100 crores (10 billion) shlokas and Brahma wanted to introduce it to Bhúloka. He searched for a good narrator and He found in Nárada... an eligible candidate." Such exaggerations are not unusual in Hindu lore when it comes to lauding great works. Such statements are not to be taken literally.

The choice of Narada for telling the Ramayana is appropriate: Narada was scholar, minstrel, spiritual soul, and traveler. The Ramayana too has scholarly and musical components. Like Narada, it has also a spiritual dimension. Like Narada again, the Ramayana has traveled to distant lands through translations in many languages (Raman, 1999).

Some Vedic hymns are also attributed to Narada. A treatise on law, the *Naradiya Dharma Shástra*, is said to have been the work of this great rishi. The Mahabharata says that Narada was also a close friend of the Pandavas whom he advised and to whom he would narrate stories.

Rishi Bharadvaja (Bharadvája)

Puranic versions of Bharadvaja's birth are, as usual, intriguing. The Vishnu Purana gives an interesting etymology of his name. It says that his mother Mamata conceived him from two fathers: her blind husband Utathya and his younger brother Brihaspati. Hence he was called bhara-dvá-jam: Born of Two (Fathers). Another explanation for the name is that this rishi was born of a Brahmin father and adopted by a royal personage, and hence had both Brahmin and Kshatriya parentage.

Bharadvajas are sometimes referred to as a pastoral people who worshipped a deity called Púshan. In due course, largely because Rishi Bharadvaja was one of the authors of the Vedas, Púshan became one of the important gods in the Vedic pantheon. Indeed, Púshan is often described as the protector of cattle. Many Vedic passages are associated with his name which is said to be derived from the root word for nourishing.

In the Mahabharata there is a question and answer session (spread to several chapters) between Bharadvaja and Bhrigu (Bk 12: Mokshadharma Parva). The former asks the questions and the latter gives answers. Here are some of the questions posed by Bharadvaja: "How did God create such diversity of life-forms?" "How did water come about, and fire, and air?" "If everything is made of the five elements (earth, water, fire, air, ether), why are these not visible in some things, like fire in trees?" "If Brahma arose from the Lotus, then should not the Lotus be called the First-Born, and not Brahma?"

The answers given to these may not be satisfactory from current perspectives, but the questions reveal a sophisticated scientific spirit of inquiry.

As with Kashyapa and Káshyapa, one must distinguish between Bharadvája (the original rishi) and bháradvája: his progeny or descendants. Thus, for example, the great Drona of Mahabharata was a Bháradvája, for he came from the loins of Bharadvája. It happened this way. One day, when Bharadvaja was on the banks of the Ganga for his spiritual practice, his eyes fell upon the voluptuous apsara Ghritáci, whose clothes were swayed by the wind. The great rishi was aroused by the sight of this sensuous enchantress. He let his vital fluid fall into a pot from where emerged in due course Drona (the *pot-born*), who was thus a Bháradvája. Passages like this may offend those attuned to Victorian prudery, and even embarrass some modern Hindus, but they are part of Hindu lore.

Drona stayed in his father's ashrama for a long time, even after the passing away of Bharadvaja. Here he studied the Vedas and became an ascetic scholar. King Prishata, whose son was the famous Drupada, befriended Bharadvaja. It is said that Drona and Drupada used to play together as youngsters. Eventually Drona married Kripi and they had a son. This child, when he was born, is said to have neighed like a horse. Hence he came to be called Ashvattáman: one with the voice of a horse. Ashvattaman was thus Bharadvaja's grandson.

Bharadvaja once lived in the court of the King of Varanasi as the royal purohit. But then, he also had ashramas in different places.

Rishi Bharadvaja was the progenitor of a gotra. (*Gotra* refers to one of the original rishi-lineages to whom dvijas trace their cultural-genealogical origin.) In Kamba Ramayanam we read that Rama and his party stopped at Bharadvaja's peaceful hermitage (Kamban, II.20 *et seq.*). The sage is described in great detail by Kamban: His tuft was plaited, a tree bark served as his loin cloth, and a deer skin covered his body. He was carrying a parasol, a jug for auspicious water (*kamandalam*) and a sacred baton (*brahmadandam*). He was so learned, it was as if the Vedas were dancing on his tongue. Rama treated him with great reverence, with flowers, prayer, and a triple prostration. Bharadvaja recognized the prince and wondered why one who could rule the whole world was there in ascetic garb. When Rama explained, the sage said it was fate that had intended all this to happen.

Then Bharadvaja offered to host the trio (Rama, Sita, Lakshmana) at his hermitage which was rich in plants, trees, fruits and sacred water. But Rama replied that the place was too close to Koshala, and would attract many citizens to come and implore him to return. Bharadvaja understood, and gave them directions to go to Chitrakoot.

In Valmiki's Ramayana we are told that when Bharata reached Bharadvaja's hermitage while he was on his search for Rama, the sage asked him bluntly: "What is your motive in looking for Rama when you ought to be busy ruling the kingdom which you have inherited as a result of your mother's demand for Rama's exile? I am rather suspicious. In your efforts to enjoy the kingdom that rightfully belongs to flawless Rama, I trust you are not thinking of harming Rama and Lakshmana" (Valmiki, II.90.10-13).

This brought tears to Bharata's eyes, and he pleaded with the sage not to speak to him thus. He informed the man of wisdom that he (Bharata) was coming to beg Rama to come back to rule the kingdom. Perhaps this dialogue is meant to heighten the drama, for one would expect a man of Bharadvaja's stature to know better. The reader (audience) is also moved to tears when they hear the noble Bharata being thus accused. Bharadvaja quickly changed his tone and said that he was aware of Bharata's intent, and that he had spoken in that way only to strengthen Bharata's resolution further.

There is a fascinating scene in (Kamban's) *Uttara Kandam* in which Rama and his entourage are traveling in the flowered aerial vehicle (*pushpaka vimanam*) on their way back to Ayodhya (Kamban, IV: 37, 162 *et seq.*). During that flight, Sita is curious about where Rama found Hanuman. In answer, like a tourist guide pointing to interesting places, Rama shows Sita as they fly over the various spots the residence of Sugriva, the kingdom of Kishkindya, the Godavari River, the Dandaka forest, the Chitrakoot Mountain, and Bharadvaja's hermitage.

The vehicle landed for a while at the hermitage of Bharadvaja. Rama prostrated at the feet of the rishi. Bharadvaja greeted him fondly and praised him for his heroic deed of ridding the world of demonic characters. Then he went on to extol the great qualities of Rama's brother Bharata who had been spending these fourteen long years virtually as an ascetic, living only on fruits and vegetables, sleeping on a bed of grass, and chanting Rama's divine name. Bharadvaja offered to bless Rama with a boon of his asking. To this Rama said: "I want the vanaras (monkeys) to live with ease, I want them to find all the fruits, vegetables and roots they need no matter where they roam." This was granted. Volket Sommer, the German primatologist who studied the sociobiology of Indian temple-monkeys for a decade, presented me with a copy of his excellent book which documents in detail how well this boon has served monkeys in India (Sommer, 1996).

As with countless other personages in India's history, one wonders who this great Rishi actually might have been. His name appears in a variety of contexts. Quite possibly, there were several great men with the name of Bharadvaja. It is said that they officiated in Vedic rituals. The Go-súkta (VI: 28) is a Rig Vedic hymn attributed to a Bharadvaja rishi. Here we read (Griffith translation):

> The Kine have come and brought good fortune: let them rest in the cow-pen and be happy near us.
> Here let them stay prolific, many-colored, and yield through many morns their milk for Indra.
> Indra aids him who offers sacrifice and gifts: he takes not what is his, and gives him more thereto.
> Increasing ever more and ever more his wealth, he makes the pious dwell within unbroken bounds.
> These are ne'er lost, no robber ever injures them: no evil-minded foe attempts to harass them.

The master of the Kine lives many a year with these, the Cows whereby he pours his gifts and serves the Gods.
The charger with his dusty brow o'ertakes them not, and never to the shambles do they take their way.
These Cows, the cattle of the pious worshipper, roam over widespread pasture where no danger is.
To me the Cows seem Bhaga, they seem Indra, they seem a portion of the first-poured Soma.
These present Cows, they, O ye Indra. I long for Indra with my heart and spirit.
O Cows, ye fatten e'en the worn and wasted, and make the unlovely beautiful to look on.
Prosper my house, ye with auspicious voices. Your power is glorified in our assemblies.
Crop goodly pasturage and be prolific, drink pure sweet water at good drinking places.
Never be thief or sinful man your matter, and may the dart of Rudra still avoid you.
Now let this close admixture be close intermingled with these Cows, Mixt with the Steer's prolific flow, and, Indra, with thy hero might.

References to Bharadvaja in varied contexts illustrate what distinguishes sacred history from fiction: The characters in it are not confined to a single story or episode. Rather, they permeate a whole body of independent, yet interconnected works. It is as if we are reading about celebrities in different magazines and newspapers.

Durvása Rishi

Different rishis were known for their different peculiarities. But this much was common to all of them: they were men of high principles and standards, and they would not easily brook any form of disrespect.

Few of them equaled, let alone surpassed, Durvása Rishi in the quickness and severity of his imprecations when he was annoyed. He is described in the Mahabharata as "the terrible Brahmana of rigid vows."

Durvasa Rishi is sometimes mentioned as a son of Atri, one of the Saptarshi. Some puranic sources also speak of him as having arisen directly from Shiva. Thus the Vishnu Purana calls him a descendent of Mahadeva. In the Mahabharata there is an episode in which Krishna says that the Brahmana Durvasa stayed with him for some time. Krishna described his complexion as green and tawny. He was clothed in rags, we read, and he carried a stick from a bilva tree. He was taller than anyone on earth. He is said to have exclaimed: "Who is there that would host the Brahmana Durvasa?" He gets into a rage when he sees the slightest transgression in the hospitality towards him. Let us recall three events where the wrath of this rishi was let loose.

First, there was the incident at Kanva Rishi's hermitage. A version of the incident is narrated in Kalidasa's play Shakuntala. Durvasa once paid a visit there while Kanva was away. He asked: "Does anyone hear me?" Shakuntala's friend Anasuya informs her that there was a guest. But Shakuntala's mind is elsewhere: She was thinking of her recent bridegroom King Dushyanta who had gone back to the capital. Durvasa became furious. "This is an insult," he screamed, and cursed that whoever was in Shakuntala's mind, that person would not remember her even when reminded, just as a drunkard cannot remember his own words when he becomes sober."

The Vishnu Purana narrates how Durvasa was responsible for the memorable episode of the churning of the ocean. [I have referred to another version of this story earlier.] It is said that once while taking a stroll, Durvasa saw a pretty woman with a beautiful garland. He wanted it, and she gave it to him. As he walked further, he encountered Indra riding on his magical elephant Airávata. Durvasa flung the garland at Indra as a gift. The latter found it to be so beautiful that he placed it on the elephant's head. The elephant wanted to experience the fragrance, and curled his trunk to the head. In the process, the garland fell to the ground. Durvasa became furious, and he hurled a curse on Indra to the effect that Lakshmi would quit his realm. And she did. This led to such disasters that the evil ones (asuras) began to assault the good ones (devas). The latter appealed to Vishnu for help. It was then that the plan for the churning of the ocean was hatched, using Mount Mandara as spindle and the snake Vásuki for churning.

In the Shakuntala story Durvasa went for a visit; and in the Indra story he was paying his respects. In a third episode, he was himself the honored guest. Lord Krishna once invited the rishi for a hearty meal. The rishi was treated to a sumptuous dinner with great regard and reverence. However, some grains of rice were not appropriately cleared after the meal, and Durvasa's rage came to the fore on account of this omission. He spelled out another of his memorable curses: that Krishna be killed by his enemy.

Durvasa also appears in the Ramayana. In the Uttara Kanda he becomes furious with Lakshmana because the latter did not give him immediate entry to see Rama. He said, "I will curse you, this kingdom, Bharata and the descendants of Rama… I cannot withhold my anger any further." Rama heard this threat, and he came out immediately. He asked the rishi what he wanted. Rishi Durvasa spoke respectfully to Rama and said that his thousand years of fasting was coming to an end that day. Therefore he wanted some food to eat. Thereupon the rishi was given a sumptuous feast. He ate to his satisfaction and moved away from the scene (Valmiki: Uttara Kanda, 105).

It may be difficult for us, in this day and age, to understand the significance of such extreme reactions to relatively innocuous misbehavior, if it was that. Perhaps these episodes suggest an important aspect of the mores of the time. Spiritual wisdom and asceticism were always held in the highest esteem. Ritualistic subservience and reverential gestures towards the sages were mandatory codes of behavior. The rishis came to expect these from everybody, including even the gods. Stories such as these served to bring home this point to the common folk in no uncertain terms. Moreover, by portraying characters like Durvasa in the popular literature, the ascetics ensured for themselves the trembling prostration from the common people: attitude and behavior that persist to this day in the Hindu world.

On the other hand, Durvasa Rishi was also generous to people who treated him with respect. One such beneficiary was Kunti. He taught her the mantra by which she could summon any of the celestials to bear her a child (Ádi Parva, 67).

This trait may be seen even today in some globe-trotting swamis of our own times. Some of them regard impatience as a god-man's prerogative, if not a virtue. In spite of their enormous learning and Vedic wisdom, quite a few rishis are known to have been rather short tempered. Once I asked privately a swamiji I happened to know why he was quick to get angry in assemblies where people were respectful of him. He told me that this was important to maintain the high pedestal in which he was held.

Fear and respect often go together, he explained. He might have a point. It became clear to me why in religious frameworks God is feared as much as respected.

Jamadagni Rishi and Parashuráma

The world of the Puranas is filled with magic and wonder. It has beings not of this world and rishis with complex genealogies. So it was with rishi Jamadagni, born to Satyavati, wife of the Brahmin Richika who was none other than the son of the great Bhrigu. The descendents of Bhrigu are said to be the Bhargavas of today.

It is said that Bhrigu presented Satyavati with a magical potion in two pots, and asked her to share one of them with her mother. The two ladies were instructed to take them, each one after embracing a different tree: the mother was to embrace a peepal, and the daughter, a fig tree. As happens in stories of mistaken identities, the ladies confused their respective assignments, and drank from the wrong cups too. So this became an error in birth-traits. For, as a result of the mistake, Satyavati was to give birth to a Brahmin child with Kshatriya disposition, and her mother was to bear a Kshatriya child with Brahminical longings. Satyavati begged of Bhrigu not to let this happen to her son; she would let her grandson be such. Bhrigu granted this wish.

The child thus born to Satyavati became the rishi Jamadagni who dedicated his life to the study of the Vedas. He led an ethical life, and at one point decided to get married. He found in Renuka, daughter of King Prasenajit, a suitable bride. In due course the couple had five sons: Rumanván, Sushena, Vasu, Vishvavasu, and Ráma (Vana Parva, 115).

At one time, Jamadagni milked his cow and kept the milk safe in a new vessel, with the intention of using it in a ritual. The deity Dharma came in disguise and spoiled the milk. Jamadagni remained unperturbed. Then Dharma took on the form of a Brahmin woman who presented herself to Jamadagni. The rishi was calm and collected, whereupon Dharma revealed himself and said that Jamadagni had given the lie to the common saying that Bhargavas were generally wrathful people.

One day when Renuka was returning from a bath in the river, she happened to see the handsome prince Chitraratha, barely clad, sporting in the waters with his lovely wives. This planted desires of a sexual nature in the heart of the Rishi's wife. [The original text describes the erotic effect on her explicit terms.] When she returned to the hermitage, guilt-ridden, the rishi detected that the luster of chastity was no longer there in her face. Enraged in true rishi-fashion, he wanted her to die. When his sons came home, he ordered them to execute their mother. All the first four shuddered at the thought of doing such a thing. For their disobedient inaction Jamadagni cursed every one of them to lose their mental faculties. But Rama, the fifth son, obeyed his father without a question. With his axe (*parashu*) he promptly severed Renuka's head. Highly pleased, the spiritual Jamadagni was now ready to grant this Parashurama anything and everything he would wish. The young man's first request was to get his mother back to life. Then he wanted his mind to forget forever the cruel act he had committed, and to be forgiven for the horrendous sin of matricide. He also wanted his brothers' sanity to be restituted. Jamadagni granted all these wishes.

Once, Arjuna, not the Pandava, but son of a king by the name of Kartavirya, stopped at Jamadagni's hermitage. Here he was well received, and his entourage was well fed. But the greedy prince wanted the principal cow in the shed. When this was refused, he and his men carried away the cow by force. When Parashurama discovered this he became enraged beyond control, and in his fury he summarily killed this plundering prince and his whole battalion. Angered by this, other men of Arjuna's army came to Jamadagni's hermitage and slaughtered the helpless rishi Jamadagni. Parashurama took an extraordinary revenge for this terrible act. He swore to exterminate all Kshatriyas on earth; indeed, he is said to have accomplished this several times over (Vána Parva, 116).

In Valmiki's Ramayana, however, when Parashurama challenges prince Rama and his party after the royal weddings, Parashurama is made to look small by the glorious Rama. In Tulsidas's version, Parashurama appears in Janaka's court to compete for Sita's hand. His angry look frightens everybody. To use Shakespeare's words, he displayed

The flash and outbreak of a fiery mind

A savageness in unreclaimed blood.

In Tulsidas's version, Parashuráma addressed Sita's father as stupid Janaka and asked him who it was that broke Shiva's bow (269:3): *kahu jada janak dhanush kai torá?* That person would be Parashurama's enemy. Sita's mother was terrified. To the frightened Sita, a mere half instant seemed like an eon: *aradh nimish kalpasama bítá.*

In historical terms, it is quite possible that the Brahmin Parashurama was one of the older, highly skilled and valiant contenders for Sita's hand who felt intensely jealous that young Rama had so easily won the contest. To satisfy his ego or to recuperate the honor he had lost by his defeat, he probably challenged Rama to contest. There are glimmers of true history hidden beneath the lines of our epics and Puranas.

Rishi Vasishtha

Another illustrious author of the Vedas and member of the Saptarshi constellation is Vasishtha, one of the greatest of classical rishis. His life and exploits suggest that he played a role in establishing the superiority of Brahmins in the Hindu social structure. As per Rig Vedic mythic visions (VII.33) this eminent personage was born of the Vedic deities Varuna and Mitra when they were aroused by the sight of the apsara Urvashi. The Mahabharata (Adi Parva: 176) describes Vasishtha as a mind-born son of Brahma and husband of Arundhati. He is perhaps the only great sage to be introduced through the wife's name.

Many monarchs performed important sacrifices with him as their family priest. The Vishnu Purana recounts that King Nimi once requested Vasishtha to be chief priest at a sacrifice. The event was to last a thousand years. Vasishtha told the king he regretted that he had prior commitments for the next five hundred years, but that he would come back after that to serve in the project. But upon his return he discovered to his disappointment that Nimi had offered the position of chief priest to Rishi Gautama. Vasishtha took this as a severe slap on the face, and cursed the king to become disembodied. Nimi, who possessed imprecating powers himself, retorted with the same curse. Losing his physical frame, Vasishtha entered the Vedic deities Mitra and Varuna, only to regain corporeality via Urvashi.

In another episode Vasishtha goes to Ayodhya, a city full of happy people. Dasharatha was not ruling at this time. After the rishi came into the palace, at the command of the reigning king, the queen united with the rishi. The rishi then returned to his hermitage. Many years after conception, a child was born to the queen. Her name was Ashmaka (Vishnu Purana: IV.4, MB: Adi Parva, 179).

It is said that Vasishtha had another hundred sons, the oldest of whom was called Shakti. One day while Shakti was walking along a path, King Kalmashapada came from the opposite direction. The king ordered the eminent rishi's son to move out of his way. Shakti said it was against the dharmashástra for a Brahmana to give way to a Kshatriya. An argument ensued as to who had the right of way. The king claimed priority on the basis of his power, the rishi's son on the basis of principle (Adi Parva, 176).

The angry king whipped Shakti. And Shakti cursed the arrogant king to become a cannibalistic rakshasa. When the curse took effect, not one, but all of the hundred sons of Vasishtha were devoured by the king-turned-cannibal.

Vasishtha had conquered ire and desire: sign of spiritual attainment in the Hindu framework. Generally, he kept his cool under the most trying circumstances. But this was news which even the great rishi could not accept with equanimity. He decided to commit suicide. He climbed to the top of Mount Meru, and took a plunge from there to the hard ground below. But the rocks where his head struck had become cotton cushions. Then he went into a forest that was ablaze, only to emerge unscathed by his passage through the flames. He bound his limbs with a sturdy rope and plunged into a swelling river, but the torrents flung him back to the bank. Next he repeated this attempt at suicide by leaping into waters infested with alligators. But the waves threw the rishi back again on terra firma. That was the end of Vasishtha's attempts to put an end to himself. Moral of the story: One destined to serve the world cannot scheme a premature death.

Perhaps we may interpret these episodes to mean that in spite of attempts to eradicate Brahminical power by others, and even when the Brahmins themselves tried to recede from their dominance in society, they have always continued to play a major role in the Hindu world, i.e. they could not and cannot be erased from Hindu culture.

In the Mahabharata there are some chapters (Anusasana Parva) where Vasishtha gives a long discourse on the qualities and significance of the cow. He describes cows as being always fragrant. They are the very source of all prosperity. They constitute the highest food. They are the best oblation for the deities. He recommends the recitation of the cow's name in morning and evening. He says that one should never feel repugnance for the cow's urine or dung. He assures us that great merit would follow those who generously give cattle as gifts. If the cow is treated with great reverence in the Hindu world, episodes like this from the epics have played no small role in establishing and fostering that sanctity.

The Puranas are not unanimous regarding the identity of Vasishtha's spouse. The Vishnu Purana says it was Urja, a daughter of Daksha. The Rishi is said to have had seven sons through her. On the other hand, the Bhagavata Purana informs us that it was Arundhati who was Vasishtha's wife. According to a story in the Mahabharata, six of the Saptarshi once abandoned their wives, all except Vasishtha. One of the stars of the Pleiades is referred to as Arundhati.

Rishi Vishvamitra (Vishvámitra)

Many ancient cultures worshiped the sun: as Shamash, Tai-Yang-King, Ré (or Ra), Sól, Helios, Súrya, and so on. But there is hardly another invocation to the sun that is held in greater reverence than the Gayatri (Gáyatri) mantra in Hindu culture. It occurs in the Rig Veda (III.62.20), reminding us that the roots of the tradition lie deep in those sacred hymns. The Gayatri is one of the earliest recognitions of the relevance of the sun, not just for physical life, but also for intelligence and awareness. It says:

    auṃ bhúr bhuvaḥ svaḥ
    tat savitur vareṇyaṃ
    bhargo devasya dhīmahi
    dhiyo yo naḥ pracodayát

In Griffith's literal translation it is as follows:

    May we attain that excellent glory of Savitar the god:
    So may he stimulate our prayers.

No translation of the serene Sanskrit in which sage-poets had uttered immortal lines can do justice to the prayerful posture and potency of any mantra, least of all the Gayatri. Nevertheless, we cannot let that precious gem of the tradition lie opaque in that esoteric tongue. So my own non-literal transcreation of the Gayatri is:

    May we achieve radiance
    Like the effulgent Sun!
    May the Sun inspire and bring light to
    All our thoughts!

The sage-poet who articulated the Gayatri mantra was one of the keenest minds in history. The authorship of the Gayatri—the jewel of sacred utterances to which every dvija is initiated early in life—is attributed to the illustrious Rishi Vishvamitra. The cultural complex we call Hinduism is rich in ironies. Some scholars have suggested that this rishi was a shudra, though this is not so according to the lore. But it really shouldn't matter. People from every strata of society have contributed to the treasures of Hindu culture in a variety of ways.

Vishvamitra—whether the traits and legends attributed to him are historical or mythological—was a most extraordinary personage. He has been described as the Rishi of Rishis. Indeed, his life, as told in the epics and the Puranas, embodies everything we may expect of an eminent rishi: He was a sage of great self-discipline, austere and given to long periods of penance, yet virile and susceptible to feminine charms, a least once. He was demanding, impatient, and adamant. Most of all, he was a scholar, poet, and deeply versed in sacred history.

Vishvamitra's sacred sacrifices were once interrupted by some demonic beings: perhaps by some tribal people who found it all to be exotic. He went to King Dasharatha and asked for Rama's assistance to rid himself of the intruders. The king hesitated, and the rishi became furious. Vasishtha, Dasharatha's spiritual counselor, advised the king to consent to the request. Rama and Lakshmana then went on to exterminate the miscreants. During this expedition, Vishvamitra taught the two brothers many things of local history (Valmiki: Balakanda, XIX *et seq.*).

Vishvamitra was Vasishtha's rival, because the latter was a brahmin, and Vishvamitra had a kshatriya lineage. His kshatriya birth happened because of an error to which reference was made earlier. Satyavati had mistakenly exchanged with her mother the magic potion that was to bring forth a Brahmin child. The mother was married to Gádhi who was a kshatriya. It was thus that Vishvamitra became a kshatriya since, in practice, caste is patrilineal.

Vishvamitra's non-brahminhood tormented him for millennia. This tension reflects a profound truth. In any society, those who are regarded as inferior—by law, convention, color of skin, or whatever—will always harbor deep resentment towards those who have a higher status. The resentment sometimes finds expression in acute ways, often by affirming one's own strength in thought, word, and deed, and in whatever other manner vis-à-vis the more powerful one.

Consider the momentous episode in which, at a time when he was a powerful king, Vishvamitra paid a visit to Vasishtha (Valmiki: Balakanda, LI *et seq.*). He was received with respect and hospitality. His entire retinue was treated to a sumptuous feast at Vasishtha's hermitage. The rich food came from the wondrous cow Sabala (a.k.a. Kamadhenu) which was a cornucopia of limitless nourishment. Vishvamitra wanted the animal for himself and promised any price for it. But Vasishtha refused. Whereupon Vishvamitra used the might of his army, summoning his hundred sons to cownap Kamadhenu. The magical animal engendered its own army. There ensued a brutal battle, at the end of which Vishvamitra's men were burnt to thin ash. The moral of the story: Material might is no match for spiritual power. Vishvamitra famously exclaimed, "*dhik, kshatriya balam, brahma-tejo balam balam!* (Fie the strength of the warrior class! It is spiritual strength that is real strength!)"

In the Markandeya Purana version of the Harischandra episode, Vasishtha cursed Vishvamitra to become a crane, and the latter was quick to retort with a similar curse. The two ornithoid rishis went at each other with earth-shaking fury until Brahma intervened and brought them back to human forms.

By intense penance, after centuries of silence, prolonged standing on one foot, months of fasting during which his body became like a strip of rotten wood, the sage finally attained the much-coveted status of Brahmarshi.

In the course of these awesome austerities he chanced to see the Apsara Menaka wading in the Pushkara Lake (Valmiki: Balakanda, LXIII). Enchanted by her physical beauty, the sage welcomed her to his hermitage and asked her to stay with him. Menaka agreed and subtly hindered his spiritual efforts. He spent ten years, enthralled in Menaka's company, before realizing what an impediment she had been to his loftier pursuits. The episode is to remind us that all the rock-like rigidity acquired by a thousand austere years can melt away when the raw fire of lust is lit. In the meanwhile, to Menaka was born Shakuntala, another beautiful heroine of Hindu lore. She was the mother of Bharata whose name is etched in the great epic and in modern India's name. Who can erase this link!

The Ramayana and the Mahabharata, the Vedas, the Brahmanda Purana, the Kalika Purana, all refer to this great Rishi, known as much for his wisdom and enormous learning as for his austerities and quick temper. Here was a hero of Vedic and puranic lore, a pillar of the Hindu world, a majestic representative of ancient Vedic culture, a rishi and name that will live forever in the cultural-spiritual core of the Hindu world for as long as the religion lives.

And yet, as with so many precious elements in the Hindu world, so little is known of historical reliability about this shining personage: where and when he was born, where he lived and died, who his descendents now are, etc.

Patañjali

The Hindu world has contributed much of significance to humanity's cultural, spiritual, and intellectual heritage. Aside from the insightful recognition of zero in computational analysis, the scientific study of human speech and syntax, inspiring hymns and grand poetry, Hindus were perhaps the first to elaborate the grand view of human consciousness as a spark of a Cosmic substratum. This is a liberating vision in itself. What is more, this was not formulated simply as a speculative hypothesis or metaphorical musing, but as an empirically verifiable aspect of

Man-Universe relationship. That empirical component of the spirituality-thesis constitutes the yoga system which has spread from India to all over the world.

The yoga system is the fruit of the most ancient exploration of inquiring humans into mind and consciousness. The epoch and place of its discovery are lost, like much of our precious past, in the mist of unrecorded events and fascinating tales of fantasy. But we do have a work attributed to an ancient rishi, which consists of succinct aphorisms on the underlying concepts of yoga. The name of that illustrious rishi is Patañjali, and his work is called *Yoga Sutra*.

The term yoga already occurs in the Rig Veda, meaning such things as yoking, harnessing, achieving the unachieved, and connection. In Vedic times austerities and celibacy, especially at certain stages in life, came to be regarded as virtues worth cultivating. The comparison of the senses to horses that need to be controlled by the horseman to reach a destination gained currency in ancient India. After the philosophical system of Samkhya was formulated, the yoga system became its empirical wing.

Without going into the details of the theory of yoga, we may say this: By following certain spiritual disciplines (sádhana), generally under the guidance of a spiritual master (guru), it is possible to attain significant control over the physical body and reach higher levels of consciousness. The physical exercises, as elaborated in texts and by practitioners of later eras, range from simple cross-legged squatting to contortions of limbs and control of the abdomen in strenuous and incredible ways. The associated spiritual exercises vary from mental repetition of specific mantras to concentration and meditation of the most sophisticated kinds.

Patañjali's *Yogasútra* is a slender volume, consisting of some 194 terse aphorisms, distributed over three principal chapters and a fourth one that seems to be appended to the three. It reads like a handbook for practitioners rather than a philosophical treatise or prescriptive manual. The first chapter deals with deep meditation (*samádhi*). The second explores the technique of yoga (*sádhana*). The third deals with the powers one obtains from yogic practice (*vibhúti*). And the last appended chapter deals with spiritual liberation (*kaivalya*). It also contains some criticisms of the Buddhist school.

Like other major works of the tradition, the Yogasutra has received many canonical commentaries, of which the one by the great Vyasa is the most prestigious. This author again is semi-legendary in that the Brahmashástras, all the Puranas and Upapuranas, as well as the Mahabharata are attributed to him. This is the equivalent of saying that all the articles in the Encyclopedia Britannica were authored by a single individual named *Arranger*.

Patañjali's classic is one of the most influential works in all of human history, though it is seldom recognized as such. It has inspired countless gurus all over India and beyond over many generations, and its fundamental theses have been expounded and elaborated by thousands of preachers and practitioners. Some of the yoga that permeated the world through marketing efforts is genuine, and some of it is spurious, some simple and others complex. But in countless instances, yoga has been found to be useful, powerful, and elevating to young students and adults, to royalty and rishis, to sports-people and housewives, and to many more. That it is efficacious is of little doubt, and its effectiveness is still a matter for scientific investigation.

According to the Tamil saint-poet Tirumular, Patañjali and he himself were instructed on the yoga along with six others by a certain Nandi Deva:

> Nandi arulpetra Nádarai Nádinom
> Nandigal Nálvar Siva Yoga Mámuni

> Mandru thozhuda Patañjali Vyakramar
> Endrivar Ennódu (Thirumoolar) Enmarumáme
> (Tirumantiram, 1)
> English translation
> We sought the feet of the Lord, blessed by Nandi.
> The four Nandis, the great Sivayoga Muni, Patañjali,
> Vyakramar and
> I (Tirumúlar) were thus eight in all.

In Hindu cultural legacy there are at least two major Patañjalis, but some scholars have maintained the two to be one and the same. The Patañjali of Yogasutra is believed to have lived in the second century CE. The other Patañjali, probably more ancient, is remembered for his great commentaries (*Mahabháshya*) on Panini's grammatical treatise. Legend has it that he fell (*pata*) as a serpent in the palm (*añjali*) of the great grammarian himself, and thus acquired his name. Fascinating, though dubious, etymology indeed!

When I was about thirteen years of age, a swamiji from the Divine Life Society in Rishikesh came to our home in Calcutta briefly. He initiated a number of us youngsters into the basic of yoga, especially pranayama (alternate inhaling and exhaling), padmasana during meditation, and shirasasana. He also initiated me to a special mantra. I practiced these regularly for about six months. Then one day, I decided to modify what I had been taught. Immediately upon waking up in the morning I began to spend just five minutes focusing on some number between one and a thousand. At the end of it I resolved explicitly each morning to show some act of kindness or say a word of affection to someone during the day, and also try to make at least one person smile. For more than seventy years now I have been practicing this every day with reasonable success.

Yájñavalkya

Rig Vedic rishis were not the only ones to receive esoteric revelation. The Shatapata Brahmana, for example, was revealed to Rishi Yájñavalkya. This work is appended to what is known as Shukla Yajus (White Yajur Veda). The Yajur Veda contains the rules and rites of rituals, and continues to play a role in Hindu sacraments. The Brihadaranyaka Upanishad, which is considered to be the most important Upanishad, is part of Shatapatha Brahmana, and thus owes its origins to Yájñavalkya also. Its middle section is known as Yájñavalkya.

In this part (Chapters III and IV of the BU) there is a dialogue between Yájñavalkya and Maitreyí: one of his two wives. This exchange is a classic passage in Hindu philosophical literature. When he offers half his estate to this wife before retiring to the forest, the keen Maitreyi asks her husband if she would attain immortality were she to possess all the wealth in the entire world. "No," replies the wise man, "there is no hope of immortality through wealth," reminding us of the Biblical line (Matthew: 19:24): "It is easier for a camel to go through the eye of a needle than for a rich man to enter the kingdom of heaven." Now the wife asks the sage to talk to her about immortality, and he is immensely pleased by this request. Then follows a discourse on the psychology of desire and its relation to the spiritual quest. Essentially the rishi says that whatever is dear to us whether husband or wife or children, whether wealth or brahminhood or kshatriyahood, the worlds or the gods or other beings, it is dear only for the sake of the átman (Self). For this reason it is important to understand what that atman is. That is why spiritual pursuit becomes primary in human life. Aside from the metaphysical-psychological question explored, this is a beautiful example of a healthy conversation between husband and wife on a serious issue.

Yájñavalkya is said to have served as high-priest at a sacrifice conducted by King Janaka (father of Sita?). Once he went to visit Janaka, and the king asked if the learned man had come there to get cows as gifts or to explore subtle matters. The rishi said, "For both, Oh King!" Then followed a series of questions and answers on the nature of Brahman, as taught by a previous teacher, and as modified by Yajñavalkya. They talked about speech, breath, sight, truth and more. The importance of speech in the oral tradition is beautifully expressed by Yajñavalkya thus: "It is through speech (uttered words) that one recognizes a friend, that one comes to know about anything: Vedas, history, lore, arts, esoteric knowledge, poetry, aphorisms, explanations, sacrifices, oblations, food, drink, this world and everything."

It is during this exchange that the Upanishadic *neti-neti*: not this, not that about the Divine is uttered. For, explains Yájñavalkya here, Brahman is inscrutable, imperishable, unattached, unchained, and immune to pain and injury. (This corresponds to the apophatic theology in Christianity where God is described in terms of what he is not.) Some of the most fundamental doctrines of the Hindu world are uttered by Yájñavalkya in the Upanishads.

Uddálaka Áruni was another major thinker of the Upanishadic age. We learn from the Bhrihadaranyaka Upanishad that Yájñavalkya was his student.

In another passage of this Upanishad, Gárgi, an illustrious woman philosopher, poses two questions about Ultimate Reality to the sage, to which he gives profound answers. In this context he says: "That which is above the sky, beneath the earth, between these two, which people call the past, the present, and the future, across space is that which is woven like warp and woof.

That is *aksharam*: the imperishable." This passage is remarkable in that here, as nowhere else in ancient thought, we find an intermingling of space and time into a single structure, such as we find only in twentieth century (Einsteinian-Minkowskian) physics. Furthermore, he describes this space-time continuum as imperishable: Brahman.

We know about this great scholar-mystic-sage also from the Mahabharata (Shanti Parva, 316) where he recounts his own experiences in which deities like Surya and Sarasvati appeared before him and gave him supreme knowledge.

Yájñavalkya is known to have been unsympathetic to Brahminical rituals and fee-mongering. Rather than pray for gold and cow, they should be asking for enlightenment, he is said to have remarked. The great seer once quarreled with his master Vaisampáyana who demanded that he return the knowledge which he had gathered from him. Thereupon Yájñavalkya is said to have spit out that knowledge. It is said in the lore that it was then that he did the austerities for which Surya and Sarasvati blessed him with the knowledge of the White Yajus.

In one of his many speeches, Yájñavalkya declared: "Liberation comes from knowledge.... Obtaining knowledge from a brahmin or a kshatriya or a vaishya or even a shudra, a person with faith must always show reverence for knowledge.... All orders of men are brahmins. All have sprung from Brahma. Everyone utters his name.... Everyone should seek to acquire knowledge.... Everyone is entitled to strive for its acquisition." Yájñavalkya was clearly one of the enlightened thinkers in a caste-framed society. But few defenders of orthodoxy quote him on this. It is unfortunate that even a thinker of that eminence could not bring about a casteless society. Such is the power of traditional religious establishment.

Concluding thoughts

There have been, and still are, countless rishis in India's long and rich history: every serious thinker who devotes his or her life to meditation and quest for knowledge of the Ultimate is a rishi. In the conceptual framework of the tradition many of them were superhuman personages who trod the soil of India and accomplished incredible things. They have had their spiritual cousins in other cultures as well. Though they are sometimes pictured as supernatural spirits that come and go in our midst, not unlike angels in other traditions, the historical fact remains that rishis in human frames have left behind a vast corpus of poetry and philosophy and anecdotal history. These authors may not have been ethereal beings who could fly, who had extra-terrestrial origins, or who wrote a hundred pages in an hour. It is difficult for people who are constrained by logic and reason to grant that those who composed the magnificent verses and engaged in sublime thoughts were the fantastic creatures reported in sacred history.

It is difficult to ignore the fact that our distant ancestors, with all their impressive achievements in thought and spirituality, in poetry and philosophy, were not meticulous record-keepers or biographers. Yet, what is impressive is that they had come up with the idea of a Chitragupta, a dossier-keeper *par excellence*. In any event, we are now left with countless classic works with attributed authors, but very few names with which definite dates and places can be associated. Valmiki and Vyasa, Vishvamitra and Vasishtha, Tirumular and Tiruvalluvar surely lived in flesh and blood at some time in some place within India, though we have lost all knowledge of the place and time of their lives.

We have to be content with the legendary narratives on them: history by no means, but interesting all the same.

There is no question but that the rishis of India are the ones who constructed the skeletal framework on which Indic culture has blossoms. But it is equally important that new rishis emerge. These rishis will not be simply scholars, rote repeaters and pious interpreters of ancestral visions, but original thinkers, critical analysts, bold formulators of new visions, and discoverers of hitherto unknown aspects of the world. Paying homage to the past is essential for the sanity of peoples. Charting new paths for the future is no less important for keeping a culture and civilization alert and alive.

IX

On the Past and the Future

Although the standard position within Hinduism doubtless equates Shruti with revelation and smriti with tradition, virtually every phase of the history of Hinduism provides some evidence that the term revelation was either actually or tentatively extended to include what we call tradition. The earliest piece of evidence comes from the Upanishads themselves, wherein no distinction is drawn between the Vedas and the Ithihasas, Puranas and so on, ...

- Arvind Sharma

Paradigm Shift in Perspectives

The above paradigm served the culture well for over a millennium, ensuring its stability, continuity, and security over the ages.

In the modern age, a reverse paradigm is trying to assert itself. Here, even shruti (revealed knowledge) is transformed into smriti (tradition). This prompts one to reflect on both shruti and smriti in non-religious, but no less respectful and fulfilling modes.

Music and dance, festivals and poetry, and other aesthetic dimensions continue to be celebrated and enriched in their classical modes, each generation adding newer elements to these. At the same time, a growing number of Hindus, both within India and beyond who are deeply connected to their culture and religion, have also been affected in profound ways by worldviews and values that have emerged as a result of modern science and technology.

Traditionalists mistakenly regard all changes in outlook as corruption caused by the West. They don't realize that Western civilization itself has been drastically affected by these very forces that have arisen from humanity's expanding knowledge about the physical, biological, and psychological world. Indeed, everyone has been affected both positively and negatively by the revolutionary discoveries of modern science to which countless people from every race and religion and nationality are creatively contributing today.

There are overt conflicts between nations and religions for sure, but it is not as universally recognized that intense tugs of war are raging within all dynamic cultures and religious frameworks between those who resist newer, more relevant, and more meaningful approaches to scriptures, traditions, and belief-systems, and those who ride with the times and themselves add to the evolving transformations that are inevitable in living systems, be they biological, cultural, or religious. In this context, traditionalists serve to preserve the best of the past, but sometimes also the worst; the new wave brings in fresh air and awakening, but it also tends to eradicate many worthy aspects of received wisdom. This is a global phenomenon.

Difficulty in the new paradigm

In the collective consciousness of the traditional framework Rama and Krishna are not simply protagonists in two epics: They are divine incarnations we pray to in sacred centers. We chant their praises in beautiful hymns and celebrate their birthdays with feast and frolic. We repeat their names in devotional meditation, and yes, in our greetings also. Rama is the ideal of the ethical man, and Krishna through the Gita is the fount of divine wisdom, the voice of the Transcendent. The names and images of all our deities bring meaning and majesty to the culture. There is the danger that they might be turned to charismatic castles in the air if we switch from religious to rational modes, from the spiritual to the secular framework. This is a troubling possibility in all traditional religious frameworks.

But it is difficult to escape the fact that when one puts on rationalistic goggles to view the sacred in scholarly terms, revered names turn from historic verities to characters in moving narratives. However, in no matter what paradigm, if one is culturally conditioned, responses to the names and images of Rama and Krishna, Ganesha and Murugan, Sarasvati and Sita will not be affected. The point to remember is that one can respect traditional approaches in some contexts, even while adopting a different mode in other contexts.

The choice and a new approach: cognitive bisonance

The conquests of the mind in matters spiritual tend to upset the ecstasy engendered by deep faith. An impeccable proof to the effect that in moments of emotional turmoil no Almighty God lovingly holds a protective hand over our heads could torment us psychologically.

Whether one should accept the persuasive evidence of facts and the logic of reasoned arguments, or respond to the tantalizing call of faith that promises psychological security and spiritual delights is the delicate dilemma that many face. Some make a decisive choice, and having done this, plead for their own preference as the right one to make. Wisdom probably lies in recognizing that there is no such thing as right or wrong choice in this matter because one is as human as the other.

The tension between scholarship and tradition is a cultural manifestation of the perennial conflict between the head and the heart. I have elaborated on this in my book *Truth and Tension in Science and Religion*. In practically every society touched by civilization and scholarship, by joy in the heart and reflection in the mind, the behavior and beliefs of traditionalists have been challenged by skeptical and inquiring minds. Such efforts often result in newer insights and understandings.

We may see in this dichotomy of human inclinations an illustration of what twentieth century physics called the *principle of complementarity* (Bohr, 1958), by which ultimate reality is recognized as consisting of apparently contradictory, but in fact mutually complementing features of perceived reality. In this view, there are two kinds of truths, small and great ones. A small truth is one whose contrary is clearly false. That milk is white is a small truth, because to say that milk is black is clearly wrong. But a great truth is one whose contrary is no less valid. To say that religions have done much good is as true a statement as that religions have done much harm.

Long before the wave-particle duality of modern physics, ancient Indian (Jain) insight had spoken of *anekánta váda* which recognized the complexity of profound problems and the multiple aspects of higher truths by stating that our view on a question will depend on the perspective from which we approach it. The grasp of a single Ultimate Truth by a single human mind is simply impossible. This is an enlightened synthesis of modesty and wisdom.

As long as we are experiencing one side of a coin, we can never appreciate the fullness of the other. But it would be a grave error to imagine that the coin has only one side. For the analytical scholar to maintain that the spiritual dimension is without significance would be as partial a vision as that of the religious devotee who does not wake up to the fact that bhajans, like namaz and the Lord's Prayer, are only enriching instruments for experiencing the Unfathomable Beyond that have evolved over the ages in different cultures.

It is to be noted that even while viewing matters from historical, and analytical perspectives, one can have reverence for traditional names, icons, and principles. One can also feel within oneself piety and home-grown humility when one hears bhajans or prostrates to icons of the Divine. Rather than cognitive dissonance, one can develop *cognitive bisonance* that enables the co-existence of spiritual responses in the heart and intellectual appreciation of the treasures of the tradition on the other. One can still experience an inner peace when one recites the shlokas of the tradition while being enlightened by a rational understanding of the sacred works as creations of great sage-poets. It is not unlike experiencing the sweetness of a candy while knowing the chemical composition of sucrose as $C_{12}H_{22}O_{11}$.

Uncertain doctrines

There are some doctrines in the Hindu world, as in other religious frameworks, whose ontological validity some people who resonate with modern science find difficult to accept. These relate to cosmogenesis, post-mortem states, and eschatology.

There is no problem imagining Brahma as a poetic metaphor for whatever gave rise to the Cosmos. One can envisage Vishnu as the totality of the physical laws that enable the world to function the way it does as also the biochemical balances that sustain life. One can also envision a principle that will ultimately heave a final sigh on all existence, and designate it as Shiva. But it is not easy for all to regard these as gods who need to be periodically propitiated with floral offerings, fruits and colorful fanfare in temples, except for the aesthetic-cultural joy they bring. Much less can they take seriously sectarian squabbles emerging from puranic tales.

Then again, some Hindus are ambivalent about the doctrine of karma. The notion that our current status is the result of previous actions on our part is an insightful way of considering the human condition. It is certainly as reasonable an explanation as any for the uneven distribution of good and ill fortunes in the world. It is also a wiser approach to difficult predicaments than pointing the finger at a God who sometimes does seem to be without mercy. Karma is also an incentive for behaving properly in order to ensure a better future, in this birth and in the next. At the same time belief in karma should not condemn the less fortunate as deserving victims of past misbehavior.

In the constrained framework of rationality, not all can accept whole-heartedly the associated thesis of reincarnation. To the question, "Do you believe in re-incarnation," some Hindus might say, "Perhaps I did in a previous incarnation, but not in the present one."

Existential Angst and some consequences

It is no secret that in the messed up world in which we live, few people or nations feel safe and secure. Terrorist attacks, new epidemics, possible collapse of financial systems, drastic changes in weather patterns and more are lurking in the background of our conscious existence.

In the midst of all this, there is a growing fear in the hearts of many Hindus that our religion is being attacked by others, that it is ill-understood and intentionally distorted by scheming outsiders who bear ill-will towards us, and that there are forces afoot to destroy Hinduism. To add to all this, the religion is being callously ignored and even decried by many of our own. At the same time, quite a few Hindus are also convinced that such fears result from exaggerated renditions of reality.

It is true that there are pronouncements on Hinduism by Non-Hindu scholars that seem to display only superficial or even mistaken understandings of the many elements of Hinduism (Ramaswamy et al., 2007). There are authors seem to intentionally present Hindu culture in negative light. Often such writings result from a lack of experiential empathy with the practitioners of the religion. Then again, the rise of extremist Islam on the world scene has had some unhappy impact within India, as it has had in many Islamic countries no less. Christian missionaries and Islamic proselytizers have been successful in drawing away large numbers of (disenfranchised) Hindus into their folds.

Then again, many Westernized Hindu youths and intellectuals tend to discard or ignore, if not trivialize aspects of their culture.

All this has made many normally tolerant Hindus uncomfortable, not to say nervous. And led to intense frustration in the hearts of a growing number of them vis-à-vis the preservation of our culture and religion within Hinduism's own land.

In theory, secularism is an enlightened format in which practitioners of all religions, as also non-believers, secular humanists, atheists, etc. are guaranteed equal rights and respect in a democratic country, and every citizen is subject to the same statutory laws. Many Hindus have been feeling for a long time that this principle is not strictly followed in India, that things are often to their disadvantage. There are provisions in the Indian Constitution which strike them as more favorable to Non-Hindus.

Furthermore, when religious thinkers speak for their heritage, secular Hindus and the media often disparage them with unsavory epithets, while the same secularists rarely engage in such language when referring to other religions in the country. Whether true or exaggerated, such perceptions are among the root causes of what is referred to as Hindu fundamentalism, has resulted in the bad name that secularism has acquired among many Hindus. [The situation is not unlike in the United States where the skewed positions of many liberal thinkers have made liberalism a bad word there.]

Some of the feelings of insecurity that Hindus are feeling are genuine and justified. Today, a growing number of Europeans feel that their culture is on the verge of being displaced from its local habitat. Not all of them are not paranoid or racist, many are realistic and patriotic. So it is with millions of reflecting Hindus in India.

The so-called Hindutva movement (which I would rather term *Bháratva*), though associated with Indian politics, is essentially a collective effort on the part of Hindus devoted to their culture to affirm and reclaim the roots of Indic civilization within India. India is as much Hindu/Jain/Sikh/Buddhist in its cultural roots as the West is largely Christian, China is Confucian, Japan is Shinto and Buddhist, Israel is Judaic, and nations like

Iran, Saudi Arabia, Indonesia, Malaysia, Pakistan, and Turkey are Islamic. This in no way implies that Muslims, Christians, Jews, Parsees, Baha'is, atheists and others shouldn't enjoy equal rights under the secular laws of India. But denying that Indic culture has been shaped and nourished for three millennia and more by Vedic visions, Upanishadic worldviews, Tamil spiritual poetry, and their offspring would be a reckless disregard for and offensive repudiation of India's deep history.

Cultural Richness

The Indian subcontinent harbors an ancient civilization with a colorful culture and rich tradition. Some enthusiastic admirers, in their deep attachment to it, fail to see any of its anachronistic aspects. They don't acknowledge it's no longer tenable tenets, practices, and beliefs. On the other hand, the secular establishment in India fails to see Indic heritage as a treasure chest of insights and values, with gems that are as relevant today as in days of yore. The educational system seems to do little to present Indic lore and wisdom in a historical framework for the edification of its young citizens. Children graduate from high-schools in India without being exposed to the Vedas, the Upanishads, the Mahabharata, the Ramayana, and the Bhagavad Gita in a systematic way. Nor do they learn about Tirumoolar, Tiruvalluvar, Guru Nanak, Mahavira, Patañjali, Kalidasa and other intellectual, spiritual, and literary giants of the tradition. The negligence of a people's cultural history in the education of its young adds to the legitimate existential Angst of many Hindus.

All through history, barring a few episodes, Hindus have been respectful of all religions. In fact, this is what made Hindus unique as a religious group. Most Hindus to this day have little difficulty showing reverence to the places and symbols of Non-Indic religions like Judaism, Zoroastrianism, Christianity, Islam and the Ba'hai faith. One inevitable, if unfortunate, consequence of the growing feelings of usurpation of Hindu centrality, if not marginalization of Hindus within the country where Hindus are thus far the overwhelming majority, has instigated many Hindus to denigrate other religions.

This is not the Hinduism in which I grew up more than seven decades ago, nor the one that was preached and propagated by the likes of Sri Ramakrishna, Swami Vivekanada, Ramana Maharishi, Swami Sivananda, Sri Aurobindo and S. Radhakrishnan. That vintage Hinduism of a distant era seems to have vanished like the glory days of genuine patriots and uncorrupt politicians who gave their lives and selfless service to Bharat Mata. Today mutual hate and abuse have replaced the understanding and reverence for all that were the core messages in the Hinduism of my youthful days. This shift from a moral high ground is claimed to be justified because tolerance and respecting others are what often landed India on the receiving end.

Hindus in the West

Though Hindus beyond the shores of India have been doing quite well, especially in Western countries and Australia, and are held in high esteem for their competence, professionalism, intelligence, and hard-work, there are many among them (especially of the first generation) who feel ignored or insufficiently recognized. They argue that Hinduism is given only marginal notice because it does not create havoc in the West; worse still, it is often mentioned only through negative references to caste, inscrutable representations of the divine, and barely clad god-men with beard and matted hair dipping periodically into muddy waters. Many Hindus in the West, who may themselves not feel at home in certain authentically traditional Hindu milieu in India, nevertheless resent such portrayals which they see as caricatures and downright wrong. Fortunately, it is neither in the spirit nor in the interest of Hindus to resort to violent actions in such contexts. So, Hindus in the West have only been writing articles, publishing protesting books, and speaking in conferences to right the wrongs. Their voices are having positive impacts in the Western world.

On my Hindu affiliation

I have already mentioned the immeasurably rich ways in which I have personally benefited from my Hindu upbringing and roots. That is reason enough for me, in spite of my discomfort with some aspects of the religion, not to abandon my heritage. Beyond that there are other factors that keep me culturally, religiously, and spiritually affiliated to Hinduism.

Few religions give its members as much freedom of thought and practice as modern Hinduism does. As a result, one can find among Hindus the most ardent believers in astrology, numerology, and miracle-mongering and also incorrigible skeptics, agnostics, rationalists, and atheists. All of them have the right to call themselves Hindus. There are any number of cult-wise authoritative spokespersons for God and for puranic visions of the hereafter, charismatic gurus and learned acharyas who tell people what to do and what not to, when to travel and whom to marry, some even performing miracles. But there is no ultimate institutionalized authority who can pronounce who is Hindu and who is not. Some venerable scholar-saints, like their counterparts in other religions, declare that those who don't subscribe to their version of God or believe in their sacred purana or diverge from their interpretations of sacred works, have no right to talk about these. But what really matters is that in the Hindu framework no saintly swami has the God given right to prosecute or penalize whomsoever they deem and declare to be errant Hindus. And if for whatever reason, a Hindu chooses to abandon his/her religion, no man or monster can call for the execution of that person. Hinduism is too civilized to make apostasy a capital crime. Efforts to define a Hindu, and subject Hindus to claustrophobic doctrinal fetters have been attempted, but not succeeded thus far, and hopefully never will.

Just over two centuries ago, when European Enlightenment thinkers were struggling to articulate the principle of religious tolerance, they did not realize that they were echoing an ancient view that is enshrined in the Vedas: *There is but one God (referred to as Truth), and That Truth is described by the learned in different ways.* Ultimate Truth, the quintessence of the Cosmic Whole, is infinite, and it appears to finite minds only as hazy glimpses. Every description of the Divine, whether from revelation or through speculation, whether from reading or by reflection, is partial. It is narrow and self-righteous to claim that one view of God is the only right one. Like the blind men who judged the nature of the elephant from their own limited perceptions, our picture of the Ultimate is never accurate, let alone complete.

Ultimate Truth is like the glitter of a gem that doesn't seem the same when viewed from different angles. Every religious tradition has something unique, meaningful, and universal to offer to humanity. To me, this is the deep message in that Vedic aphorism, and this affirmation of multiple approaches to the Divine is the most significant contribution of Hindu insights to humanity. It is of greater relevance today than ever before.

In other words, the message of Hinduism is that for the enlightened heart and mind God can be seen in the Star of David as in the Christian Cross, in the contemplation of the Buddha as in the Crescent of Islam, in the Adi Granth of the Sikhs as in the abstract sound of the sacred Aum of the Hindus, and in other places still. It is this Hindu spirit that inspired me to write the following reflection when I drove to the Cape of Good Hope in South Africa in December 1999, while I was attending the Parliament of World Religions in Cape Town:

Universal Reflections

In striving to recognize the primacy of Fire and Light.
I feel kinship with my Zoroastrian sisters and brothers.
In striving to respect the Ten Commandments,
I feel kinship with my Jewish sisters and brothers.
In striving to be kind to neighbor and the needy,
I feel kinship with my Christian sisters and brothers.
In striving to be compassionate to creatures great and small,
I feel kinship with my Buddhist and Jaina sisters and brothers.
In striving to surrender myself completely to the Divine,
I feel kinship with my Muslim sisters and brothers.
In the recognition that religious wisdom flows from the Masters,
I feel kinship with my Sikh sisters and brothers.
In the recognition that serving fellow humans should be the goal of all religions,
I feel kinship with my Bahai sisters and brothers.
In my reverence for plants and trees, for lakes and mountains,
I feel kinship with my Native American sisters and brothers.
In my respect for those who see the world only as natural phenomena arising from physical laws,

I feel kinship with my religious naturalist sisters and brothers.
In feeling that all these and more are all paths to the same Unfathomable Mystery,
I feel kinship with my Hindu sisters and brothers.
In my love and laughter, joy and pain,
I feel kinship with all my fellow humans.
In my need for nourishment and love, and instinct to live on,
I feel kinship with all beings on the planet.
In my spiritual ecstasy with this wondrous world,
I feel kinship with the Cosmic Whole.

Concluding thoughts

Mine is one of millions of voices that incompletely sing the song of Indic culture. They do this in different ways. I am blessed to be part of this tradition because it offers many fulfilling visions of the Unknown Beyond; it enables me to reflect on these from my own limited perspectives. It has made cultural experiences abundant through the pleasing poetry, profound philosophy, magnificent music and colorful dances. The poetry of Kabir and Kamban, the spiritual longings of Andal and Manikkavasakar, the philosophies of Shankara and Ramanuja, the ecstatic music of Shri Chaitanya and Saint Thyagaraja, the aesthetics of Bharata Natyam and Manipuri dance are but some of the countless elements that have made my life as a Hindu extraordinarily rich.

I have not mentioned the considerable scientific achievements of classical India in mathematics and medicine, in astronomy and alchemy; nor about the solid contributions of Indians to modern science and mathematics (Raman, 2006). Notwithstanding these matters of which the people of India can be legitimately proud, some modern (?) Hindus make claims to the effect that their forefathers knew about quarks and quantum mechanics, deigned planes and nuclear weapons. Most informed Indian scientists are embarrassed by such unfortunate pronouncements.

I have said nothing of the joyous feasts and festivals that are marked on the Hindu almanac, or about the sculptures and frescos in the land, or about culinary delights that Indian cuisine offers. Oh, there is so much more to say!

There is little doubt that in the course of this century, India will play a more important role in world affairs, and Hinduism will grow to become a stronger and sounder religion, cleansed of its blemishes, and with as yet unimagined visions. It has the potential to serve as a beacon for religious harmony in this complex world of ours.

In 1994, for the inauguration of Mayor William Johnson of Rochester, NY I composed a prayer based on Hindu visions, and adapted to the modern world:

> A wholesome society has people with diverse interests and talents:
> There are those who study, meditate, and reflect: the thinking ones.
> There are those who manage and govern: the administering ones.
> There are those who engage in commerce: the trading ones.
> There are those who work and produce: the laboring ones.
> None is more important, and none any less.
> None is more exalted, and none too lowly:
> All are essential for the well-being of society.

May each person follow the path of one's own talent and inclination.
May knowledge and wisdom come to those that strive for it.
May caring and compassion come to those that make the laws.
May fairness and honesty be with those who trade.
May commitment and just recompense be part of those that labor.
May there be appreciation for each other's contribution.
May there be respect for each other's work and profession.
May all act in accordance with the laws of the country.
May the laws of the country be fair and just.
May justice always prevail.
May our children grow under the guidance of caring parents.
May our young people have respect for teachers and elders.
May there be unconditional love in every family.
May there be joy and harmony in the community.
May there be happiness in the whole world.
May there be peace, peace, and peace in the world.

Om shanti, shanti, shantihi!

Select Bibliography

Agarwal, Satya P., *The Social Role of the Gita*, New Delhi: Motilal Banarsidass (1998).
Aiyar, P. S. Jagadisa, *South Indian Shrines*, Calcutta, Rupa & Co. (2000).
Aiyar, V. V. S, Kamba Ramayanam: A Study, Delhi Tamil Sangam. (1950).
Allen, Charles, *The Search for the Buddha: The Men Who Discovered India's Lost Religion* (Illustrated) (2003).
Andal, *For the Love of God: Selections from Nalayira Divya Prabandham*, Australia: Penguin classics, (1996).
Asher, R.E., T. C. Kumari, T.C., *Malayalam*, Routledge, (1997).
Ashley, Mike, *The Mammoth Book of King Arthur*. London: Running Press, (2005).
Azhvars, *The holy lives of the Azhvars, or the Dravida saints*, Ananthacharya Indological Research Institute, (1982).
Bahirat, B. P. *The Philosophy of Jnanadeva*, Bombay: Popular Prakashan, (1956).
Bhatt, G. P. (ed.), *The Vāyu Purana*: Pt.1 (Ancient Indian Tradition and Mythology) New Delhi: Motilal Banarsidass, (2005).
Bhatt, N. R., *Shaivism In The Light of Epics, Puranas and Agamas*, Varanasi: Indica Books (2008)
Bhattacharya, Bhabani, *Gandhi- The Writer*, New Delhi, National Book Trust (2002).

Bhattacharya, D., *Love Songs of Chandidas*, London: Allen and Unwin (1969).

Bhave, Vinoba, *Talks on the Gita*, Varanasi Sarva Seva Sangh Rajghat, (1964).

Bofman, Theodora Helene, *The Poetics of the Ramakian*, Celler Book Shop (1984).

Bohr, Niels, *Atomic Physics and Human Knowledge*. Ox Bow Press. Wiley Interscience (1958 ed.)

Bromley, David G., Shinn, Larry D., *Krishna Consciousness in the West*, (1989).

Brown, C. P. (tr.), *Verses of Vemana*: In the Telugu Original With English Version, New Delhi: AE, (2007).

Bryant, Edwin, *The Quest for the Origins of Vedic Culture: The Indo-Aryan Migration Debate*, Oxford University Press, (2001).

Chakrabarty, Bidyut *Local Politics and Indian Nationalism: Midnapur (1919-1944)*. New Delhi: Manohar (1997).

Chaturvedi B.K., *Agni Purana*, New Delhi, Diamond Books, (2004).

Chaudhuri, Nirad C, *Hinduism: a religion to live by*, Oxford India (1999 ed.)

Chenchiah, P., Raja Bhujanga Rao. *A History of Telugu Literature*. India: Oxford University press. (1988)

Civachariyar, Kacciyappa, *Civacariyar aruliya Kanta Puranam: Mulamum telivuraiyum*, Varttamanan Patippakam (2000).

Coburn, Thomas B. *Encountering the Goddess: A Translation of the Devī-Máhátmya and a Study of Its Interpretation*. Albany, N.Y.: State University of New York Press, (1991).

Cross, Milton, *Milton Cross' Encyclopedia of the Great Composers and Their Music*, Vol. I, Doubleday & Company, Inc. (1962)

Das, R. K., *Temples of Tamilnad*, Bombay: Bharatiya Vidya Bhavan, (1964).
Das, Suranjan *Communal Riots in Bengal, 1905-1947*, India: Oxford University Press, (1991).
Debrov, Dipavali, *The Linga: Purana*, Delhi: Books for All, (2000).
Deshpande, N. A., (trans.), *The Padma Purana*, (Ten Volumes), Delhi: Motilal Benarsidass, (1992).
Dutt, M. N., *Rediscovering India: Garuda Purana*, Bel Air, CA: Hesperides Press, (2006).
Dutt, Romesh Chunder, *The Ramayana and the Mahabharata: the great epics of ancient India condensed into English verse*, London: J.M. Dent and Co., (1929ed.)
Fabri, Charles Louis, *Discovering Indian Sculpture: A Brief History*, Affiliated East-West Press (1970).
Feuerstein, Georg, Kak, Subhash, Frawley, David, *In Search of the Cradle of Civilization*, Ill: Quest Books (1995, 2001)
Gandhi, M. K. *The Bhagavad Gita According to Gandhi*, Berkeley, CA: Berkeley Hills Books, (1998)
Gandhi, M. K. *Young India*, (1925)
Ganguli, Kisari Mohan, *The Mahabharata: Translated from the original Sanskrit*, Delhi: Munshiram Manoharlal, (1981ed.).
Gansser, Augusto, et al., Himalayas. *Growing Mountains, Living Myths, Migrating Peoples*, New Delhi: Bookwise (1987).
George (ed.), K.M., *Modern Indian Literature, an Anthology*, New Delhi, Sahitya Akademi (1992).
Ghose, Sarat Chandra, *Life of Dr. Mahendra Lal Sircar*, Calcutta: Hahnemann Publishing Company, (1935).
Gogoi, Lila, *The History of the system of Ahom administration*, Calcutta, Punthi Pustak, (1991).
Goswami, Dr. Karunamaya, *Evolution of Bengali music*, The Independent, (8 June 2002).

Graves, Kersey, *The World's Sixteen Crucified Saviors: Christianity Before Christ*, 1875, Adventures Unlimited Press, (2001ed.).
Griffith, Ralph T. H., *The Hymns of the Rigveda* (1890)
Hopkins, Edward Washburn, *Epic Mythology*, Orient Book Distributors, (1986).
Ishwaran, K, *Speaking of Basava: Lingayat religion and culture in South Asia*. Boulder, Colo: Westview Press (1992).
Iyengar, BKS, *Light on the Yoga Sutras of Patañjali*, New Delhi, Harper –Collins Publishers India, (1993).
Iyengar, Kodaganallur Ramaswami Srinivasa (ed.), *Asian Variations In Ramayana*, New Delhi: Sahitya Akademi, (2003).
Iyengar, P. R. Srinivasa, *History of the Tamils: From the earliest times to 600 A.D.*, Asian Educational Services (1995ed.).
Jackson, John G. Krishna and Buddha: *Black Gods of Asia. African Presence Early Asia* (1996)
Jacob, Judith M., Reamker (Ramakerti): *The Cambodian Version Of The Ramayana*, Routledge/Curzon, (2002).
Jayaraman, P., Sant Vani, Vani Prakashan (2011).
Jindal, K. B., *A History of Hindi literature*, Kitab Mahal, (1955).
Joshi, K. K. (ed.), *Matsya Maha Purana : An Exhaustive Introduction*, Sanskrit Text, English Translation, (2 Vols-Set), Delhi: Parimal Publications, (2007).
Kahn, Charles H., *Anaximander and the Origins of Greek Cosmology*. New York: Columbia University Press, (1960).
Kak, Subhash, *The Astronomical Code of the Rigveda*, Delhi: Munshiram Manoharlal Publ., Pvt Ltd (2000).
Kakati, Banikanta, *Assamese: It's Formation and Development-a Scientific Treatise on the History and Philology of the Assamese Language*, Guwahati. LBS Pub., (2007).
Kamath, Suryanath U, *A concise history of Karnataka: from pre-historic times to the present*. Bangalore: Jupiter books, (2002).

Kanda, K. C., *Masterpieces of URDU GHAZALS: From the 17th to the 20th Century,* Sterling Publishers Pvt.Ltd (1998).

Karandikar, M. A., *Saint Namdev,* New Delhi: Maharashtra Information Centre, (1985).

Kidwai, Sadiqur-Rahman, *Gilchrist and the 'Language of Hindoostan',* Rachna Prakashan, (1972).

Knapp, Stephen, *The Vedic Prophesies: A look into the future,* Detroit, MI: World Relief Network, (1998).

Krishnamurti, B., *The Dravidian Languages,* Cambridge, Cambridge University Press, (2003).

Kumaradoss, Y. Vincent, Robert Caldwell: A Scholar-Missionary in Colonial South India, Delhi: ISPCK, (2007).

Lal, Mohan (ed.) *Encyclopaedia of Indian literature,* Volume 5, New Delhi, Sahitya Akademy, (1992).

Lal, B.B. *The Saraswati Flows on: the Continuity of Indian Culture.* New Delhi: Aryan Books International (2002).

Long, Jerrery D. A Vision for Hinduism: Beyond Hindu Nationalism. I. B. Taurus (2007).

MacDonell, Arthur Anthony, *A Sanskrit Grammar for Students,* Oxford: Oxford University Press, (1927).

Mahadevan, T. M. P., *Invitation to Indian Philosophy,* Arnold-Heinemann, New Delhi, (1980).

Majumdar, R.C., *The History and Culture of the Indian People,* New York: The Macmillan Co., (1951).

Mani, Vettam. *Puranic Encyclopedia.* 1st English ed. New Delhi: Motilal Banarsidass, (1975).

McLeod., W. H., *The Sikhs: History, Religion, and Society,* M.Y. Columbia University Press, (1989)

Medhi, Kaliram *Assamese Grammar and the Origin of Assamese Language.* Guwahati: Publication Board, (1988).

Meduri, Avanthi (Hrsg.), *Rukmini Devi Arundale (1904-1986), A Visionary Architect of Indian Culture and the Performing Arts.* Delhi: Motilal Banarsidass, (2005).

Mehrotra, S. R., *Towards India's Freedom and Partition*, New Delhi: Rupa & Co., New Delhi, (2005).

Menon, Ramesh, *Bhagavata Purana*, Kolkata: Rupa & Co.

Mohanty, Prasanna Kumar, *The History of: History of Odiya Literature*, Odiya Sahityara Adya Aitihasika Gana), (2007).

Müller, Max, *India, What can it teach us*, Lecture IV, (1882).

Mugaḷi, Raṃ Śrī, *History of Kannada literature* New Delhi: Sahitya Akademi (1975).

Nagar, Shanti Lal, *Hanuman - In Art, Culture, Thought and Literature*, New Delhi, Sundeep Prakashan, (1995).

Nagar, Shantilal, *Sri Ranganatha Ramayana : Rendering into English from Telugu*, Delhi, B.R. Publishing (2001).

Nagaswamy, R., *Mahabalipuram (Monumental Legacy)*, U.S. Oxford University Press, (2008).

Nair, C. N. Sreekantan, and Joseph, Sarah, *Retelling the Ramayana : Voices from Kerala*, New Delhi, Oxford University Press, (2005).

Nakanishi, Akira, *Writing systems of the world: alphabets, syllabaries, pictograms*, Tuttle Publishing, (1990).

Nandakumar, Prema, *Makers of Indian literature: Bharati*, New Delhi: Sahitya Akademi, (1989).

Narla, V. R., *Vemana*, New Delhi, Sahitya Akademi, (1969)

Nathani, Sultan,*Year: Intekhab-O-Lughat*, New Delhi: Nathani Trust, (2002).

Nikhilananda, Swami, *The Gospel of Sri Ramakrishna* Vol. I, Ramakrishna Math, (2000 ed.)

Omvedt, Gail, *Dalit Visions: The Anti-caste Movement and the Construction of an Indian Identity*, Orient Longman (1995).

Palakeel, Thomas, *Malayalam Literature: A Brief Survey*, www.shelterbelt.com/KJ/malayalams.

Pande, Rupanarayan S. P., *Goswami Tulsídaskrt Bálabodhini tíká lavakush kánd sahit*...Lucknow: Tejkumar Press (1974)

Pandeya, Avinash, C., *The Art of Kathakali*, New Delhi: Munshiram Manoharlal (1999).

Parekh, Manilal, *Brahmarshi Keshab Chunder Sen*, Rajkot: Oriental Christ House, (1926).

Parthasarthy, Professor Rajagopal, (trans), *Cilappatikaram of Ilanko Atikal: An Epic of South India*, New York: Columbia University Press, (1992)

Percival, P., *A Collection of Proverbs in Tamil, with Their Translation in English*, Nabu Press, (2010 ed.)

Pillai, M. Narayana, *Civaka Vcintamani*, Puram (1981).

Pillai, M. S. Purnalingam, *Tamil Literature*, New Delhi/Madras: Asian Educational Services (1994).

Pillai, Sivaraja K. N., *Agastya in the Tamil Land*, New Delhi: Asian Educational Service (1985)

Prabhupada, A. C. Bhaktivedanta Swami, *Srimad-Bhagavatam: Bhagavata Purana* (18 Volumes) Los Angeles, CA: ISKC, (1999).

Prabhupada, His Divine Grave A. C. Bhaktivedanta Swami, *Bhagavad-Gita As Is*, New York: Collier Books, (1975)

Premchand, *Nirmala*, Alekh Prakashan (2008).

Puligandla, R., *That Thou Art: Wisdom of the Upanishads*, Freemont, CA: Asian Humanities Press, (2002).

Raghavan, K. S., *The Date of the Mahabharata War*, Srinivasanagar: Srirangam Printers, (1969).

Raghavan, V, *Tyagaraja - Life and Lyrics.*, New Delhi: Oxford University Press (1979).

Rai, Amrit. *A house divided: The origin and development of Hindi-Hindustani*. Delhi: Oxford University Press, (1984).

Rajagopalan, Usha, *Pánchálí's Pledge*, India: Everyman's (2013).
Raman, V. V. *Sivapuranam*: A Mystic Poem, XLibris, (2011).
Raman, V. V. *Tirukkural*, Chennai: Manimekalai Prasuram, (2000).
Raman, V. V., *Satanama: Hundred Names From India's Past*, Bombay: Popular Prakashan, (1989).
Raman, Varadaraja V., (2006). *Glimpses of Indian Scientists*, New Delhi: Samvad India Foundation.
Raman, Varadaraja V., Glimpses of Indian Scientists, *New Delhi: Samvad India Foundation* (2006)
Raman, Varadaraja V., *Indic Visions in an Age of Science*, New York, NY: Metanexus. (2011)
Raman,V. V., *Reflections from Alien Shores*, Mumbai: Bharatiya Vidya Bhavan, (2000).
Ramaswamy, Krishnan et al. *Invading the Sacred, An Analysis of Hinduism Studies in America*, New Delhi: Rupa & Co. (2007)
Ranade, Ramchandra D, *Tukaram*. New York: SUNY Press, (1994).
Rao, S. R. *Lost City of Dwaraka*, New Delhi: Aditya Prakashan, (1999)
Rao, V. S. Narayana, *Mokshhagundam Visvesvaraya*, New Delhi, National Book Trust.
Robinson, Catherine A. *Interpretations of the Bhagavad-Gītā and images of the Hindu tradition*, Oxon: Routledge, (2006)
Roy, Indrani Basu. *Kalighat: Its Impact on Socio-Cultural Life of Hindus*, New Delhi: Gyan Publishing House, (1993).
Sar Desai, ManoharRai, *A History of Konkani Literature* New Delhi: Sahitya Akademi, New Delhi, (2000).
Sarkar, Jadunath, *Shivaji And His Times*, Calcutta: Orient Longmans, (1992 ed.)

Sastri, Sivanath, *History of the Brahmo Samaj*, 2d ed. Calcutta, Calcutta University Press, (1974)
Seely, Clinton B., *The Slaying of Meghanada: A Ramayana from Colonial Bengal*, New Delhi: Oxford University Press, (2003).
Sen, R.N., *The Brahma-Vaivarta Puranam*. AMS Press, (1974).
Sengupta, Arputha Rani, *Manimekalai: Dancer with a Magic Bowl - Buddhist Epic in Tamil*, Regency Publications, (2008).
Shapiro, Michael C., *Hindi,* in Garry, Jane & Carl Rubino, An encyclopedia of the world's major languages, past and present, New England Publishing Associates, (2001).
Sharma, Arvind, *Classical Hindu Thought: An Introduction*, Oxford University Press (2000).
Sharma, Arvind, *Modern Hindu Thought: An Introduction*, Oxford University Press (2005).
Sharma, Arvind, *New Focus on Hindu Studies*, Delhi: DK Print World (2005).
Sharma, Arvind, *A Hindu Perspective on the Philosophy of Religion*, New York: St. Martin's Press, 1991.
Sharma, S. R., *Life and Works of K. M. Munshi*, Book Enclave, (2008).
Shastri, P., *Introduction to the Puranas*, New Delhi: Rashtriya Sanskrit Sanstha, (1995).
Siegel, Lee, *Gitagovinda: Love Songs of Radha and Krishna*, New York: New York University Press, (2009)
Singh, Gurmukh, *The Rise of Sikhs Abroad*, New Delhi. Rupa & Co, (2003).
Smith, Vincent A., *The Oxford History of India*, Oxford: The Clarenden Press, (1967 ed.).
Sommer, Volker, *Heilige Egoisten: Die Soziobiologie indischer Tempelaffen*, München, München Beck (1996).

Steever, Sanford B, *The Dravidian Languages*. Taylor & Francis, (1998).
Swaminathaiyaravargal, Dr. Oo. Vé. *En Charittiram*, Besant Nagar: Dr. Oo.Vé., S. Nilayam (1990).
Tagare, Ganesh Vasudeo (tr,), *The Kurma Purana*, New Delhi: Motilal Banarsidass, (1998).
Tagare, Ganesh Vasudeo (tr.) *The Nārada Purana*, Delhi: Motilal Benarasidass, (1998).
Tagare, Ganesh Vasudeo, *Studies in Skanda Purāṇa*, Delhi: Motilal Banarsidass, (1996).
Tagore, G. V. (ed.), *Brahmanda Purana*, South Asia Books, (1986).
Tagore, Rabindranath, *Gitanjali*, Booksurge Classics, (2009).
Talib, Gurbachan Singh, and Singh, Attar ed., *Bhai Vir Singh: Life, Times and Works* Chandigarh, (1973)
Tapasyananda, Swami, *Srimad Bhagavad Gita (The Scripture of Mankind)*, Kolkata, Sri Ramakrishna Math (2005ed.)
Thapar, Romila, *Recent perspectives of early Indian history*, Mumbai, Popular Prakashan, (1995).
Thomas, Edward J., *The Life of Buddha as Legend and History*, Kissinger Publishing, (2007).
Thongthep, Mechai, *Ramakien*, Bangkok, Naga Books (1993).
Thurston, Edgar, and K. Rangachari, K., *Castes and Tribes of Southern India*. Clarendon Press (1909).
Tilak, Bal Gangadhar (Tr. Bhalchandra Sitaram Sukthankar) *Srimad Bhagavadgita Rahasya Or Karma-Yoga-Sastral*. Reprint. Delhi, Low Price, (2002)
Tirumular, *Tirumantiram: A Tamil Scriptural Classic*, Chennai: Sri Ramakrishna Math (2002).
Tolkappiyar, *Tolkappiyam: The earliest extant Tamil grammar : with a short commentary in English*, Kuppuswami Sastri Research Institute; 2nd edition (1999)

Valmiki, *Srimad Valmiki-Ramayana*, Gorakhpur: Gita Press (1992).
Van der Veer, Peter, *Ayodhya and Somnath, eternel shrines, contested histories*, (1992) Rao, S. R., The Lost City of Dvaraka, Aditya Prakashan, (1999).
Vanmikanathan, G. (Translator), *Periya Purana by Sekkizhar*, Chennai: Sri Ramakrishna Math (1985)
Varadarajan, Dr. M., (Trans, E.Sa. Viswanathan), *A History of Tamil Literature*, Sahitya Akademi, New Delhi (1988).
Vas, Eric A., *Subhas Chandra Bose: The Man and His Times*, Lancer Publishers, (2008).
Warrier, A. G. Krishna, Bhagavad Gita Bhasya of Sri Sankaracarya (Shankaracharya): With Text and English Translation (Sri Ramkrishna Math (2002)
Wilson, H. H. *The Vishnu Purana: A System of Hindu Mythology and Tradition.* Cambridge: Read Country Books, (2006).
Winternitz, M. A History of Indian Literature. Oriental books, New Delhi, (1927ed.)
Yocum, Glenn E., *Hymns to the dancing Siva: A study of Manikkavacakar's Tiruvacakam*, Heritage (1982).
Zellior, Eleanor, and Mokashi-Punekar, Rohini, *Untouchanble Saints: An Indian phenomenon*, New Delhi: Manoha, (2005).
Zvelebil, Kamil, *1972. The Smile of Murugan: On Tamil Literature of South India,* Leiden: Brill (1973).

www.ingramcontent.com/pod-product-compliance
Lightning Source LLC
Chambersburg PA
CBHW021437070526
44577CB00002B/203